Jim Nickelson

Fine Art Inkjet Printing:

The Craft and Art of the Fine Digital Print

rockynook

Fine Art Inkjet Printing: The Craft and Art of the Fine Digital Print
Jim Nickelson
www.jimnickelson.com

Editor: Joan Dixon
Project manager: Lisa Brazieal
Marketing coordinator: Mercedes Murray
Layout and type: Hespenheide Design
Cover design: Aren Straiger

ISBN: 978-1-68198-206-9
1st Edition (1st printing, June 2017)

Rocky Nook Inc.
1010 B Street, Suite 350
San Rafael, CA 94901
USA

www.rockynook.com

Distributed in the U.S. by Ingram Publisher Services
Distributed in the UK and Europe by Publishers Group UK

Library of Congress Control Number: 2016944451

This book is printed on acid-free paper.
Printed in China

To Heather, for encouraging me to begin printing seriously;

to Becky, for supporting me in everything;

and to Eliza, for inspiring me to do it all.

About the Author

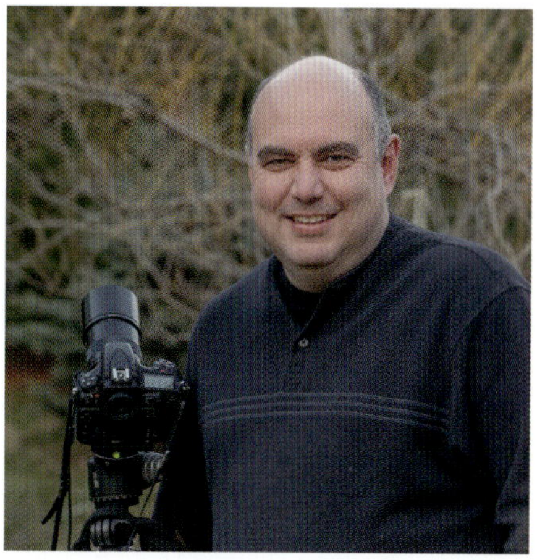

Jim Nickelson is a photographer whose work is driven by a sense of wonder of the natural world and its underlying science. Jim works full time as a fine art photographer and custom digital printer, and he teaches workshops on photography and digital printing both privately and through Maine Media Workshops.

Jim has received numerous awards for his photography, and his work has been exhibited widely. His work resides in museums, as well as in public, corporate, and private collections across the United States and Canada. Jim makes his home in Camden, Maine, with his amazing wife and daughter. He can be found online at jimnickelson.com and at nickelsoneditions.com.

Table of Contents

Introduction

Fine art inkjet printing continues to increase in popularity as its quality now surpasses many traditional types of printing and as acceptance into the art world is essentially complete. Inkjet printing has finally come of age.

Over the past decade, I've worked as a custom fine art printer for clients across North America. I've also been pursuing my own fine art photography career and have been navigating the gallery world during that time. I'd like to share some of what I've learned about fine art printing and, in particular, printing with the intention of working with fine art galleries.

I wrote this book to provide a different perspective from a more traditional technical book and to spend more time discussing how to realize your artistic intent with a print as well as special considerations for the art world.

Before we jump into printing, let's talk about what this book covers. In this book we'll talk about the basics of creating your own fine art prints using inkjet printers, including details about both hardware and software. We'll also talk about more subjective aspects such as choosing a suitable paper and how to realize your artistic intent in the print. Later chapters will address preparing your work for presentation to fine art galleries and emphasizing the print as an object, along with many other topics.

Throughout the book, standalone "Print Mastery" articles provide more advanced information for those wishing to take their printing to the next level. For beginning printers, feel free to skip these sections until you feel the need for more information and are prepared to tackle them.

Over my years of printing and teaching I have developed basic principles that underlie my decision-making throughout the editing and printing process. I've identified these Principles of Printing throughout the text and gathered all of them in the Appendix for your convenience.

I focus on Adobe Lightroom and Photoshop for digital darkroom software and on Epson inkjet printers for hardware, because these are the most commonly used tools for processing and printing. My goal, however, is to make these materials generally applicable by providing principles that can be used with different types of software, computer platforms, and printers.

Finally, I often refer to photographic prints and photographers, but the lessons and tools in this book are equally applicable to making digital prints of any type of artwork, such as reproductions of paintings or digitally created artwork.

Enjoy, and happy printing!

1 Fine Art Inkjet Printing

In this chapter, we'll discuss my overall philosophies for creating fine art inkjet prints as well as why it's such an exciting time to be working with inkjet prints. We'll also cover what makes a fine print and how best to realize your artistic intent for an image in a physical print.

The Craft and Art of the Fine Digital Print

> *Art stands on the shoulders of craft,*
> *which means that to get to the art*
> *you must master the craft.*
> —Ann Patchett

My philosophy for creating the fine digital print derives from a simple concept: the creation of a fine digital print requires excellence in both *craft* and *art*. Mastery of the *craft* of printing is a necessity for mastering the *art* of printing. I will of course address mastery of both in this book.

The **craft** in making a fine digital print is the development and implementation of the necessary skills to create prints that are *without noticeable flaws* and that take advantage of the inherent properties of the materials. Part of the craft of printing is developing your skills and workflow so that you can *consistently* produce prints that look as you intend. Learning the craft of printing requires learning both about the printing hardware as well as the editing software used to prepare an image for print.

The **art** in making a fine digital print is embodied in the inherent aesthetic decisions to craft the image itself and the resulting print to further the actual *intent of the artist*. Art is involved in making decisions of how to change the look of the image and print to improve its ability to convey your artistic intent.

Craft without art may give you good and solid results, but you will find that making consistently great prints will prove elusive. Having the tools to subtly modify a file for printing is useless without knowing where to go.

Art without craft will result in interesting prints that suffer from distracting flaws. It is only through mastery of craft that we have tools that we can use to produce the art. Knowing what you would like to do in a final print but being unable to achieve it will only produce frustration.

> *My aim is not to exhibit craft, but rather to submerge it, and make it rightfully the handmaiden of beauty, power and emotional content.*
> —Andrew Wyeth

It is the combination of the **art** of knowing your artistic intent for your image and the **craft** of being able to realize this artistic intent in your final print that results in prints that are special and meaningful. While you may not achieve these results with each and every print, it is what we should strive for each time we create a print as printmakers in this new world of inkjet printing.

Be the Director of Your Final Print

> *I have often said that the negative is similar to the musician's score, and the print to the performance of that score. The negative comes to life only when 'performed' as a print.*
> —Ansel Adams

Most photographers have likely seen Ansel Adams's quote (or one of its many variations) regarding printing being a performance and it has become something of a cliché. And yet, his words still contain immense power in describing both the reason and the nature of printing your photographs, at least implicitly.

A photograph, to both Adams and myself, is not complete until it is an *actual physical print* (**Figure 1-1**). In addition, the photographer and their **artistic intent** should dictate how that print is actually performed (i.e., made).

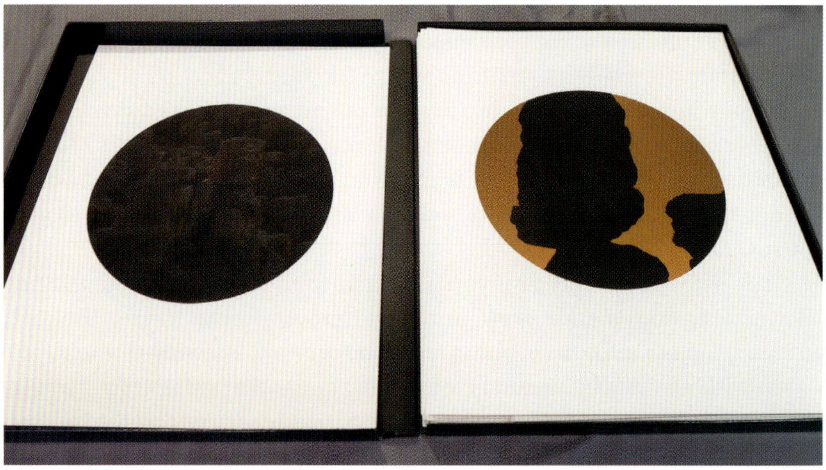

Figure 1-1: Fine art prints from my *East of the Sun, West of the Moon* series created for a portfolio. The images are 12" across and the paper is 17" × 22", allowing for a generous border.

The idea of the photographer dictating how their final print looks underlies my operating principle that each photographer should be the director of his or her final print. Just like the director of a play or movie, or the conductor of a symphony, each photographer should take control of the printing process so that each print embodies their artistic intent. The best way to do so is for a photographer to do his or her own printing, but the same principles also apply if a photographer is working with somebody else, whether a distant Internet-based printer or a local custom printmaker.

To successfully direct your final print, you need to know both what constitutes a good print and also what sort of tools are available to create a good print. You also need to know what your artistic intent is for your photograph. I hope to provide the knowledge and tools necessary so you can be the director of your final print.

Print Mastery: Digital Prints as Performances

Ansel Adams, of course, was referring to printing in a traditional darkroom where dodging and burning were done by hand and each print was a unique performance (and thus a unique object).

This same principle applies to printing digitally when the idea is expanded to each photograph rather than each individual print. While a properly functioning inkjet printer will produce print after print that are effectively identical, most of the creative work of printing instead occurs before and up to the time of printing. I think of the "performance" inherent in the detailed editing of an image for print to be effectively recorded when I save the file, and a printmaker can repeat this saved performance for future prints.

The fact that the creative performance of preparing an image for print does not need to be performed from scratch for each print does not eliminate its performance aspect. Indeed, since the edits for print need only be performed once, many printmakers perform more sophisticated edits than they would have ever dreamed of in a traditional darkroom, knowing that their efforts could be leveraged over many copies. I believe this to be one of the key advantages of digital printing when compared to traditional methods.

Options for Printing

> *I consider it essential that the photographer should do his own printing and enlarging. The final effect of the finished print depends so much on these operations. And only the photographer himself knows the effect he wants.*
>
> —Bill Brandt

Once you have decided to print your work, you must choose from one of three options. The first choice, and not surprisingly my recommended choice, is to print yourself. Printing yourself will give you control over the complete artistic process, which provides a significant advantage in having your final print realize your artistic intent. I believe that printing for yourself, and learning how decisions in the field can impact the final print, can also make you a better photographer.

Printing Ourselves

While printing yourself is a great choice, it does come with some disadvantages. First, equipping yourself with a high quality-printer and materials can be very expensive, particularly equipment suitable for large-format prints (**Figure 1-2**). A printing setup also can take up a large amount of space, limiting the number of people who can pursue this route.

Moreover, mastering printing requires the dedication of time and mental energy, which is something that not every photographer wants to invest. Each of us involved in photography quickly realizes that every moment spent printing, marketing, designing a website, updating computers, doing business taxes, or the like is a moment that we are not photographing. No one can be an expert in everything, so each of us must decide for ourselves how we wish to spend our valuable time.

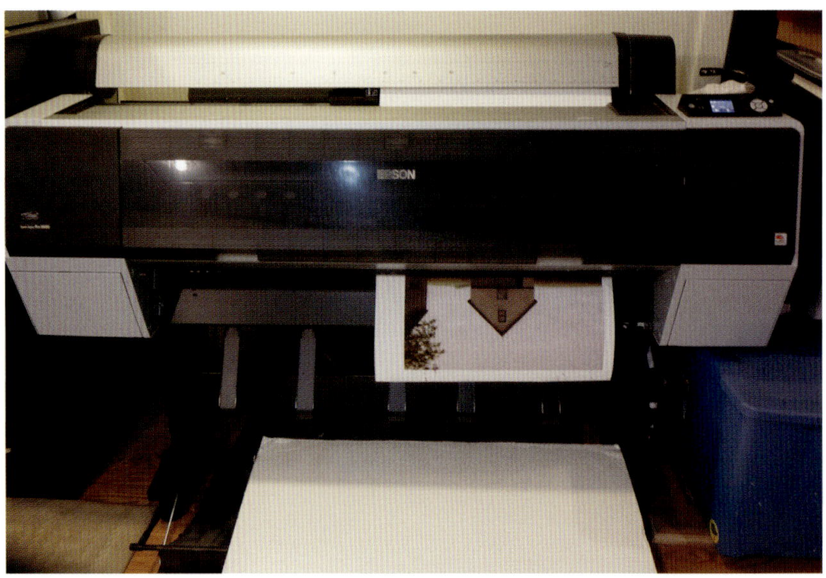

FIGURE 1-2: My Epson 9900 large-format printer. These 44" carriage width printers require a significant amount of space (shown is a 24" wide roll of paper printing to provide a sense of scale). Image Courtesy Linden Frederick.

Working with a Custom Printer

Working with a custom printer is another option for printing your work. A custom printer can work with photographers individually to help them realize their artistic intent, and can utilize their specialized expertise and equipment to do so. I interpret Bill Brandt's words that lead off this section to mean that all photographers should direct their final print regardless of whether they push the print button themselves, as much of the creative and subject aspect of printing has moved to the digital darkroom rather than the mechanics of printing itself.

Many photographers make their own small prints themselves and work with a custom printer for larger prints. For many photographers, this is a wonderful solution that allows them to gain the majority of benefits of printing themselves without the higher investment of money and space required for a large-format printer for the occasional giant prints.

Working with a Non-Custom Printer

The third option is to work with a non-custom printer, such as online print services. This is usually the most cost-effective option and can provide very good results. In this case, it's up to the photographer to fully prepare their files, as customized attention will of course be lacking.

If you are working with a third party such as a custom or non-custom printer, much of the materials in this book will still apply to your process. Regardless of who is doing the printing, a better file should result in a better print.

For all of these options, you still can be the director of your final print. The essence of this concept is determining your artistic intent and making the relevant decisions in accordance with this intent.

Artistic Intent

> *To convey in the print the feeling you experienced when you exposed the film—to walk out of the darkroom and say: 'This is it, the equivalent of what I saw and felt!'. That's what it's all about.*
> —John Sexton

Your artistic intent for a particular photograph or other work of art is related to the reaction you wish to achieve from a viewer. The artistic intent can be the look or feel of the final print, or it can be an emotion or message that you wish to convey with the print.

Artistic intent is by definition *subjective* to the artist. In other words, the feeling, thought, or emotion you wish to evoke with a print is entirely up to you. For example, if you desire a dark and moody feel for your print, then a successful final print should convey this feeling, such as by producing a final print that is darker and with deeper shadows. Someone else cannot successfully opine whether the final print is too dark or too light without knowing your artistic intent for the image. How dark your print should be is entirely up to you as the artist, as it is with all meaningful decisions about your work. Below you will find an example of how the "feel" of a photograph can be quickly and easily varied in light of the artistic intent of the photographer (**Figure 1-3**).

The photograph on the *left* is the processed photograph that was made consistent with my artistic intent for the photograph. The *middle* photograph is a modified version of the first, made significantly darker by lowering the exposure, and the result makes the entire image feel more like night, with the stars becoming more prominent compared to the darker surrounding sky. The version on the *right* takes the original version and moves the white balance more toward blue, making the image feel more like night in a different way, via color.

Figure 1-3: The original photograph, a darker version, and a bluer version, each of which could represent the photographer's artistic intent. This night photograph is from Acadia National Park in Maine.

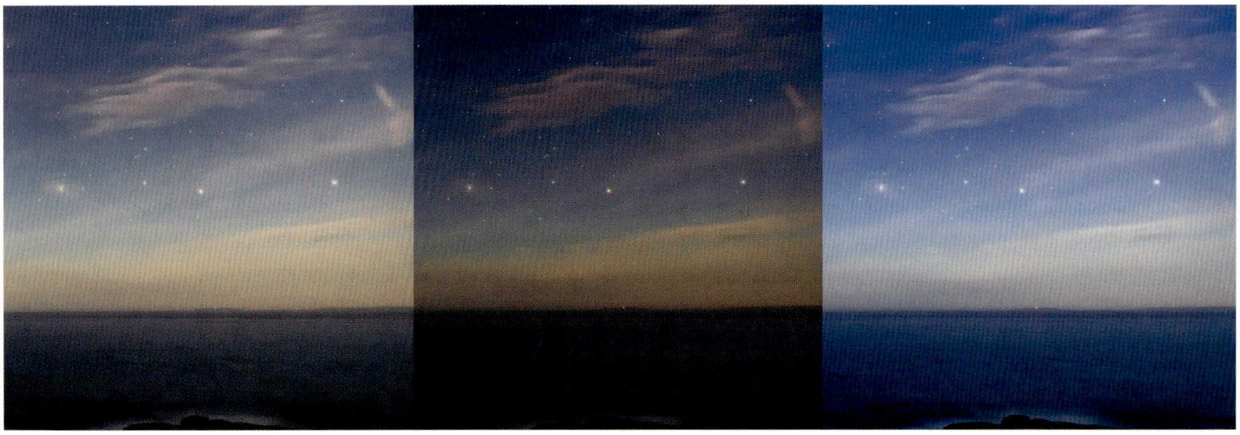

Principles of Printing #1: Artistic Intent Should Drive Your Decisions

Your artistic intent for your work should drive your decisions throughout the entire printing process. Everything from how you process an image, how large you print it, and what paper you use for the print should be guided by your own artistic intent.

Each photographer has a purpose for choosing to shoot a photograph and then for choosing to print that particular photograph. A fine print helps any photograph realize its fullest expression, and the nature of that expression depends on the artist. By taking control of the process, the artist can serve as the director of his or her final print.

Any of these three versions of this photograph would be acceptable interpretations of the scene as realized in print. The one that is "best" should entirely be at the discretion of the artist, who chooses the interpretation most consistent with the mood and feel he or she desires to convey to the viewer of the print.

Many of the decisions you will face as a printmaker will be subtler than the choices presented here, but the need to make such choices will inevitably arise. I do believe, though, that there is no one "right" answer and that the resolution of these decisions should be based on the desires of the artist.

A nonexhaustive list of artistic intentions you can have in editing an image for print (and possible means of achieving them in editing for print) include the following:

- Dark and moody (darker and/or more contrast)
- Light and airy (brighter and/or less contrast)
- Feels like night (bluer white balance, darker, more blacks)
- Consistent with feeling artist had at time of photographing scene
- Re-create scene as closely as possible to reality (being sharp and showing detail in shadows, perhaps)
- Dream-like (soft-focus, gauzy)
- Intensely saturated and contrasty
- Desaturated and without intense colors
- Feeling of warmth (warmer white balance)
- Feeling of coolness (cooler white balance)
- Consistency with other prints in same project (i.e., the print statement for a portfolio)

What Makes a Fine Art Print?

> *The fine print represents, to me, an expressive object of beauty and excellence. The difference between a very good print and a fine print is subtle and difficult, if not impossible, to describe in words. There is a feeling of satisfaction in the presence of a fine print—an uneasiness with a print that falls short of optimum quality.*
>
> —Ansel Adams

What makes a good print? What makes a great print? These questions are notoriously hard to define, and for many experts it comes down to a paraphrase of U.S. Supreme Court Justice Potter Stewart's definition of pornography, "I know it when I see it." My own attempt at answering these questions a bit more objectively follows.

A *good print* is a print that looks like you want it to look, conveys what you want it to convey, and does not have any problems that detract from the image. Problems such as objectionable noise or over-sharpening will take a print out of the category of good prints as they distract the viewer and are indicative of poor craftsmanship. I know that for me, once I see a flaw in a print (whether my own or someone else's) I have a hard time seeing anything else.

A *great print* is a print that captures your intent perfectly and has impeccable craftsmanship. A great print has a presence about it that allows the physical print to transcend the image itself. Often with a great print, someone who doesn't respond to the artistry of your work will still appreciate the craftsmanship. To perfectly capture your intent with a print, you will often have to interpret your image in the digital darkroom to emphasize or de-emphasize various relationships within parts of the print or interpret the print is in its entirety.

Another hallmark of a great print is that whatever editing or other machinations you performed to make the print sing will be invisible to the viewer. The viewer will recognize it as a great print but will be unable to pinpoint exactly why it is so: they will just appreciate the print itself.

Once we are past the threshold of a good print and have solved any craftsmanship issues, it is in the digital darkroom and through the choice of paper that we can adjust the image through emphasis, de-emphasis, or other modifications to create a great print that perfectly captures our artistic intent.

What's in a Name?

> *What's in a name? That which we call a rose,*
> *by any other name would smell as sweet.*
> —William Shakespeare

One of the most common questions I receive from clients, photographers, and collectors is what to call these beautiful prints that we make using our inkjet printers. If you begin to investigate this issue, you will quickly find that there are many different answers to this question.

A once-popular name for these prints that has now fallen out of favor in the fine art world is *giclée* (see the sidebar for more about this word). With that word no longer being a suitable choice in the fine art world, there is no consensus on what name to use instead.

Inkjet prints is a name you occasionally see, and it has an appeal because all of the prints in this category do indeed come from an inkjet printer. Inkjet prints are a bit over-inclusive, though, covering both dye-based and pigment-based inks, and many inkjet printers are not suitable for fine art prints because of archival concerns or print quality. There is an artistic heritage in embracing the mechanical printing device used to make a print, such as etchings, lithographs, engravings, and the like. Many do not like this name because they feel that the word *inkjet* still has negative connotations with viewers.

Pigment prints (or archival pigment prints, or pigment ink prints, or other variations) have become one of the most popular choices for a name for these prints. At present, the best choice for printing using inkjet printers is using pigment inks so this a natural choice. Combining pigment prints with an identification of the substrate, such as *pigment print on cotton rag paper,* also harkens to artistic tradition. Many other types of artistic prints that do not involve inkjet printers also use pigment inks, though, making the name much less precise.

Digital prints (or fine digital prints, or fine art digital prints) is the most common name I see today, but it also suffers from being over-inclusive in that many prints may use a digital image but are not inkjet prints. Photo labs often print digital image files on aluminum using dye-sublimation processes or using a wet-based process for a digital C-print, two very different processes than inkjet printers. The qualifier of "fine" or "fine art" helps distinguish pigment inkjet prints from the less archival alternatives.

Perhaps the best current choice for a name for these prints is *digital pigment prints* or a variation on this such as *archival pigment photographic prints*, which combine the materials and the process into one name. While this name seems to be rarely used, I believe it will continue to become more popular as the problems with other choices become more evident. It is not perfect, but it conveys the nature of the printing process and the physical object without being too over-inclusive.

Astute readers will note that I use the name *Fine Digital Print* on the cover of this book in deference to what I believe is the most commonly used name today. In the interest of convenience I will use this phrase or *pigment prints* throughout this book for times when the word *print*—the most elegant and simple of all names—will not suffice.

What about Giclée?

One word for a digital print that you almost certainly have come across is *giclée*. The word giclée was first used by Jack Duganne, one of the earliest digital printmakers, for fine art digital prints made in Iris inkjet printers. Many have (and still do) embrace this term for all digital prints because it has marketing appeal and avoids early negative connotations associated with words such as *digital* and *inkjet*. Others also use the term for certain classes of digital prints, such as prints on canvas, prints on watercolor paper, or reproductions of other artwork.

Regardless of its origins, the name is seen by many in the fine art world as being overly pretentious and it is widely disliked. My experience in the art world is that the vast majority of fine art galleries and museums do not like the term and I do not recommend using it. I personally associate it with prints made using the original Iris printers and thus consider it not applicable to modern inkjets, but it will likely still have life for years in many markets.

Why Print?

I'm often asked by friends, family, and even other photographers why I bother printing my work when the whole world seems to be moving digital. For me, the answer is simple: *creating a fine art print is my primary purpose in making photographs.*

The Fine Print

> *...the ultimate end, the print, is but a duplication of all that I saw and felt through my camera.*
>
> —Edward Weston

As is likely becoming obvious, I am a strong proponent and champion of the *fine print*. If you are a photographer, I think it is essential to eventually print your work. You can do it yourself or have someone else do it, you can create a fine digital print or something equally and differently wondrous like a silver gelatin or platinum print, and you can print at whatever size that makes you happy. The exercise of selecting a photograph for print, performing any necessary preparation, and seeing how it actually looks once off the screen can be extremely valuable.

While I love how the Internet has made it possible to disseminate images electronically, I do believe that there is something special about an *actual physical print*. Perhaps it is the presence of a fine print as an object. Perhaps it is the implication that you care enough about the photograph to actually create a physical print, or perhaps it is the fact that so many photographs just look different (some better, some worse) on paper rather than on a backlit LCD monitor or iPad screen. Whatever the reason, I find that nothing in the world of photography compares with seeing a wonderful print of a photograph (**Figure 1-4**).

Making a print of your photograph, and putting care into doing so, is putting a stake in the sand for your artwork, a way of saying "this is important" and "this is what I'm trying to say."

Advantages of Printing

Printing your work has numerous advantages over a digital-only existence for your photographs, such as:

- Creating a final art object that can be displayed, shared, or sold. You can also create exclusivity by limiting the number of prints you make of a particular image. For the fine art gallery world, physical prints are still a necessity.
- For many, a photograph is not a completed work of art until it is embodied in a physical print.
- Owning a physical object that provides security in case of loss of digital files without having to worry about backing up, file formats, and migrating to new media.
- Physical prints and portfolios are much more likely to be saved and treasured, held or donated to collections, or sold to collectors than digital files. This is vital also for any considering your legacy.

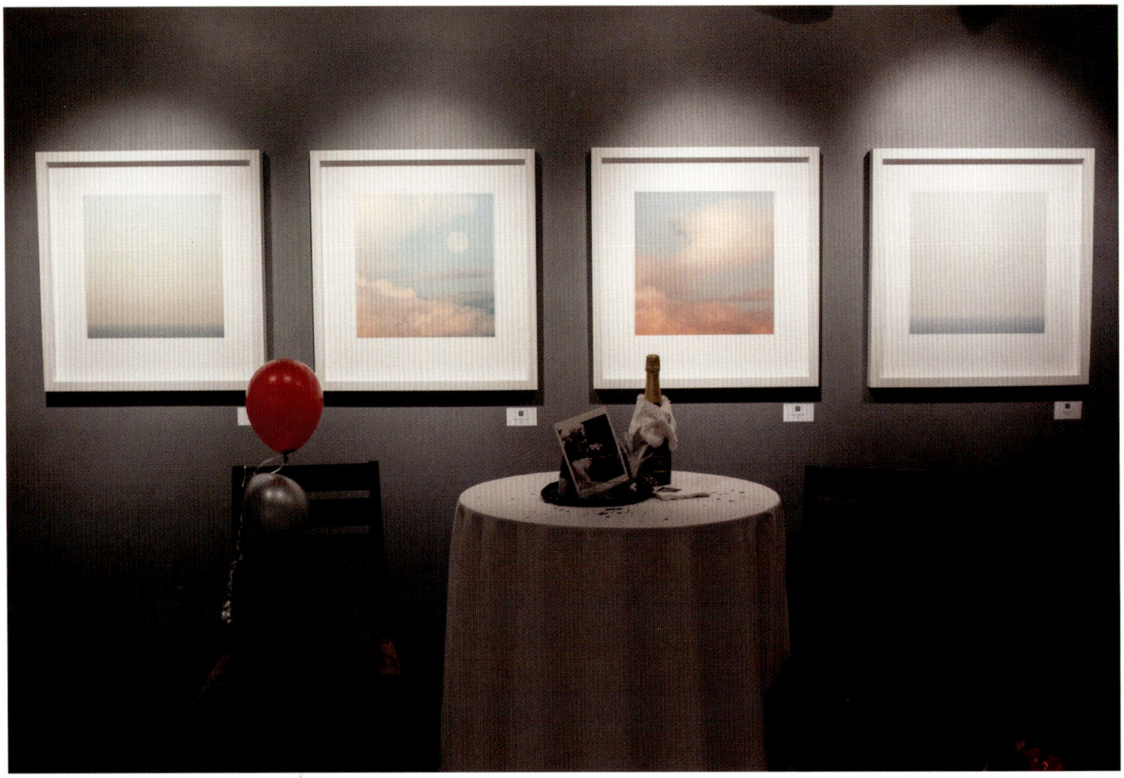

Figure 1-4: The author's photographs hanging on the wall at an opening. Courtesy 555 Gallery, Boston, MA

- Facilitating more careful study of the image by being firmly fixed in a physical object and also by providing more detail and substance. Digital images are often viewed very quickly, and a physical print is more often enjoyed at leisure.
- Allowing artists to more precisely control the final look and feel of their work without having to worry about what phone the viewer is using or whether their display is too bright or not calibrated. You can choose the precise paper that best matches your artistic intent. Printing gives you control over scale and lets you present your work large, two things that are almost impossible to accomplish with digital display using current technology.
- A carefully displayed print, with great presentation and lighting, can be a much more significant and powerful experience than viewing

the same image digitally. A fine print can be almost sensual, and careful viewing of a physical print is more likely to evoke an emotional response in the viewer.

- Prints subjectively look better. A backlit display has drama, but a print is more beautiful. Subtlety is much easier to achieve in a print than in a digital image.
- Learning to print your photographs, spending more time with them during editing, and learning what works best (and what doesn't work at all) will make you a better photographer as you internalize these lessons.
- Deciding what to print will help you learn to edit your photographs, something I find to be among the most difficult and elusive of skills for all of us creating photographs.
- Some photographs work far better in print than they do on the screen, and you won't know this about a particular photograph until you try.
- Zigging when everybody else is zagging. There are millions of photographers out there seeking attention on digital platforms, and one way to distinguish yourself from the others is to create fine prints of your photographs.

Printing in a Digital World

> *I view this flood of (digital) images as a type of visual communication, which I look at and use, but which in the context of art has no bigger meaning for me. The physical presence of a printed photograph still has an enormous influence on me. It allows me to access a photograph in a sensual, even physical way. I could imagine that this approach is going to become more important for other people as well. The photographs stored on my cell phone are not going to be printed, and they thus remain immaterial. They are fleeting—like falling stars…*
>
> —Thomas Weski

I am convinced that the future of photography on the whole will be digital distribution and display of imagery. Most people at some point in the future will enjoy photography that is displayed electronically as their entire photographic experience, whether it be advertising imagery, a wall-mounted monitor in their living room with rotating landscape images or family portraits, checking out galleries and websites on their tablet or cell phone or whatever device comes next, or the like.

I believe this despite the fact that modern printing methods, particularly for color, are as good if not better in almost every way than the printing methods that have come before, including superior color fidelity and range, longevity, and the ability to selectively control every aspect of the image. The advantages of electronic images, in terms of cost, availability, and flexibility, are just too overwhelming.

Fewer and fewer people are likely going to want to buy or display an actual physical print and hang it on their wall. Fewer and fewer, however, does not equate to zero. I absolutely believe there will remain a passion and desire for physical fine art prints, just like there is such an interest in many other types of art (or other displaced technologies such as LP records for music) that were long ago considered outdated.

The challenge, then, is to educate people on what a print can be and to make those prints as amazing as possible. If you want to defeat something that is cheaper and more convenient, you had better be offering something that is unequivocally better. Make your prints better than people have ever seen. Make a handmade book of your photographs that you've printed and bound yourself that tells a compelling story. Make your work so interesting or beautiful or important that people don't want to live without it. Do something great. That is our challenge as photographers and printers in this new world.

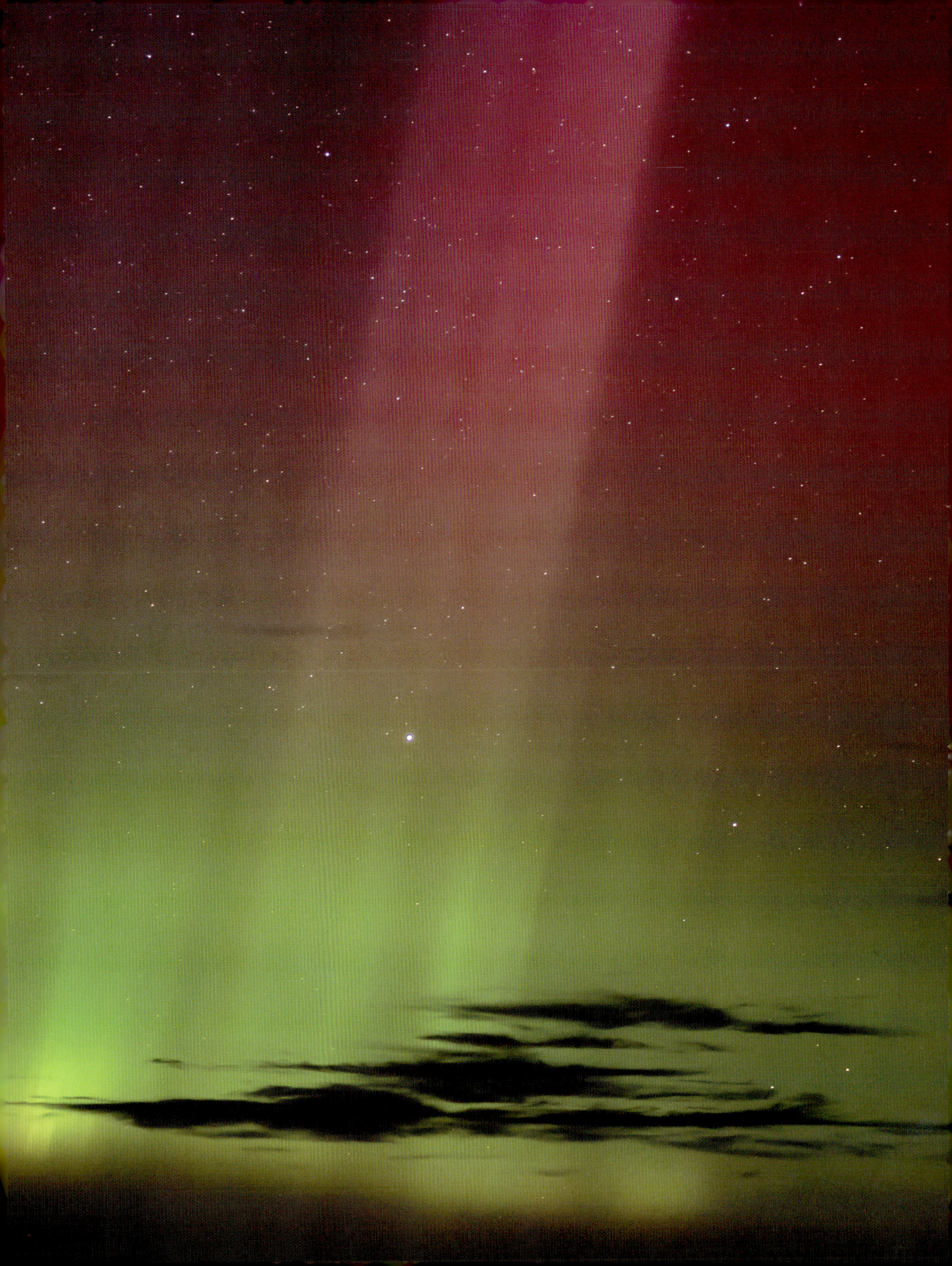

Printing Hardware and Environment

2

A digital printing system includes three basic hardware components. A computer, a display device, and of course a printer are necessary to make fine digital prints (**Figure 2-1**). Careful selection of each will allow you to have a more pleasant, productive, and consistent printing experience.

> *The thing that is ironic is that the new digital technologies, to my mind, are far and away the finest printing processes that have ever existed.... I find myself very, very excited to use this new technology that is going to destroy photography to make the best versions of it I've ever seen.*
>
> —Richard Benson

Choosing a Computer

There is no single best computer platform for digital printing, and both Apple and PC computers (i.e., computers based on the Microsoft Windows operating system) are widely and successfully used to create fine art digital prints. I used PC computers for many years and then switched to Apple computers a few years ago, and the difference was not as significant as I expected. There are a few pieces of specialized software that are only available on one platform or the other, but generally speaking, everything you need to do you can do on either platform.

Apple computers have the benefit of being the dominant player in the photography and printing world, which results in them frequently being the platform of choice for workshops, online instructional videos, and books like this one. It is easier to find helpful information when a Mac is your platform of choice as there is a large community of support already existing.

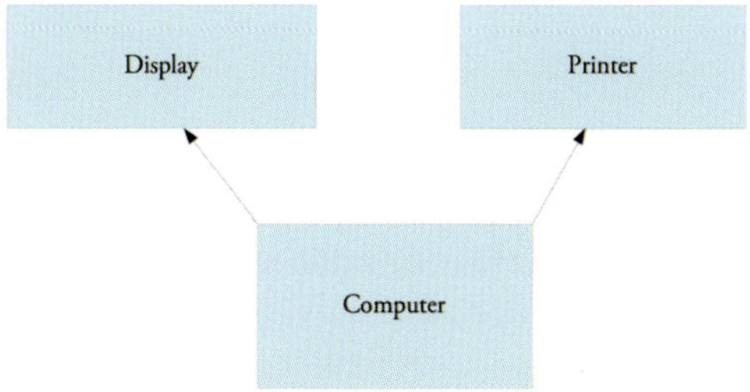

Figure 2-1: Basic hardware components of a digital printing system

Whichever platform you choose, you'll have a more productive experience if you have sufficient computing power to run your chosen software at an acceptable level of performance. Technology has improved enough that most computers would be fine for purposes of image editing and printing, but better specifications will allow you to work more quickly and efficiently.

From my experience, the area of computer specification that will have the most direct application to what you will do printing digitally is memory (RAM). If you are buying a new computer or upgrading an old one, investing in more memory will give you the best bang for your buck for printing. A faster hard drive (such as a solid-state drive, or SSD) can also have an enormous impact on performance relevant to printing because it can make opening, editing, and saving files quicker.

If you already have a computer, I suggest giving it a try for digital printing as it very well may be good enough in performance, leaving you free to invest in printers, paper, and ink. If you decide you need a new computer, I recommend focusing on the aspects noted above when deciding what computer to purchase.

Choosing a Display Device

A display device such as a computer monitor serves as your interface with your image during the editing process and therefore plays a vital role in the digital printing process. The display device should be able to convey to you as accurately and consistently as possible the information that exists in your image file. Ideally, the display would also be consistent in brightness and color from top-to-bottom and side-to-side.

Below are factors relevant to choosing a display for printing (besides price, of course):

- **Size** – I recommend a monitor with sufficient size (usually 24" or over) so that you can effectively and efficiently edit your images. Image editing benefits from a large screen so that you can display as many of your tools as possible along with a reasonably sized image.
- **Controls** – When calibrating a monitor, the best results are achieved if you can control color using the separate Red, Green, and Blue channels. Regardless of whether you can control color, I strongly recommend choosing a monitor that at least lets you control brightness and contrast.
- **Surface** – Matte displays are better than glossy displays for printing and other color-critical work. Glossy screens can give you false views of your image by showing colors as too saturated or too sharp. Reflections are a potential issue with glossier displays, too.

- **Gamut** – Wider gamut displays (i.e., those that can show something more like Adobe RGB color space rather than the sRGB color space) are great. They can potentially show a wider range of colors on a particular image and give you a better idea of what information is contained in your image, making it more likely you will put some of the wider gamut to paper (**Figure 2-2**). A modern digital camera can contain a wider range of colors than even a wide-gamut display can show, and it is advantageous to show as much of this range as possible when editing so that you do not accidentally throw subtleties of color away.

  While I would certainly rather have the benefits of a wide color gamut if given a choice, I do think the benefits are often a little overstated. You can do high-quality work using a display without a wide color gamut, and its benefits will be primarily limited to those images where you are actually taking advantage of that larger gamut. Wide-gamut displays are usually very good displays, however, so they will usually have other benefits as well. I recommend a wide-gamut display but it is not an absolute requirement.

- **Calibration** – Hardware-based calibration provides the best results in ensuring that your display accurately displays your image. Software calibration is an important additional step described in more detail in chapter 3, but the ability to calibrate the hardware itself is a significant advantage to the higher-end displays (such as those from Eizo and NEC) that provide this capability.

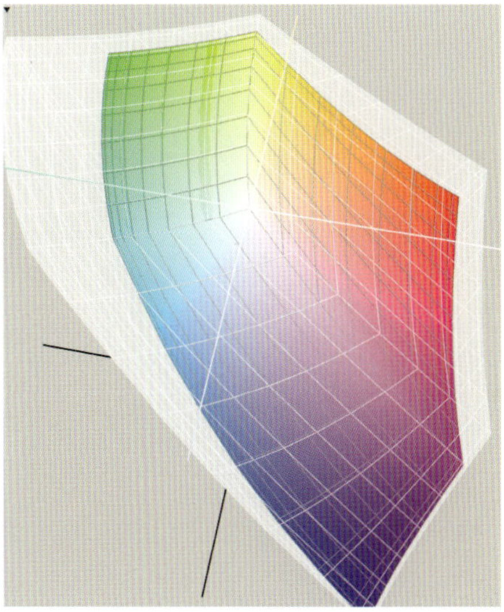

Figure 2-2: A comparison of the gamut of Adobe RGB (the grayscale) and sRGB (the color wireframe) to illustrate the difference between a wide-gamut display (near Adobe RGB) with the smaller gamut of a monitor with only an sRGB gamut. In this three-dimensional representation of Adobe RGB and sRGB color spaces, the gray wireframe area outside of the color wireframe area represents color beyond the capability of sRGB and within the capability of Adobe RGB.

LCD and (increasingly) LED displays dominate the market as of late 2016, and of the different types of these displays I recommend the In-Plane Switching (IPS) type since they are more consistent in color across the entire display.

If you are looking for a higher-quality LCD or LED display, I can confidently recommend the NEC Multisync PA series and Eizo monitors. In late 2016, you'll need to spend a little less than $1,000 or so to buy a high-quality, large, wide-gamut display. At the higher end, the Eizo displays are still considered the gold standard for color-critical work.

Avoid a laptop screen for your primary monitor. They just don't have the quality, controls, and size, even the new Apple Retina displays. You can use your laptop display but your path will be more difficult. Apple desktop displays are generally well regarded and I have had good experiences with them, but they are not high gamut and newer ones tend to be extremely glossy and thus harder to use for editing.

One possible solution for many people is to use a smaller higher-end display as a second display. By, say, adding an external NEC or Eizo monitor to your laptop or iMac, you can use the higher-quality display for image editing and printing while keeping your regular display for browsers, Photoshop tools and palettes, and anything else that does not require critical color. In this scenario you can buy a smaller (and thus less expensive) high-quality display since you do not need to fit all of your programs on it at once.

Whatever display type of monitor you decide to use, be sure to calibrate it using an external calibration device (as described in chapter 3). Calibration is important for color-critical work, and even the best displays can be hampered by improper calibration.

Choosing an Inkjet Printer

At its most basic level, an inkjet printer will receive as input an image file, translate the information in the image file to instructions for nozzles of the printer, and then use the nozzles to lay down tiny drops of colored ink that together form a continuous image when viewed by the human eye.

Looking at an inkjet print through a high-powered loupe or a microscope will reveal that the image is made up of thousands of tiny color dots. By carefully managing the size, placement, and color of the dots, the printer is able to create a print that appears as a continuous tone print when you view the print with your eyes.

At present, there are two primary methods to apply ink onto paper: thermal technology and piezoelectric technology. Thermal inkjet printers (such as those from Canon) work by using tiny heating elements to eject ink droplets from the nozzles. Piezoelectric printers (such as those from Epson) apply current to a Piezo element so that it flexes and forces a drop of ink out of the nozzle. Regardless of which method your printer uses, the material in this book should be applicable.

Making the Choice

Important things to consider when shopping for an inkjet printer are the type of ink it uses and its size, as well as its speed of printing and its feature sets.

Pigmented Inks vs. Dye-based Inks

The threshold choice for choosing an inkjet printer is whether you wish to have dye or pigment inks. Because of archival considerations, I strongly recommend a **pigment ink printer**. Early dye printers were able to produce more colors and deeper blacks than pigment printers, but pigment-based printing technology has advanced to almost eliminate that gap. Pigment-based printers remain the best choice for long-lasting prints and are generally accepted as superior to dyes in terms of archival characteristics.

Printer Size

The actual physical size of your printer, and the maximum size of print that you can make, are defined by the printer's **carriage width**. Carriage width is the maximum width of paper that a printer can handle (printers with large carriage widths are often called large format printers) (**Figure 2-3**). The maximum width essentially defines the short end of your maximum print size.

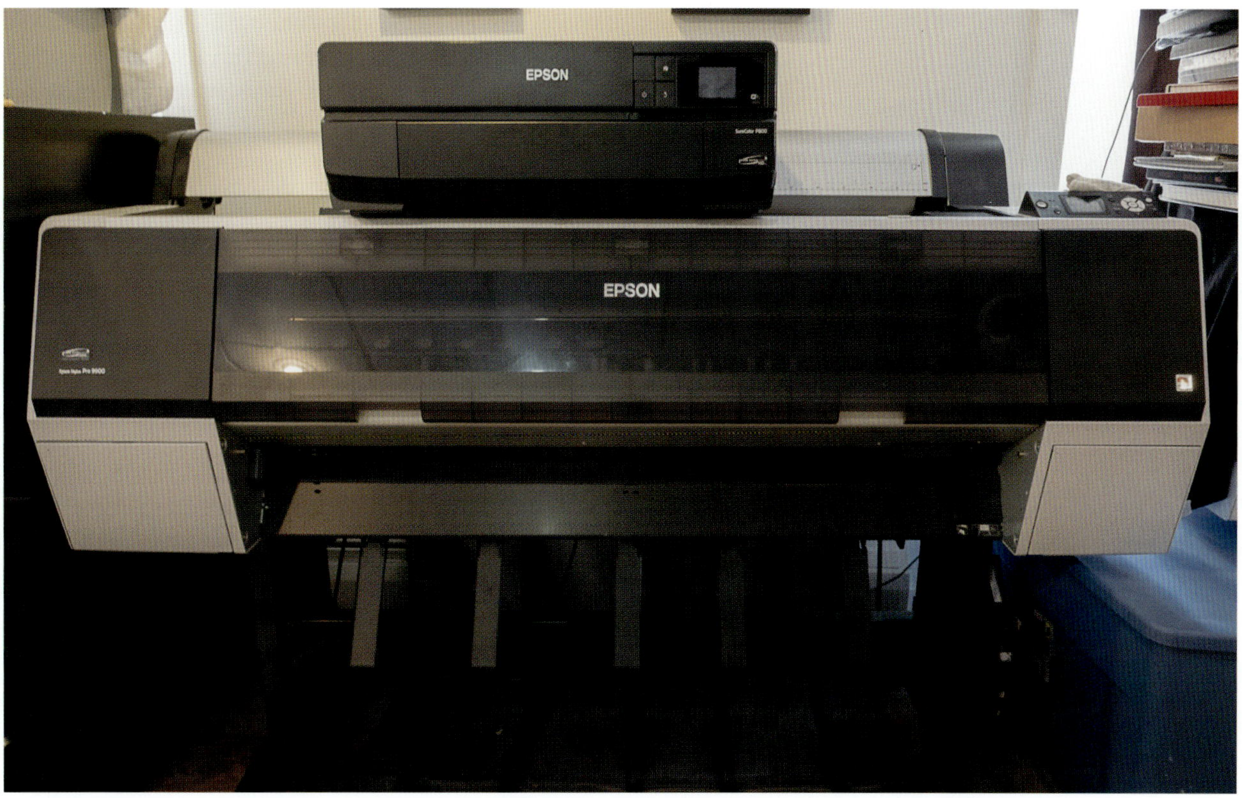

Figure 2-3: My 17" Epson P800 compared to my 44" Epson 9900. Please note that these are not in their usual positions!

A 13" printer, for example, can print on paper that is 13" on the short end, such as the commonly available 13" × 19" paper. Most inkjet printers suitable for fine art printing are 13", 17", 24", 36", 44", or 60" in carriage width.

Generally speaking, as the carriage width goes up, the physical size and cost of the printer also goes up, while the cost of the ink (the operating cost) goes down. The ink cost goes down as larger printers can take larger cartridges that hold more ink and that are less expensive on a per-milliliter basis. Accordingly, I recommend getting the largest printer you can afford given your space constraints and maximum anticipated print size.

For many photographers, the 13" and 17" printers are the sweet spot for home printing with reasonably sized ink cartridges and without taking up massive amounts of space. Many also find that once they start printing they would like to print larger than they originally anticipated, so buying larger than you need at first can prevent you from having to upgrade. If space or funds are limited, you can use a smaller printer for your own prints and send out your larger prints to a print shop.

Larger printers are often built to a higher quality level and with tighter tolerances than smaller printers, as they are intended for a more professional audience. I have also found that with my Epson printers, my larger 44" printers need to be used more frequently than my 17" printers to avoid clogs. These larger printers are meant for heavy usage, so if you are going to print infrequently, you may run into maintenance problems with wide-format printers.

Many larger printers can handle roll paper in addition to sheet paper. Roll paper has its own handling issues but can be more cost-effective and can also provide longer, more panoramic printing options. Most, but not all, papers only have cut-sheets available up to 17" × 22", so for larger prints roll papers are often a necessity.

Choosing Your Printer

Both Epson and Canon provide many different high-quality pigment-based inkjet printers geared toward the fine art market and are suitable for creating fine digital prints. Even the last generation or two of Epson and Canon printers provide great image quality, because technology has reached a point of sufficiency for fine art printing. The newest printers can provide improvements in image quality, printing speed, and feature sets, but having the absolute latest technology is not a requirement.

Considerations of which printer to get will depend on feature sets, printer carriage width, and familiarity with the brand. I use Epson printers ranging from 13" to 44" carriage width and I've been generally happy with them. I can vouch for the great image quality with Epson printers and the quality of service available under their warranties. I have limited experience with the Canon printers, but from the samples I have seen and from my conversations with other fine art printers, I believe that inkjet printers from either manufacturer can create wonderful fine art prints.

Printing Environment

You should give consideration to your printing environment. Attention given to ambient light and environmental conditions in your studio can pay big dividends in terms of more efficient workflow and reduced printer issues.

Ambient Light

Ambient light in your digital darkroom can wreak havoc with the accurate display of color and contrast on display devices. Below are a few tips for controlling the lighting in your editing environment to make it consistent and appropriate. You need not follow every suggestion, of course, but each should provide some degree of improvement in your digital darkroom. Tips include:

- Avoid having any windows or bright lighting in your editing environment. Extraneous light changes the apparent contrast and color of the screen and can also add distracting reflections. If you have a window, consider a blackout curtain or even a piece of cardboard to block the light while you are editing.
- Use a monitor hood to at least partially shield your screen from extraneous light (**Figure 2-4** on the next page). Higher-end monitors can include a hood, but third-party hoods are also available for popular monitors.
- For better control of color, consider painting nearby walls a neutral gray, changing your desktop background to a neutral gray, and removing colored items from the area. I've even seen many recommend wearing neutral gray clothing, too, so that the color from your shirt does not reflect onto the screen. These sort of recommendations are definitely in the realm of diminishing returns, and I will be the first to admit that I have not implemented this group of recommendations myself, but these are steps you can try if you are having issues.

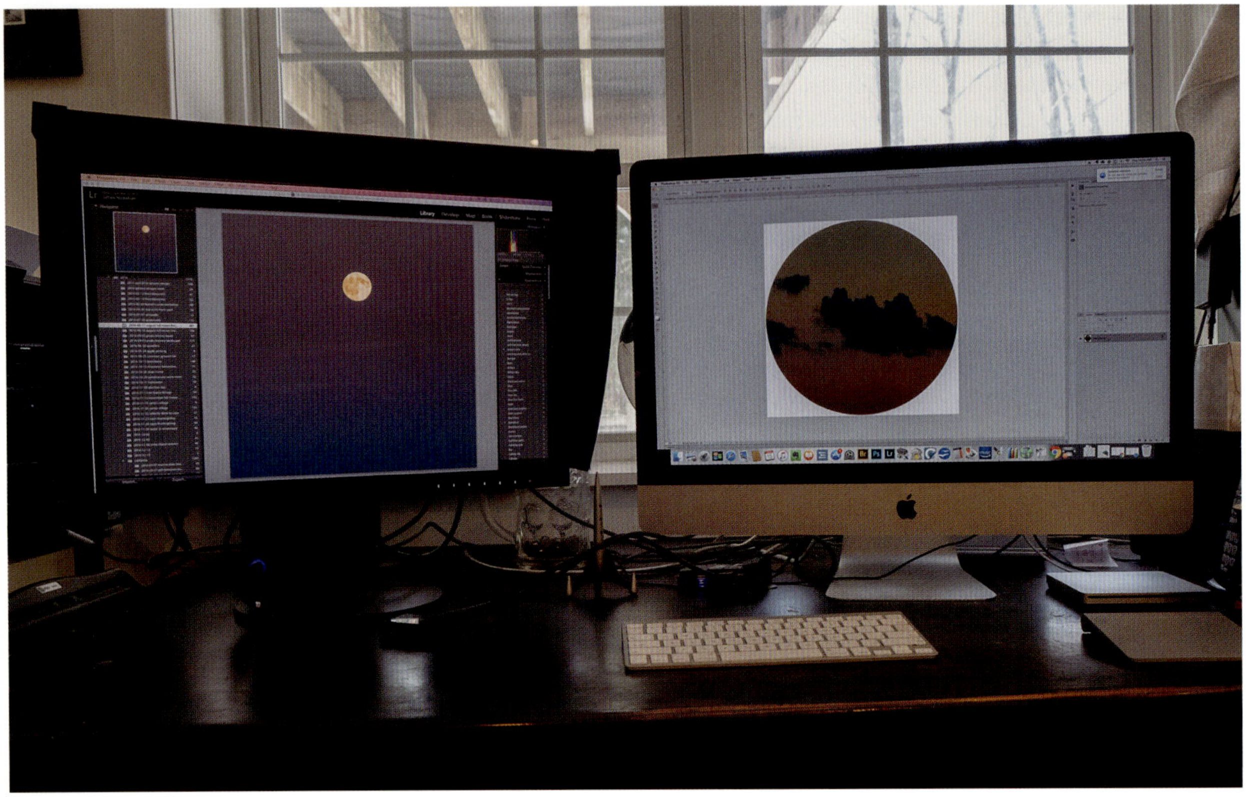

FIGURE 2-4: My Eizo CG2420 second display connected to my iMac. I normally use the Eizo for image editing and the iMac for everything else. The Eizo monitor has its own hood and it is very effective with this screen. My old Apple Thunderbolt monitor had an extremely glossy screen and a hood was essential (and still not enough). And if you insist on putting your screens in front of a bright window like I do, I recommend covering the window with curtains or a piece of cardboard while editing to control the lighting.

Environmental Conditions

Sometimes we take modern inkjet printers for granted because of their competence and reliability. Modern printers, though, are incredibly complex machines, particularly with respect to the printheads. Each printer and its printheads are designed for a particular range of environmental conditions, including temperature and humidity. For most home printing situations, humidity is more likely to be an issue as temperatures in most houses and studios stay within a relatively tight range. Epson printers have a recommended humidity range of 40% to 60% for optimal operation. Dryer conditions can result in the printheads not staying moist enough to produce consistent ink droplets with their Piezo technology.

Does this really matter in the real world? In short, yes. My personal experience, and that of many others, is that operating one of these printers outside this range (particularly at lower levels of humidity) can result in much more frequent clogs and, as a result, wastage of ink from nozzle cleanings and wastage of both ink and paper from ruined prints.

I recommend purchasing a hygrometer (**Figure 2-5**) to measure the humidity in your print studio. They are pretty inexpensive and can provide you with insight as to the actual conditions in your studio and how it compares to the optimal range.

Over time, once you know your humidity level, you can decide what approach to take. My printing studio is in a basement on the coast of Maine and the humidity as I type this is about 47% and within specs, which is typical for the winter with my setup. In the summer, however, the humidity skyrockets (I do not have air conditioning) and I use a dehumidifier all summer and fall to keep the humidity to acceptable levels. Many people in other parts of the country end up instead buying a humidifier to raise the humidity in their printing area, which I would recommend doing if your environment dictates this.

Canon printers can accommodate a wider operating environment according to their specifications (the Canon imagePROGRAF Pro-100 is rated at 10% to 80% relative humidity) and thus appears to be less susceptible to varying humidity because of its different head technology. I have found, though, that papers often curl more in higher humidity, and that paper curl can cause loading or other problems on any printer, so humidity control is desirable even for printers with wider operating ranges.

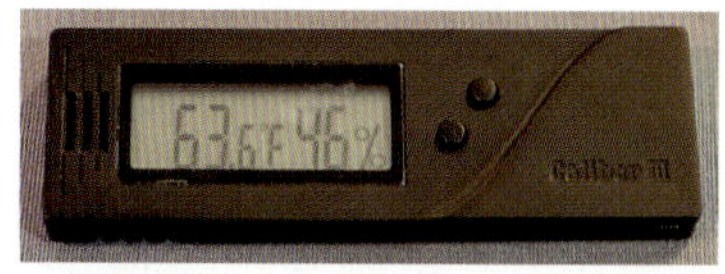

FIGURE 2-5: A Caliber III hygrometer that measures temperature and humidity, a little worse for wear but still functional. A new one should cost less than $30.

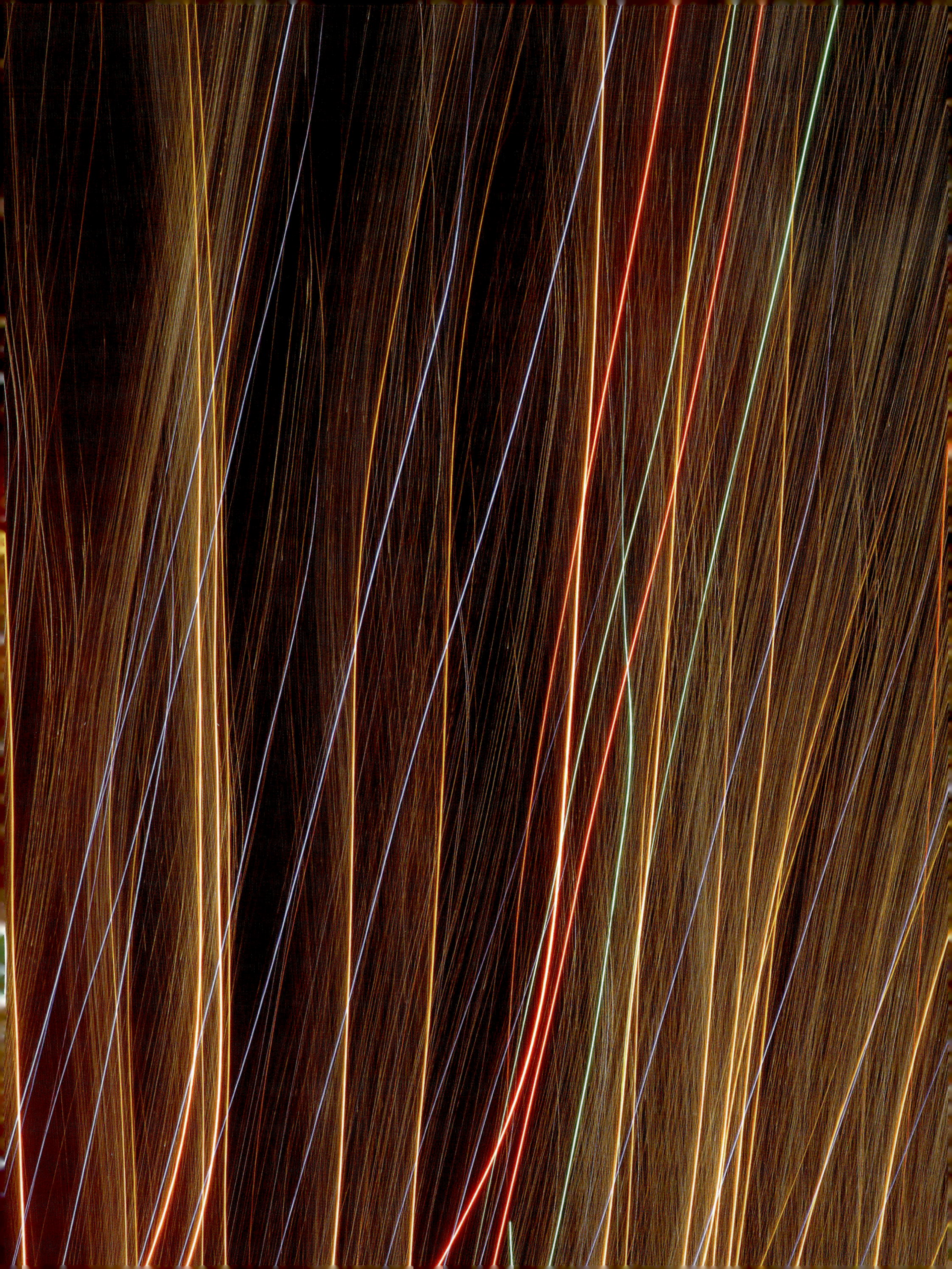

Color Management for Printing

3

Color management for digital imaging and printing remains a source of consternation for many photographers. Proper color management is essential for creating fine art digital prints that consistently match your creative vision. In the interest of brevity and clarity we will only address the aspects of color management that I see as important to typical digital printing and will not try to address every detail of color theory.

Introduction to Color Management

> *It is important that we know where we come from, because if you do not know where you come from, then you don't know where you are, and if you don't know where you are, then you don't know where you are going. And if you don't know where you are going, you're probably going wrong.*
> —Terry Pratchett

In order to understand color management and to apply it to our goal of making fine art prints, we need to discuss the basics of the system and how the components interact with each other.

The Color Management System

What is color management? It is a system for maintaining a consistent and accurate appearance of colors across a wide range of devices. To do so, we have to convert (more than once) between one set of color capabilities to another. For digital printing, the most essential devices are the display device you use to edit and the printer itself **(Figure 3-1)**.

The two primary goals of color management for printing are:

- **Accurate displays** – Ensuring that your display accurately displays the colors of your image as embedded in your file so that your edits are based on a true representation of your image

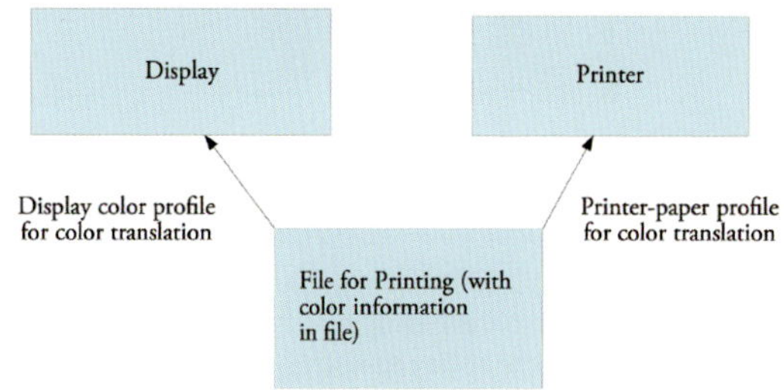

Figure 3-1: A very high level description of the color management system. A display profile will translate the information from your image file to instructions used to present the image on your display. The printer-paper profile will normally be used to translate the image file to instructions suitable for your printer. Errors on *either* of these translations can result in your print not matching your intentions.

- **Accurate lay down of inks** – Directing the printer to accurately lay down inks on paper to achieve colors that match those of the file as closely as possible

The combination of these two goals will give you more consistency in printing, will reduce the number of wasted prints, and will also facilitate working with someone else who is printing your work. Failure to properly account for *both* of these goals will result in a final print that does not match your artistic intent for the image.

Color Models and Spaces

Color models are a way of turning colors into numbers using a mathematical formula. The RGB color model used by digital cameras and monitors, for example, allows for the color in a particular pixel of an image file to be represented as a combination of red, green, and blue values (the three additive primary colors).

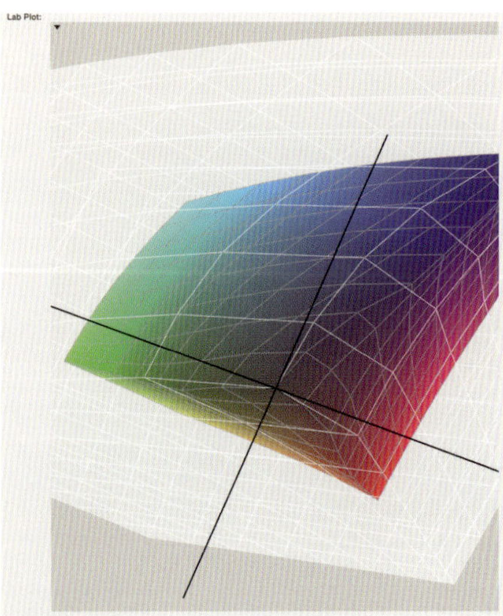

Figure 3-2: The ColorSync Utility on the Mac provides the ability to visually compare two color spaces. This is a comparison of the ProPhoto RGB color space (the gray wireframe) with the sRGB color space (the color wireframe). The ProPhoto RGB color space is quite large and includes many nonvisible colors, and it dwarfs the relatively small sRGB color space in terms of the attainable colors.

A specific implementation of a color model is called a **color space**, which is a computer model of possible colors. Color spaces are about the *theoretical* colors that are possible, not what is actually in an image file. A larger color space, such as ProPhoto RGB, could include more theoretical colors than a small color space such as sRGB (**Figure 3-2**). At its highest level, a color space can define how far the reds can go, how far the blues can go, how far the red-blues can go, and so on.

Working color spaces such as Adobe RGB (1998), ProPhoto RGB, and sRGB are color spaces particularly suited to editing tasks (you might also see these described as *editing spaces*).

A file should have a particular working space associated with it (i.e., the file is "tagged" with the color space) so that programs such as Photoshop know how to translate the data in the file for other purposes. In other words, it is hard to translate something if you don't know what language from which you are starting.

The color space that is associated with an image file tells us what colors could theoretically be in the image, but it does not tell us what particular colors are represented in the file in reality.

Color Profiles

Color profiles are often considered to be a type of color space, which is true to some extent, but it is more useful to think of them as a description of how a particular device deviates from a pure color space. A color profile is a computer file that contains information about *how a particular device renders colors*. The color profile effectively *translates* color information to its related device. So, for a given input such as the contents of an image file, the color profile describes how the device will take that input and translate those into the actual colors the device will reproduce.

The following types of device-specific color profiles are relevant for fine art printing:

- Display profiles
- Printer-paper profiles

When you are looking at a display device that is displaying a photograph or other digital file, Photoshop or Lightroom will use whatever **display profile** you have selected to convert the information in the file to colors that are displayed on your monitor or other display. The display profile can be thought of as a *translation* of colors from the file and into instructions to physically show colors on your display. A **custom display profile** is created by using the characteristics of your particular display device and is thus more accurate than a generic display profile.

If your file has colors that you desire, then a proper **printer-paper profile** will give you as close to your desired colors as that printer and paper combination can produce to that ideal. The printer-paper profile converts the colors in the image file into a language usable by the printer and designed to look correct on that particular paper with that particular ink and printer (as depicted in figure 3.1). If you use the wrong printer-paper profile, the colors in the print will not accurately portray the colors in the file itself.

Diagnosing Color Management Issues

We can use what we've learned so far about color management to diagnose many of the most common issues that arise in printing. Referring back to Figure 3-1, there are two essential translations of color that occur when editing a file for print: the translation between the file and your display

Principles of Printing #2:
You Have to Know Where You Are to Know Where to Go

Consistent and accurate color management is essential to successful printing. If you are not looking at an accurate version of your file, your edits will give you results in the print that you don't expect.

(managed by the display color profile) and the translation between your file and the printer (managed by the printer-paper profile). If your prints are coming out with colors that do not match your display, the problem could be in either (or both!) of those translations. My first step in diagnosing these issues is to try to narrow it down to one of these translations, if possible.

In other words, for you to get prints that replicate the colors you are expecting, both the display color profile and the printer-paper profile need to be correct. If you edit using a display with an incorrect profile, your file will have the wrong color and it will print with the wrong color; if you print a file with correct color but use an incorrect printer-paper profile, the print will come out with the wrong color.

Incorrect Display Profile

If your display profile is incorrect, then the image displayed on the screen will also be incorrect and will not accurately show you what is in your file (i.e., it will not be translated correctly). If, for example, your display color profile is too warm in color, then any image displayed on the monitor will not be displayed accurately and will instead appear warmer than it really is.

To test for an incorrect display profile, try having that file printed with an outside print service or just with a friend who has a printing system that is working properly. If you send that file to someone else to print for you and the print comes out looking differently than your display (and hopefully close to what your printer is giving you), the problem is likely that your display profile is giving you a false view of your file.

For example, if the print comes out cooler than you expect (with not enough warmth), your display profile is likely giving you a false indication of warmth, encouraging you to edit the image to take out some of the warmth (when you are really making it too cool).

If the print you receive back looks like your display but does not match what your printer is giving you, the problem is more likely in the printing half of the color management situation, such as a printer-paper profile or incorrect setting, as discussed below.

Incorrect Printer-Paper Profile

If you use a different printer-paper profile or printer and get different results, something in the printing part of the chain is likely the culprit, such as the printer-paper profile or incorrect settings. After double-checking your settings, one way of testing this is to use the profile of a similar paper just to see if the results are better. If so, something is likely wrong with your printer-paper profile. Make sure you are using the one that is actually for your printer (a mistake I've made many times!), and consider having a new custom printer-paper profile made if you decide that what you have is not working well.

Calibrating and Profiling Your Display

Creating and setting a profile for your display is one of the most important steps in color management for printing. When someone is having trouble getting accurate color in their prints, I've found that this is most likely a big part of the problem.

Generic vs. Color Profiles

A *generic* color display profile is one provided by the device manufacturer and describes the typical behavior of an average device. A *custom* display profile is a color profile generated for your actual monitor and is thus very likely more accurate than a generic profile.

If you are on a Mac, you can go to System Preferences > Displays > Color, and you will see what color profile is currently selected for your system (**Figure 3-3**). You can select various profiles from the list on the left to see the effect of different profiles. Generic profiles are profiles such as sRGB, color LCD, Apple Cinema Display, and the like.

Almost everyone will recommend that you need to create a custom display profile for your monitor for best results, and I agree. While most high-quality monitors have reasonably good color out-of-the-box, and drifting of colors (a problem with CRT monitors) is largely a thing of the past, I still *strongly* recommend that you calibrate and profile your display. The tools for doing so are relatively inexpensive, and the payoff in peace of mind, consistency, and accuracy is worth it.

Figure 3-3: The display profile on my iMac is a custom display profile called "iMac_D65-aug31-2014.icc." It's a bit old (I put information such as the target color and date in the name), but this is not the monitor I use for accurate color (though it still looks pretty good).

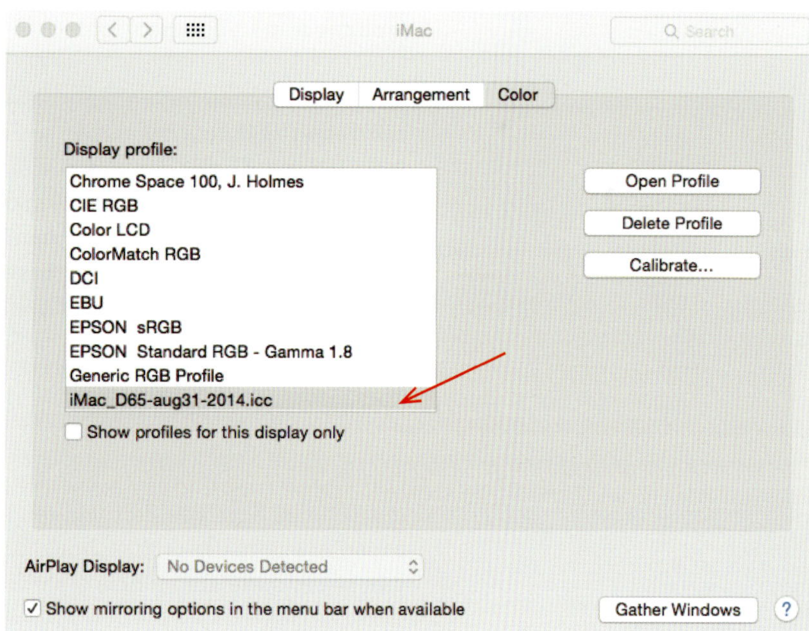

Profiling vs. Calibrating

Profiling your display means creating a monitor color profile that describes how the colors actually are displayed on your monitor. *Calibrating* your display means actually adjusting your display to a set of standards, such as the luminance or brightness of the monitor white, the color of the monitor white, the gamma value (tone response curve of the display system), or the luminance of the monitor black. Typically when you are calibrating your monitor a profile is also created as part of that process. Monitors that can perform hardware calibration are the best choice, but profiling to create a display profile custom to your monitor can and should be done with any monitor.

When calibrating a display, you need to calibrate to a standard. I recommend D65 (for the color of the monitor white, or the target white point) and a gamma of 2.2 with a luminance of the same brightness at which you are going to be working (about 80–100 Cd/m2).

Monitor Calibration Recommendation

- D65 (for the color of the monitor's white, or the target white point)
- A gamma of 2.2 with a luminance of the same brightness at which you are going to be working (about 80–100 Cd/m2)

Profiling and Calibration Tools

Many wide-gamut, high-quality displays come with their own profiling and calibration tools, and if you have one of those monitors you simply use those tools. If you are using a monitor without included tools, I recommend a calibration package like the ColorMunki or any of the many Spyder products. Many of these products are less than $200 and can produce very good results for monitor profiling. Software-based calibration is inadequate for color-critical work, so hardware-based solutions such as these are necessary.

Printer-Paper Color Profiles

Printer-paper color profiles, also known as printer profiles, are designed to characterize how a printer will render various colors on a specific type of paper. A well-made profile should accurately describe (in a language computers can understand) how a particular color in an image file will be rendered in ink on a piece of paper. Because each type of paper is different in color and how it handles ink, these profiles are specific to a combination of *printer* and *paper*. If you accidentally use a profile for a different type of printer than the one you have, the results will not be good.

Most paper manufacturers provide free printer-paper profiles for their papers and popular photo printers, and my experience is that, generally speaking, the profiles now have become consistently pretty good. This is particularly true for the wide-format professional printers as the manufacturing tolerances of these more expensive printers tends to be tighter, making generic profiles more accurate. These profiles will usually have useful instructions, as well, because they inform you of the settings they used to make them as well as where to install them.

My recommendation is that if you are a beginner printer, or if you are not having any problems, then simply use the printer-paper profiles provided by the manufacturer. Profiles typically come with instructions and recommended settings and, unless you have a specific reason to do otherwise, I suggest following their recommendations on settings.

Custom profiles for your specific printer and your choice of paper are also available. Since your printer might deviate from the "average" printer of its type, a custom profile can provide more accuracy for your machine. There are companies that provide this type of service for a fee, and if you use just a few papers, that route may be worth considering. You can make your own profiles using printer-calibration hardware, too. I can recommend the ColorMunki Photo package as a relatively low-cost option for doing so.

Printer-paper color profiles live in the following folders:

- Mac OS: Library > ColorSync > Profiles
- Windows 7, Vista, or XP: Windows > system32 > spool > drivers > color

Once you've installed your printer-paper profile, you may have to exit out of Lightroom or Photoshop for the new profile to be visible and selectable.

Print Mastery: Finding the Profiles Folder on the Mac

Apple has made it much more difficult to find the proper Profiles folder in which to place any download. The Library folder is now hidden by default. To reveal it so that you can go there, select Go on the menu bar while in Finder and, while the list of locations is visible, hold down the Alt-Option key. This will reveal the Library folder for as long as you hold the key down, so you can then select and go to the Library folder to install your profile.

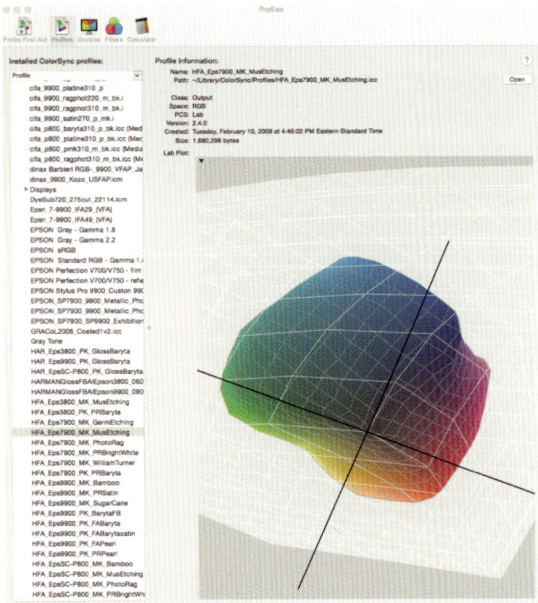

FIGURE 3-4: The 3D representation of the printer-paper profile for Hahnemühle Museum Etching on the Epson 7900 and 9900 printer is shown. This is a model of all of the colors that can be printed on the printer-paper combination. If your file to be printed has a color beyond this range, it is considered out-of-gamut.

Gamut and Rendering Intent

Gamut is a term that is used to describe the portion of a color space that can be reproduced by a particular device. Gamut is often represented by a three-dimensional plot of hue, saturation, and luminance so that the gamut can be better visualized.

If an image is "out-of-gamut" in a particular color space, then that means that there are some colors in the image file that extend beyond the gamut and thus cannot be perfectly reproduced on that device (**Figure 3-4**). In this case, when the image is translated into the too-small color space, a *rendering intent* is used to translate the out-of-gamut image into the available space within the color space.

For fine art printing, I recommend that you choose between **Relative Colorimetric Intent** and **Perceptual Intent** as the best choices for accurate colors for inkjet prints. No rendering intent will be the best for every image, so *soft-proofing* how a rendering intent will work on each particular image is recommended (we'll talk more about this in chapter 7). Rendering intents are only relevant, of course, when there are out-of-gamut colors, so the rendering intent does not matter on images that are entirely within gamut of your printer-paper combination.

Print Mastery: Conversions of Color Space via a CMM

All files should have an attached color space, which is the particular color model being used for the data in the file. Whenever an image is converted from one color space to another (from a *source* space to a *destination* space), a **Color Management Module (CMM)** is used to map, or translate, the colors of the image from the first color space to those of the second color space. One example of this is that whenever an image is sent to a device like your monitor or the printer, the color space of the image must be converted to that of the device.

Sometimes when an image is converted by the CMM from the source space to the destination space, there are colors from the source space that are not reproducible in the destination space (i.e., they are out-of-gamut). When this happens, the CMM will use a rendering intent to determine how to handle those colors that are not reproducible.

I recommend that you always include an embedded color space with an image. Often during the saving process Photoshop will ask you whether or not the color space should be embedded, and you should agree to the embedded color space.

In Photoshop, you can convert from one color space to another using Edit > Convert to Profile rather than Assign Profile. Convert to Profile does a much better job of preserving the appearance of an image, and I only recommend using Assign Profile (at least on an image that already has a profile) if you really know what you are doing and have a specific reason for doing so. One common reason to use Assign Profile is when you have a file that is untagged with a color space and you wish to assign a color profile to it.

Relative Colorimetric Intent vs. Perceptual Intent

Relative Colorimetric Intent preserves the colors that are in-gamut and clips any out-of-gamut colors to the closest reproducible value. If, for example, there were saturated reds that were out-of-gamut, the Relative Colorimetric Intent would represent accurately all the reds that were in-gamut and all of the reds that were too saturated to be in-gamut would instead be represented as the most saturated red available. I find that most often this is the best intent for photographic images, particularly those with natural colors.

Perceptual Intent will compress the full color gamut of an image to fit into the new color space so that colorimetric accuracy is preserved. Perceptual Intent is concerned with preserving the *relationships* between different colors, and in doing so all of the colors in the image may end up shifting. Perceptual Intent is also commonly the best intent for printing images, especially for images where the relationship between colors, particularly saturated ones, predominates. With high-saturation colors, Perceptual Intent can preserve gradations in those areas whereas Relative Colorimetric treats them all as maximum in saturation.

Print Mastery: Other Rendering Intents

In Photoshop you will see two other rendering intents available beyond Relative Colorimetric and Perceptual. I do not recommend using them for printing fine art images, but it is useful to know a bit about them.

Absolute Colorimetric Rendering Intent is based on the Relative Colorimetric Intent but uses the media white-point to calculate its data, and is mostly used for preparing images for reproduction on printing presses and the like.

Saturation Intent is similar to Perceptual Intent but maintains the saturation of colors at the expense of hue and lightness of colors. Saturation Intent will not commonly be the best option for digital printing of photographs, but is often the best choice for prints of graphs or charts where maximum saturation is desired.

Setting Up Color Management

Setting up color management in your application can be tedious, but it is important for the color management process. You should only need to do it once, but occasionally I'll find that an upgrade will reset settings to their defaults, so I recommend checking after implementing any upgrades to make sure nothing has changed.

Photoshop

To set up color management in Photoshop, select Edit > Color Settings, which will open up a panel where you can set Photoshop's color settings (**Figure 3-5**).

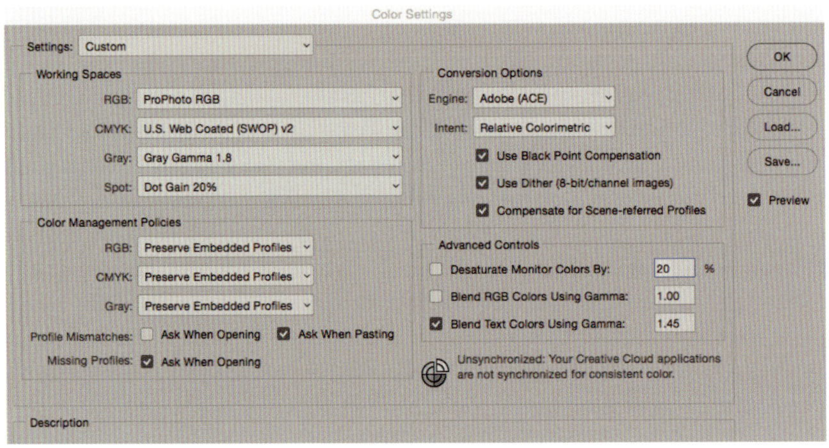

FIGURE 3-5: Photoshop's Color Settings panel

Here is what I recommend and why for the settings that I change from the default (I'll only list the ones that matter for our printing purposes here):

- **Working Spaces, RGB** – ProPhoto RGB (Adobe RGB as a second choice). I recommend ProPhoto RGB because its large size encompasses the capacity of current digital cameras (and most likely on future models as well), but Adobe RGB is not a bad choice.
- **Working Spaces, Gray** – Set at 1.8 if using ProPhoto RGB, 2.2 if using AdobeRGB. Here we should choose a grayscale working space that has a gamma that matches the color space for any color images we are working with as they may be converted to black-and-white. Therefore, your decision for RGB impacts what you should choose here.
- **Color Management Policies** – Confirm that Preserve Embedded Profiles is selected for all cases. This allows any file you open to keep its color space when you work with it in Photoshop, unless you choose otherwise. I recommend only changing color spaces using the Convert to Profile command in the Edit menu.
- **Profile Mismatches** – Deselect the Ask When Opening box. Since we are preserving the embedded profiles and not converting to the working space, this will just give you annoying warning messages when you open files with different color spaces. For Ask When Pasting,

I prefer to check that box so that I get a reminder if I'm pasting in something to another file that is the wrong color space.

- **Missing Profiles, Ask When Opening** – We want a profile associated with every image file, so a warning and an option to assign one is preferred.

Lightroom

Basic color management is handled seamlessly by design and without user input in Lightroom, which I consider a very good thing. Where color management does come into play is when you leave Lightroom, either by exporting the file or by opening a file in an external editor such as Photoshop.
One way of leaving Lightroom is to use as an external editor such as Photoshop, so if you do this, go to Lightroom > Preferences > External Editing to manage what sort of file you will send to your external editor (**Figure 3-6**). I recommend choosing TIFF (or Photoshop/PSD, if you prefer), ProPhoto RGB Color Space, and a Bit Depth of 16-bits. I also recommend setting a resolution of 360 ppi (if you are using Epson, 300 otherwise).

When exporting a file out of Lightroom, the appropriate settings will depend on usage. If you are exporting a full-size file for additional editing in Photoshop, I again recommend selecting ProPhoto RGB color space and 16-bits at the time of export.

Recommendations for Leaving Lightroom

When leaving Lightroom to open an image in another editing application, I suggest going to Lightroom > Preferences > External Editing. Then choose the following settings:

- File Format: TIFF (or Photoshop/PSD, if you prefer)
- Color Space: ProPhoto RGB Color Space
- Bit Depth: 16-bits
- Resolution: 360 ppi (if you are using Epson, 300 otherwise)
- Compression: None

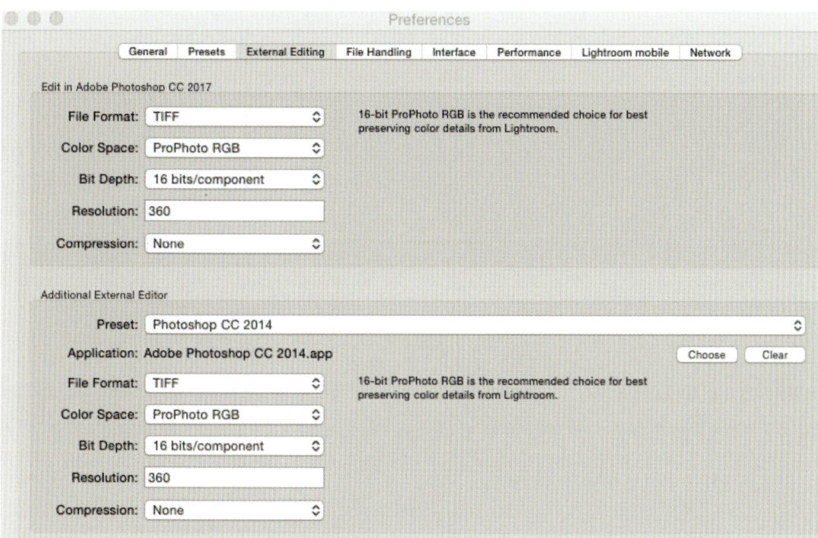

Figure 3-6: This panel shows my recommended choices for color settings in Lightroom. Most importantly, I recommend ProPhoto RGB for Color Space and 16-bit Bit Depth.

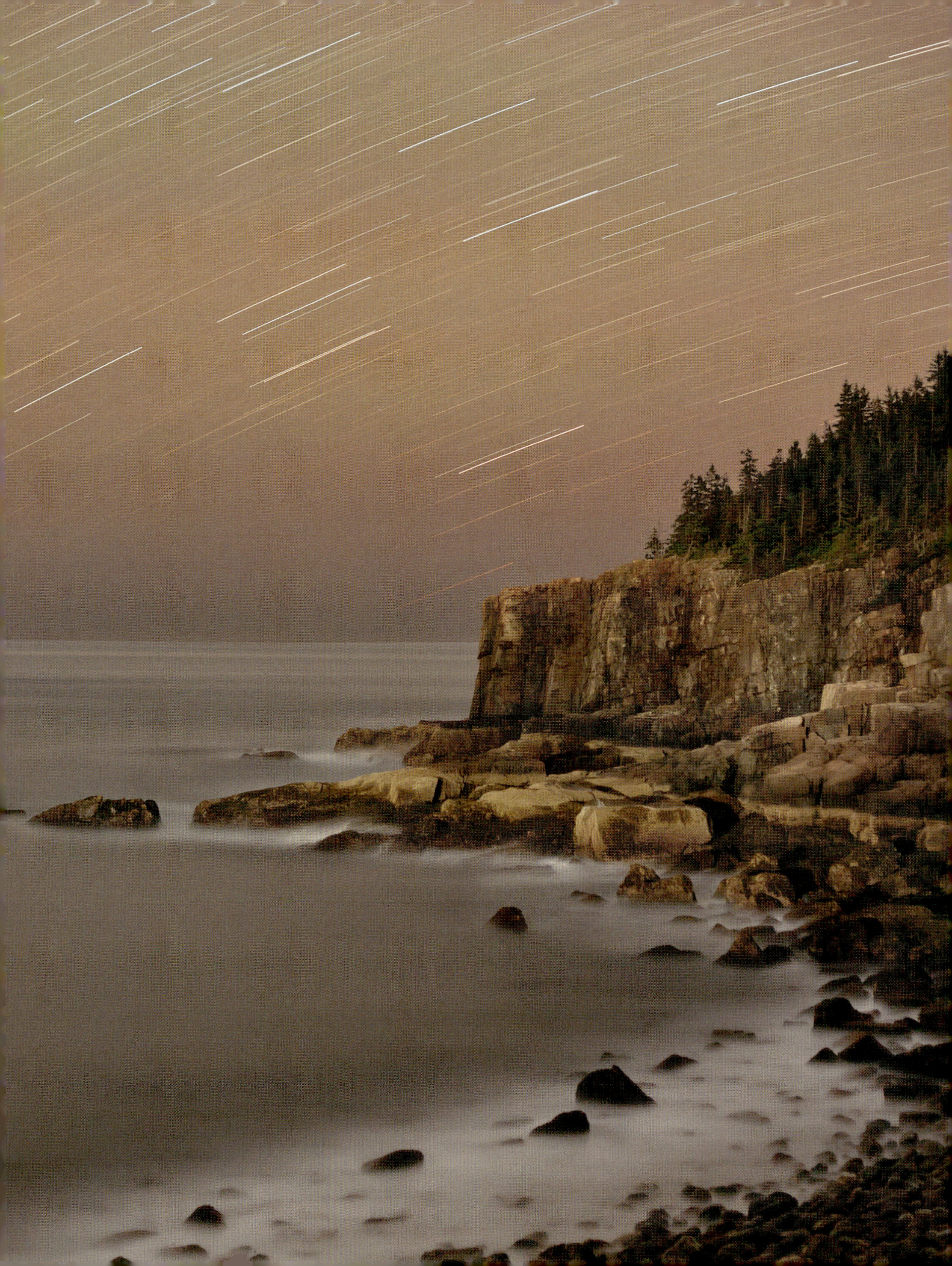

Optimizing Your Workflow from Capture to Print

4

Optimizing your workflow from capture to print can provide benefits in efficiency of time and materials, peace of mind in knowing that all of your changes are safely preserved and are also reversible, and improved results in your final prints.

In this chapter we'll discuss how to make sure you are capturing the highest technical quality photograph possible, how best to retain the valuable information in your file using nondestructive editing techniques, and best practices in file management and backup.

Optimizing Your Photographic Capture

> *They say my prints are bad, darling they should see my negatives.*
>
> —Lisette Model

Optimizing your photographic capture is an important first step in creating great prints. The quality of your original file can play a significant role in the achievable quality of the final output. Simply put, the better your original file, the better your final print can be.

You can certainly create great prints from less-than-great photographic captures, so please do not take this as an absolute requirement. Improving your capture will potentially give you a higher image quality with less effort, but with sufficient work and appropriate creative choices we can successfully print even flawed photographic captures. Throughout this book I will provide techniques for improving your final print, regardless of whether the original was technically perfect or technically challenged.

Even if we can achieve a successful print with a flawed file, it is still advantageous to start off from the best possible starting point, as you can save significant amounts of time in the digital darkroom. When you start with a superior image file you won't need to spend time fixing problems and instead can focus on the creative side of printing. If you plan on printing large, all of your problems will be magnified, making it even more beneficial to get it right in camera.

Principles of Printing #3: Optimize Your Starting Position

The better the quality of your original file, the better off you will be with your final print. Faults in your original capture can result in problems in your final print or in significant time spent trying to overcome those faults during image editing and printing.

Printing photographs you've already taken is not relevant for this section, as "it is what it is" in terms of technical quality of these existing photographs, so the suggestions here only apply going forward. I certainly recognize that many shooting conditions—and styles—don't lend themselves to practicing all of these techniques, but the more fully you embrace the goal of improving your photographic capture, the better off you will be in the digital darkroom and in achieving great prints.

Let's look at a simple example of a properly exposed photograph and one that is severely underexposed by about 3 stops (**Figure 4-1**). The underexposed one on the right can be recovered in the digital darkroom by increasing the exposure the appropriate amount, but by doing so any noise in the image will be dramatically increased (and a clean image will have noise introduced). We can use noise reduction to try to remove this increased noise, but we'll have the trade-off of reduced sharpness and less detail. With some effort we can ameliorate the problem, but only at the cost of time and some loss in image quality that may show up in print.

So how do you optimize the technical quality of your original capture? There is no one answer as to how you should best operate your camera to maximize image quality, and much will depend on the conditions. There are many, many books and tutorials out there on this topic, so I will just summarize here the primary things I recommend to maximize image quality for

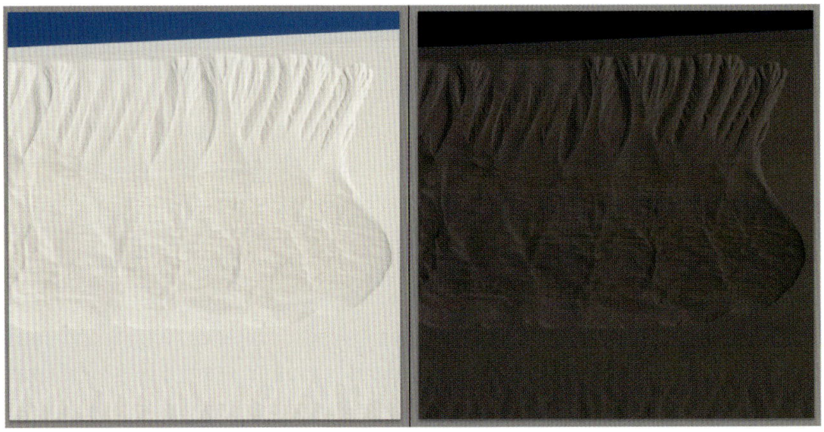

FIGURE 4-1: Two versions of a photograph from White Sands National Monument in New Mexico. The version on the left has a typical exposure and the one on the right is 3 stops darker. On the darker version, the data is there and can be recovered, but only at the loss of image quality.

printing based on issues I've seen with printing my own photographs and those of my clients.

To maximize image quality for print with your original capture I recommend:

- **Shoot in RAW** – This is my strongest image quality recommendation: it provides the most options in the digital darkroom for making changes to the image without affecting image quality. Files shot in JPEG format can allow for fewer edits before breaking down and don't allow for good recovery of highlights or shadows.
- **Improve sharpness** – A lack of sharpness is difficult to correct for print, so a sharper original image can make a big difference. Use a tripod if your type of shooting allows (street photographers, feel free to ignore this one). And since you are using a tripod, you should also use mirror lockup to minimize or eliminate any camera shake. If you can't use a tripod, use image stabilization to help prevent camera shake, or faster shutter speeds to help reduce camera shake as well as subject motion blur.
- **Low ISO** – Use the lowest ISO possible (down to your camera's native ISO) to minimize noise. To be more precise, use the lowest ISO possible consistent with your needed aperture and shutter speed settings.
- **Gear matters** – Larger sensor sizes will give better image quality, all else being equal. Using better lenses, and using any lens under its optimal conditions, will also give you better results. Technology is leveling out, but newer cameras generally improve on the image quality of their predecessors. (If you don't have fancy gear, don't worry! Great prints are still possible, just a little more challenging.)
- **Increase exposure** – Get as much exposure as possible without blowing your highlights. If you have to bring up your exposure for print, you will be at a heightened risk of introducing noise or other artifacts. (See sidebar, "Expose to the Right.") Shooting RAW will help prevent losing highlights due to over-exposure, though it can still happen.
- **Printing big** – Everything matters much more if you want to print big, so doing everything you can to maximize image quality is even more essential.

Print Mastery: Expose to the Right

Expose to the Right (ETTR) is the theory that the captured image should be as bright as possible without burning out any highlights. The *right* nomenclature refers to how things look on a histogram (which we'll cover next), as an image that is brighter will have more data toward the right side of the histogram than on the left side. The reason for this is simple—the way data is stored digitally allows for more data to be stored in the highlight areas of the file rather than the shadow areas of the file (and will thus have a better signal-to-noise ratio). A proper ETTR exposure will provide a cleaner, less noisy file than a similar darker exposure of the same scene when both exposures are adjusted to the same point. In other words, it is better to darken an exposure in post-processing rather than to brighten one.

Optimizing Your File

Whenever we leave the RAW file format, we'll want to make sure that we preserve image quality as much as possible, so understanding more about file formats and how to handle them throughout the imaging process is important.

Understanding Your File

To know how best to manage your file, you must have a good understanding of how files work and how they contain data.

Image Data and the Histogram

A digital image file we use for printing consists of a variety of types of data. An image file has a height and width in pixels (e.g., an image may be 4000 pixels in width and 3000 pixels in height), forming a grid of pixels. The bulk of the data in an image file is a description of what image information is contained at each pixel, essentially an identification of a color or a shade of gray.

The **histogram** is an essential tool both in the field and in the digital darkroom for understanding the nature of the data in an image file. The histogram is a visual representation of the data in your image based on a statistical analysis of where values fall between pure white and pure black. It is a graph of luminance levels of your image and therefore gives a very good representation of the type of data that makes up your image.

A histogram skewed to the left indicates a darker image and with more information toward the shadows, whereas a histogram skewed to the right indicates a brighter image with more information in midtones and highlights (**Figure 4-2**).

As you edit your image in Lightroom or Photoshop, you can see how the histogram itself changes. Pushing up your exposure, for example, pushes the data in your histogram to the right. You can play with this yourself by taking an image and moving the exposure up and down to see how the histogram reacts. As you continue to gain experience, the histogram will become an essential editing tool.

One crucial use of the histogram when shooting or editing is determining when a limit is reached either with shadows or highlights. When the histogram reaches the right edge, that means pixels are starting to become blown out as pure highlights; when the histogram reaches the left edge, pixels are starting to become pure black (**Figure 4-3**). The histogram can thus serve as an excellent way of making sure your editing doesn't unintentionally lose data either on the highlight or shadow end.

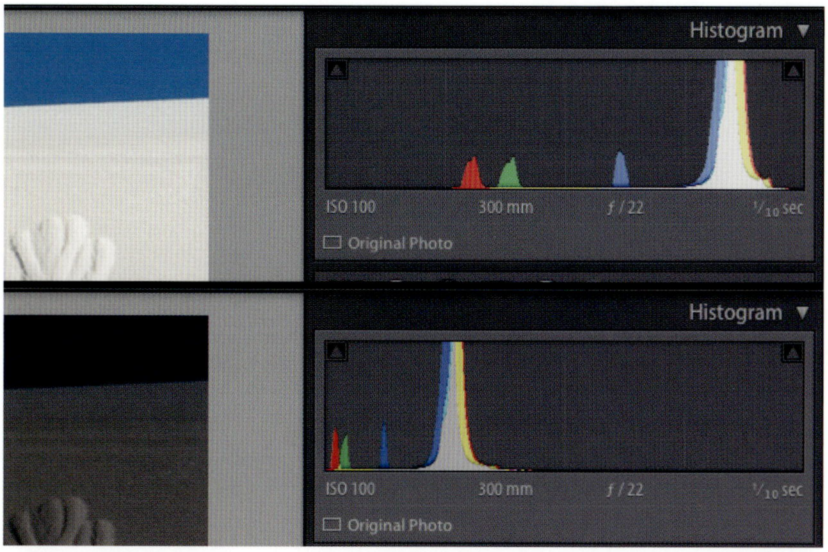

Figure 4-2: The histograms from the photograph versions from Figure 4-1 show the differences in exposure, with the brighter image having the histogram skewed to the right and the darker image having the histogram skewed to the left

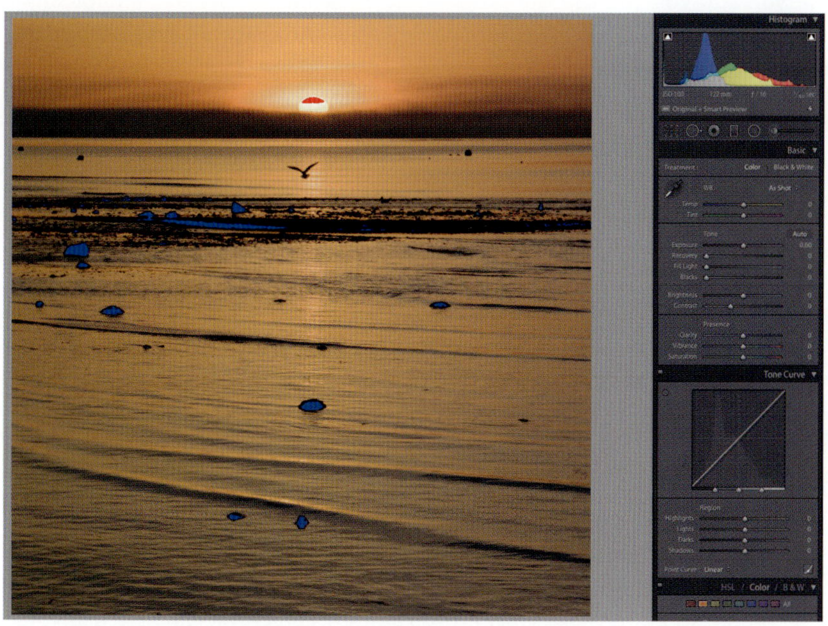

Figure 4-3: The histogram reveals that small areas of this image are pure black (the spike on the left end of the histogram) and blown out in the highlights (the small bump on the right side of the histogram). In Lightroom, you can click on the triangles in the upper corners of the histogram and Lightroom will superimpose color in those pure black/blown-out areas, blue for pure blacks and red for blown-out highlights. Sometimes having pure blacks or blown-out areas are not a bad thing. In this image I don't mind that the rocks are pure black, for example.

Dynamic Range

Dynamic range is a number representing the ratio of the maximum and minimum levels of light that can be recorded in a single image, and it represents the maximum range of the image from the deepest shadows approaching pure black to the brightest highlights without burning out. Dynamic range is camera and sensor dependent, and generally speaking, cameras with larger sensors and newer technology will be able to capture a larger dynamic range. Not every image requires a large dynamic range, but the larger the dynamic range, the more *potential* range of tones you can capture in a single image.

File Formats

Now that you understand some of how files work, let's talk about the differences between file formats and which ones to use.

Recommended File Format

If you are shooting RAW files, I recommend keeping your image in RAW format as long as possible. If you are using Lightroom, this is taken care of for you and you can use the program normally. If you are using Photoshop, I recommend staying in Adobe Camera Raw (ACR) for as long as possible before moving into Photoshop proper.

So what file format should you use for editing an image for print? TIFF or PSD, 16-bit, ProPhoto RGB. If you'd like more details on why I recommend these options, please continue reading the next Print Mastery sidebar.

Don't Use JPEG Files for Editing

The most common file formats used for image files (besides RAW files) are Photoshop files (.psd), TIFF files (.tif), and JPEG files (.jpg). Photoshop files and TIFF files use *lossless* compression to keep file sizes reasonable, which means that data is not lost upon saving any edits.

JPEG files are very popular because they are relatively small in size and are readable by almost any piece of software. This convenience comes at a price, however, because they use *lossy* compression to manage files sizes, and therefore, some data is lost during editing. Each time you save a JPEG file

Print Mastery: TIFF or Photoshop/PSD Files?

For most purposes TIFF files and Photoshop files are interchangeable and both will work great as an image format. They are similarly sized and almost every application out there used for image editing can work with either one. If you do use TIFF files, I recommend using Lempel-Ziv-Welch (LZW) as the compression method seems to be universally accepted. If you are using Photoshop files, I recommend using Maximize Compatibility to make the files more accessible to other applications such as Lightroom (but at the cost of some increase in size).

Both formats also allow for saving Photoshop layers. TIFF files with layers have an option for layer compression, also, and for that I recommend using the run-length encoding (RLE) option if given that choice. Because of Adobe's recent switch to cloud-based subscriptions, many have considered moving to TIFF files in the interest of preserving capability for a future where they may not be using Adobe products, because Adobe does not own that format. I suspect both will be equally compatible in the end.

it re-compresses the data and you lose some amount of data. The amount of data lost will depend on your compression settings and the nature of the image. As long as your intention for a JPEG file doesn't involve editing (e.g., a file for your website or to share digitally with others), JPEGs can be a very good choice.

It may take multiple saves of a JPEG file to see a visible loss in quality, but it will happen eventually. Moreover, JPEG files are generally limited to 8-bit rather than 16-bit, providing additional downsides that will be explained shortly. Therefore, I highly recommend using TIFF or PSD files for all image editing.

Even in situations where you are working with a JPEG original file, such as if you are printing images from an iPhone or a point-and-shoot camera, I recommend resaving the file as a TIFF or Photoshop file to prevent further damage from any additional modifications and saves of the file. Switching formats doesn't recover information that is already lost, but you can at least stop the bleeding.

Using an editor like Lightroom with JPEG files can be successful because Lightroom doesn't modify the original file, so you can avoid those damaging compressions every time you change the image.

Choosing a Color Space for Your File

There are a few times during the image editing process where you might need to select a color space for your file. If you are shooting RAW (as I would recommend), you need to choose a color space whenever you export out of your RAW processing program (e.g., exporting out of Lightroom into Photoshop or finishing with Adobe Camera Raw and "opening" your file for further editing). If you are shooting JPEGs or TIFFs in your camera, you also must set a color space in your camera's settings.

I would rank the common color spaces in the following order, with the most desirable for editing and printing listed first:

1. **ProPhoto RGB** – I consider this to be the most desirable color space to use.since it is significantly larger than even Adobe RGB, and many modern cameras produce colors that cannot be described with the Adobe RGB color space. ProPhoto RGB can hold all of the colors that a camera can capture and all the colors that a printer can print, and other commonly available color spaces such as Adobe RGB do not. If you are using the latest cameras and are using Adobe RGB, you are likely throwing away some of your color information for some shots. ProPhoto RGB does require you, practically speaking, to use 16-bit files because the space is so large that banding or posterization can result when using 8-bit images.

   ProPhoto exceeds the gamut of human vision and is pretty future-proof, so your images will be able to take advantages of future advances in printer technology.

2. **Adobe RGB** – Even though it has limitations, Adobe RGB is still a good general-purpose color space that is a reasonably good fit with modern cameras, monitors, and printers. However, there are some colors that can be captured or printed that will be outside the gamut of Adobe RGB and that will thus result in loss of data.

3. **sRGB** – As the lowest common denominator and the color space of the Internet, sRGB is ubiquitous. It is much smaller than Adobe RGB and will definitely result in lost colors with some images, particularly in the reds. Many online printers require you to send them files in this format. It is also the best choice for mailing small images to people or for using on your website, since everybody's system can handle this type of file.

As we discussed in chapter 3, I recommend setting ProPhoto RGB as your default color working space in Photoshop. Lightroom uses this internally by default and it cannot be changed (not that you should want to), but you should choose ProPhoto RGB in the export dialog (where you can control things) if exporting for future editing.

Now, you likely cannot see all the colors that ProPhoto RGB gives you since your monitor has a relatively limited color space (most good monitors are in the ballpark of Adobe RGB). Much like the 16-bit vs. 8-bit discussion, though using the larger color space gives you more headroom or insurance to make changes.

Print Mastery: Switching Between Color Spaces

When switching between color spaces, unless you have specific reasons for doing so, always choose to convert from one color space to another rather than *assigning* a new color space from within Photoshop. If you do not do this, your colors will change, often dramatically and unpleasantly.

If your file is already in, say, the Adobe RGB color space, there is no benefit to converting it to ProPhoto RGB, even if it started out that way. Like with bit depth, once the data is lost, it is lost, and the choice is most relevant for the beginning of the editing process. John Paul Caponigro describes this in terms of a bucket of water—if you pour a full large bucket into a small bucket it will overflow, and if you pour the small bucket back into the larger one that overflowed water is lost. You should use smaller spaces only for specific output purposes, like web images or images being sent to some online labs.

8-Bit or 16-Bit?

For image editing, I strongly recommend working with 16-bit files rather than 8-bit files. The bit depth determines the number of possible color values for each pixel in the image. A particular color channel of an 8-bit file can represent one of 256 color combinations whereas a particular color channel of a 16-bit file can represent one of 65,536 combinations, resulting in an improvement of many orders of magnitude of descriptive ability. Much of this extra capacity is not actually used for most cameras—which may only capture 14 bits or 12 bits of data—but even those levels are much improved over 8-bit files.

Why does it matter if you keep your images in 16-bit format and have this extra data? Simply put, 16-bit files are more robust and are better able to handle manipulation. You can perform more manipulation on a 16-bit file before you see degradation, and if you are performing heavy manipulations, whatever degradation you do get is reduced. You can see this effect in, for example, the loss of smooth gradations of tone or color. Black-and-white images are even more dependent on smooth gradations of tone than are color images; therefore, using 16-bit files for that type of image is even more critical.

If you are using RAW files and want to use 16-bit files, it's easy—they are 16-bit by nature, and using Adobe Camera Raw or Lightroom keeps them in 16-bit mode during the entire editing process. If you are using Photoshop, I recommend using 16-bit files throughout the entire editing process.

Print Mastery: Why Would You Use 8-Bit Files?

Eight-bit files have the advantage of being half of the size as 16-bit and require less storage space and less processing power. Using modern computing platforms with plenty of processing power and with hard drive storage being relatively inexpensive, the case for using 8-bit files is not very compelling.

It is certainly the case that for many images, particularly ones that are not manipulated to a large extent, the tone and color is smooth enough with an 8-bit file that the differences will not be evident in print. There are many images where that is not the case, and it is beneficial to have the extra manipulation capability as a sort of insurance policy. Since you never know which images you may want to later edit or convert to black-and-white, it is prudent to use 16-bit files.

Another reason to use 8-bit files is because you have to do so. There are still plug-ins, features, and applications that require 8-bit files. In these cases, I recommend performing as many edits as possible before you get to the point where you have to convert to 8-bit.

If your image started as an 8-bit file, there is no benefit to switching to a 16-bit file. Once that additional data is lost, it is lost and it doesn't matter if you then put it in a larger container. So if your file has been 8-bit at sometime in its existence, you can safely leave it as an 8-bit file throughout the editing process.

Once you are finished editing (including resizing and performing output sharpening), you can usually convert to 8-bit without visible loss. The benefits of 16-bit are mostly in the editing and manipulation processes rather than the printing process, at least with current technology, as I will discuss in more detail in chapter 7.

Print Mastery: Very Large Files

If you are working with very large files (more than 2 gigabytes), such as when you are printing scans from medium or large format or large digital files with many layers, then file format can come into play again. Regular Photoshop files only work up until 2 gigabytes whereas TIFF files can usually be used with files up to 4 gigabytes in size. Photoshop also has a Large Document Format option to save .psb files rather than .psd, and that has a very large limit.

To enable the Large Document Format in Photoshop, select the appropriate box for .psb files found in Preferences > File Handling.

Nondesctructive Editing – "Do No Harm"

Principles of Printing #4: Do No Harm

Don't do anything to your file that you can't reverse in some way.

An important part of a good printing workflow is to never do anything that will permanently damage your original file (what I like to call "Do No Harm"). What we are trying to accomplish is retaining the ability to undo any changes you make to your file, even if doing so requires going back to your original file. Nondestructive editing preserves the ability to reverse any changes you've made.

For a RAW file this is easy, since RAW editors are designed not to jeopardize or change the image content of your original file. So, to *do no harm* to your file in Lightroom, just use Lightroom normally. Lightroom is designed is to be a parametric editor—which means that no changes are made until you export the file in some way, so that changes aren't "baked-in" until you leave Lightroom; perfect for nondestructive editing.

To *do no harm* to your file in Photoshop, I recommend working with layers. You can use duplicate layers for pixel-level edits (such as removing dust spots or noise reduction) and adjustment layers for most other types of changes. This gives you the ability to go back and undo any changes by editing or removing layers, making everything you do reversible. I also recommend doing your layer edits on a second copy of the file from your original file so that you don't accidentally edit my original file.

File Management and Backup

A detailed discussion of file management and backup is beyond our scope here, but there are some aspects that are relevant to preparing and printing images. In this section, you'll find a few suggestions for file management and backup in Lightroom and Photoshop.

Backup

I strongly recommend, of course, that everyone have a robust backup solution for valuable image files, whatever that solution may be.

Briefly, here is what I do to protect my data:

- All my data is stored on a RAID (redundant array of independent disks) drive in my studio, which automatically and seamlessly backs up each piece of data to two separate hard drives.

- I frequently back up my entire RAID to an external hard drive that I also keep in my studio.
- I less frequently take that backup external hard drive to a safe deposit box and swap it out with another identical one, and then I refresh the backup on that drive once I return to my studio. By doing this I always have one reasonably fresh off-storage copy of everything.
- For my best and final images, I upload them to cloud storage. I'd love to use cloud storage for everything, but the files are just too numerous and large for that to work well with current solutions.

No backup system is invulnerable, but a similar system may work for your data as well.

Lightroom

If you are printing with Lightroom, the changes you make to an image, including any changes you make after soft-proofing to correct an image for print, are stored in what is called *metadata* in your Lightroom catalog. Changes to the metadata are automatically stored in the Lightroom catalog, and most users also have at least an occasional backup of the catalog, giving some backup protection. But this still leaves you subject to loss of data if your *catalog* becomes corrupted or lost.

What I recommend doing is to have Lightroom automatically save metadata into the XMP file for each image, too. This provides an additional level of backup in case of catalog loss or corruption, and it allows other applications (such as Adobe Bridge or Camera Raw) to access this information as well. To change Lightroom away from its default to start doing this, simply go to Lightroom > Catalog Settings > Metadata on the Mac, or Edit > Catalog Settings > Metadata on the PC, select the Metadata tab, and then make sure the box is checked in front of "Automatically write changes into XMP," as well as the "Include Develop Settings" box preceding it (**Figure 4-4**). Now, your data will be automatically saved in two locations rather than just one.

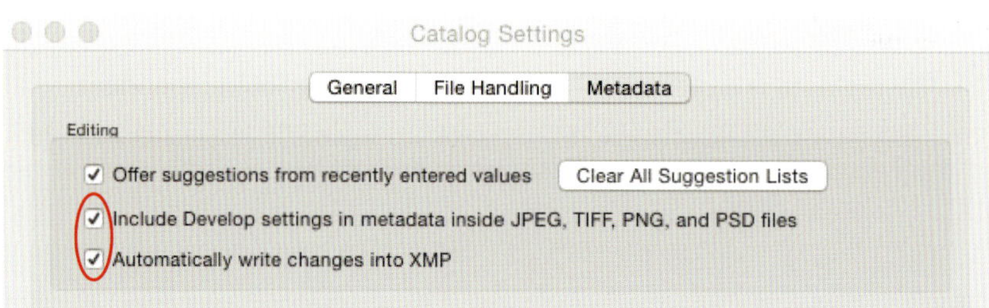

Figure 4-4: Selecting the second and third boxes in the Editing panel of the Metadata section will give you extra backup protection in cases of having a lost or corrupted Lightroom catalog

Just to be safe, after I first make this change, I select all my images in the Library Module, go to the Metadata menu, and select Save Metadata to Files, to make sure that every image in my catalog that has already been edited has metadata saved to the XMP file as well.

A Portfolio, or Final Selects, Catalog

My workshop students often ask me how I organize and format my own files. I'm always a bit hesitant to respond because I use a pretty idiosyncratic setup, but one part of it that many of them have adopted is having a separate set of "final" files for my best images. For my best images, I convert the master Photoshop file with all of its possible layers to a final, flattened TIFF file. I also rename this final file with my selected title for the photograph and store all of these files in one discrete folder. As a final step I'll import the final image into a separate Lightroom catalog that contains only final images.

For me, this setup provides a number of advantages. Having all of my final images in one place lets me easily duplicate select ones to take with me on a trip or for uploading to remote storage. I also love being able to see all my final images in one place without being distracted by the also-rans. I use this database of final images to make JPEGs to use for my website or marketing, to send to galleries, and to easily review when I'm looking for something specific.

Another benefit is additional future proofing. I end up with a Photoshop file with layers and a flattened TIFF, one with maximum information in layers and another with maximum compatibility as a flattened TIFF.

Something similar could be done by using just one Lightroom catalog and keywords or collections, but I like the cleanness of this solution.

Photoshop

If you are editing and printing from Photoshop, I recommend working with a master file. A master file is a file (either TIFF or PSD) that contains all of your edits to a particular file, with as many of those edits as possible in layers for maximum reversibility and preservation of image quality.

Once you have a master file, I recommend making a *separate file* for each size print you will make from this master. Simply flatten the master file, resize as appropriate, perform output sharpening, check for any issues, and then save this file as a print version of the file to keep it separate from your master file.

The most important thing is to not to lose your master file, which this method accomplishes, and a separate resized and saved print file can also save you effort in the future. A saved print file also makes consistent prints from various printing sessions easier to accomplish.

For practical purposes, the way I keep track of things is my master files have names that end with "-mst" and my print files have names that end with "-prt-size," such as "-prt-8×8" or "-prt-16×16." The nomenclature doesn't matter as long as you are consistent and as long as it makes sense to you. I often save my print files as TIFFs to further distinguish them from my master PSD files, and as a very optional additional level of backup just in case one format of the two becomes unavailable in the far future.

For a portfolio image where I might create prints in different sizes, I will end up with quite a few files (**Figure 4-5**). I retain the original file, a master Photoshop file, and then whatever print files I've created. Here they are depicted adjacent for ease of viewing, but I store the files in various locations (print files in one place, master files in another, and so on).

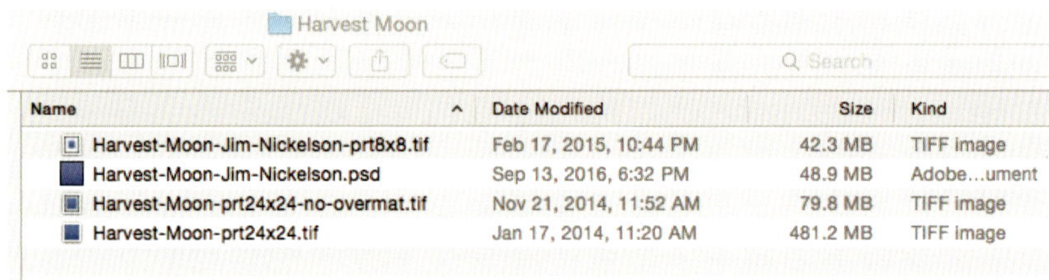

FIGURE 4-5: An example of my storage of a master Photoshop file and various TIFF files prepared for print of one image

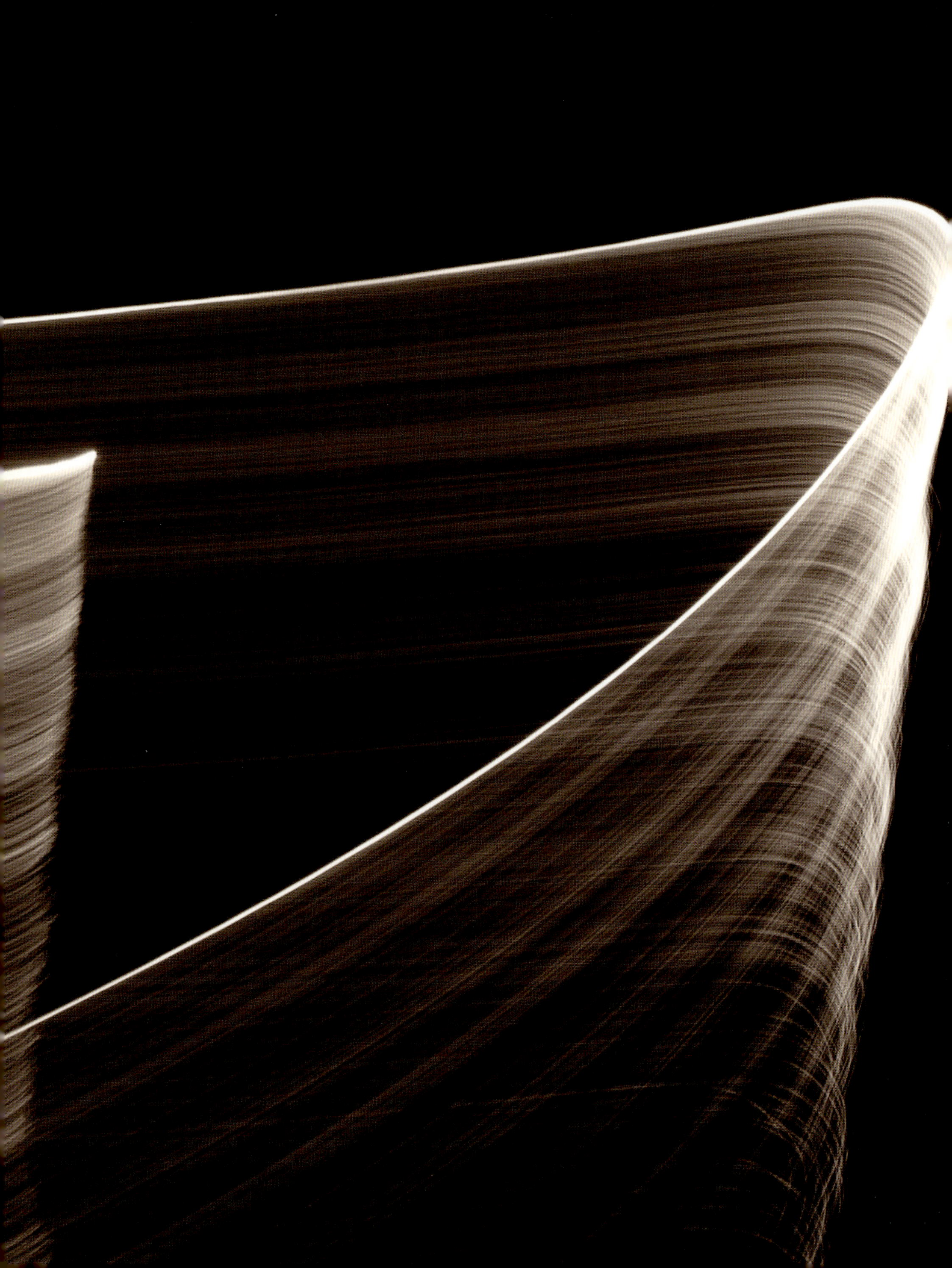

Image Editing

5

Editing your image to prepare it for print is perhaps the most important step in the printing process. The editing step also happens to be the most interesting part of the process as well, since it is where most of the aesthetic decisions will be made and because there are so many options available to accomplish each task.

In this chapter we'll cover the basics of image editing as well as introduce the idea of *print interpretation* as a way of thinking about how you want your final print to look. Keeping in mind your print interpretation for a particular image is essential as it can underlie all of your editing decisions.

After we've discussed image editing and print interpretation, we'll move on to what I consider the first steps of the editing process: cropping, defect correction, sharpening, and noise reduction.

> *There is a considerable amount of manipulation in the printmaking from the straight photograph to the finished print. If I do my job correctly that shouldn't be visible at all, it should be transparent.*
> —John Sexton

Image Editing Overview

The choice of image editing software is an important one, though most of the concepts here will apply no matter what software you use. We'll also cover my personal workflow in both Lightroom and Photoshop, as well as the steps necessary to make sure your own workflow is nondestructive to your images.

Choice of Software

The first question for image editing is the choice of which tool to use. There are myriad choices for editing both RAW files and image files more generally, and covering all of them is beyond our scope here.

For RAW files, many use software that comes from their camera manufacturer or dedicated RAW processing software such as Adobe Lightroom,

Adobe's Camera Raw that is built into Photoshop, the now-discontinued Apple Aperture, PhaseOne's Capture One Pro, or DxO Optics Pro. For more general image editing (for those who need something beyond what the RAW processors offer), many use Adobe Photoshop, Adobe Photoshop Elements, or the shareware program GIMP. More and more people are avoiding these options altogether, too, and are doing all of their photo capture and image editing on their smartphones. Photographers have a wealth of choices, and I encourage you to look into these many options, and based on their particular strengths and weaknesses, decide which is best suited for your camera and workflow.

For purposes of this book, however, we will be discussing Adobe Lightroom (and Adobe Camera Raw as part of Photoshop) for RAW processing and Adobe Photoshop for image editing more generally. We will also address printing from both Adobe Lightroom and Adobe Photoshop as each offers its own advantages and has its adherents.

Why Lightroom and Photoshop? Because these two programs are the two most commonly used editing programs, they are what I use myself, and they both do a wonderful job of editing, preparing, and creating great fine art prints. Because of their popularity, there is also an extremely large community of support for these programs, and many workshops, online videos and articles, and books like this one use these programs, too, for the same reason.

The principles and ideas in this book should be general enough that you can apply them to your program of choice. If you use, say, Capture One Pro for RAW processing, the same basic ideas will apply as we will discuss regarding Lightroom, and you may apply these ideas to the specific tools available to you (and of course any Photoshop discussion, evaluating prints, paper choice, and the like will apply without modification).

Principles of Printing #5: There Are Many Ways to Get There from Here

I'm a firm believer that with today's tools we have many good ways of performing our tasks in editing and printing, and you should choose what works best for you. For editing software, I think Photoshop and Lightroom are both great, but you may find that other programs give you better results for your particular camera or type of print, or they just make more sense to you in terms of workflow. Go for it.

Lightroom and Photoshop are immensely powerful and flexible tools, and there are always multiple ways you can accomplish any particular task. I often joke with my workshop students that you can do anything in Photoshop 20 different ways, and 18 of those ways are good. Some methods may be better than others in terms of the impact on image quality or ease of use, but I believe photographers should work with the methods with which they are most comfortable. I always recommend experimenting with other methods to see if they offer improvement over what you are doing, but also don't feel the obligation to use every recommended technique if what you are doing is working fine.

Lightroom vs. Photoshop

Both Lightroom and Photoshop, individually or in tandem, can be used for the production of fine digital prints, so personal preference as to which one you like to use and their relevant strengths and weaknesses will dictate your choice. Where appropriate, I will discuss how to perform each task using both.

Lightroom is easier to use for both image editing and the mechanics of printing. Image editing in Lightroom is optimized to be quick and easy, and the printing workflow is much less complicated, particularly if you are printing multiple images at once (such as for proof prints or contact sheets) (**Figure 5-1**). Lightroom also has output sharpening for print built right in (something that requires a third-party plug-in or extra work in Photoshop) and its enlargement routines seem at least as good as Photoshop's, if not better.

So what is not to like about editing and printing in Lightroom? Simply put, there are some things that you just *cannot* do in Lightroom that you *can* do in Photoshop, and there are some things where Photoshop is just more powerful. One technique I often use that is only available in Photoshop is the ability to precisely and controllably blend or merge two separate files.

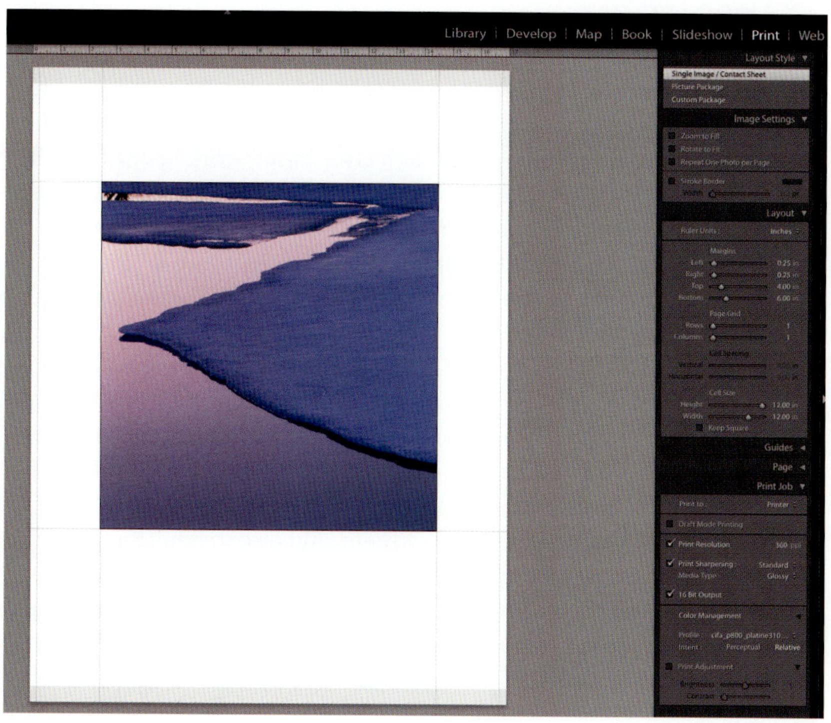

Figure 5-1: Lightroom's Print Module is an elegant and powerful tool for printing images

Another crucial example is that Photoshop is still superior in the ability to make masks for complicated local adjustments (though each iteration of Lightroom improves this aspect). Photoshop is also still superior in the ability to make pixel-level corrections to an image.

Lightroom continues to add new features and each generation seems to close the gap, but Photoshop is likely to remain ahead in absolute capability. Lightroom can certainly be used as an exclusive piece of software, but there will be things you cannot do if you choose that path. For most photographers and most prints, I believe Lightroom's powerful capabilities are enough, and you can make great prints using only Lightroom.

I, like many others, choose the path of using both. I do all of my initial editing in Lightroom, and perhaps my first hard proofs, but I export from Lightroom to Photoshop for final tweaking and for any more difficult edits. Many use Photoshop as an external editor from Lightroom to use any necessary tools, and then they continue to work on the image in Lightroom after the Photoshop edits are complete so they can take advantage of Lightroom's workflow and printing features. For most photographers, though, Lightroom will provide all the capability they need, but Photoshop provides an additional step up in ability and control.

Workflow and Editing Order

As we discussed in chapter 4, I recommend using nondestructive editing methods to implement any changes, whether it be by the parametric edits of Lightroom or Adobe Camera RAW or a layer-based workflow within Photoshop. Image editing is iterative, and you often have to go back to tweak earlier steps after making later changes, and you are better positioned to do so with a nondestructive workflow. This is particularly true for printing, as making your print look as you intended will likely require additional edits.

When working with a RAW file, the order in which you apply your edits doesn't matter to the program itself, so you are free to edit in whatever order makes sense for you and your images. With a RAW editor such as Lightroom or Adobe Camera Raw, all the changes you make are saved and then executed optimally by the program whenever you leave the program by printing, exporting, or opening in Photoshop. This flexibility allows all users to develop a workflow that works best for them, and also to iterate and experiment without damaging image quality.

Next, I will present my preferred order for performing steps for editing and printing. I hesitate to call it *optimal* as that word does not allow for either subjective preferences or the fact that my workflow is based on what works for me and what I have been able to ascertain from publicly available information, and I do not know the inner workings of the underlying code of Lightroom or Photoshop. But I do believe mine is an intuitive workflow that also takes advantage of the characteristics of the programs.

Your workflow should be considered iterative, and changes down the line can necessitate changes to earlier edits, so consider the order to be a rough guideline of how to edit rather than a required path. For example, you may perform the first five steps and then decide that the third step should be adjusted a bit, so go back to the third step, make a change, and then continue again from there.

Principles of Printing #6: Consistency, Usually

Work toward your goal in a consistent fashion, but don't be afraid to veer off the path, either. I typically perform the same basic edits to each image in a particular order. I do this to establish a routine and because it is an editing order that makes sense to me, but there is nothing magical about the order in which I personally edit. Using a consistent approach also reduces the probability that you will forget something.

My order is generally as follows:

1. Capture sharpening
2. Cropping
3. Correcting any dust spots
4. Noise reduction (adjusting sharpness as needed)
5. Performing global changes (adjust white balance, exposure, contrast, saturation, etc.)
6. Performing local changes (dodging and burning, localized color/contrast/saturation)

Once I've completed a pass through the image, I'll then tweak some of the earlier items as necessary. By performing edits in a relatively predictable order, I believe that you can better anticipate the effect of a change on the final image, as you will be more experienced with the changes further down the processing path that impact your current edit. If you are modifying saturation without yet having modified contrast, for example, your "eye" might not be able to anticipate how later changing the contrast will change your saturation if you normally modify contrast first.

Lightroom supports a similar order in editing as it is designed for your workflow to be from left-to-right through the modules, and then top-to-bottom within each module (such as the Develop module). That is not to say you cannot edit things in whatever order you choose, but the designers have outlined that as a preferred order. It is an order that works pretty well for me, and I suggest giving it a try as you seek out your own consistent pattern of editing.

The editing order can make it easier or more difficult to perform various edits—an image that is off on white balance, for example, can give misleading results in saturation that will become evident when you finally do correct the white balance. Because of Lightroom's parametric editing, the final image will not vary based on the order you perform edits; the edits, when they are actually made at export, are done simultaneously in an optimal fashion regardless of the order in which you made them.

Even though I have a preferred order, I sometimes will stray drastically from that order. If an image is way too dark, I'll jump right to brightening it up via exposure so that I can better make other decisions, such as color balance and cropping. Nothing is set in stone in terms of order, which is one of biggest advantages of the parametric editing of Lightroom and the layer-based editing of Photoshop.

My Workflow

This is not the "best" workflow by any means. Many of these steps may be modified based on personal preference without loss of quality in the final print, but it is what I consider to be a best practice in terms of quality as well as an intuitive way of approaching the printing process, and I believe it utilizes the best of both Photoshop and Lightroom. This workflow contains some of my idiosyncratic practices such as wanting to have a precise and repeatable border around the printing, which is something not everyone will find necessary. We'll discuss these steps in detail throughout the remaining chapters.

1. Import photo into RAW processor (Lightroom)
2. Perform capture sharpening and any other preset adjustments
3. Perform lens corrections in Lightroom (if available)
4. Decide on artistic intent for image and final print
5. Crop
6. Correct any defects (dust spots, etc.)

7. Noise reduction (adjusting sharpness as necessary)
8. Adjust white balance
9. Perform global tone corrections (exposure, white point and black point, contrast, highlights, shadows)
10. Perform global color corrections
11. Perform any local edits using selective adjustment tools such as the Adjustment Brush
12. Reassess noise reduction in light of global and selective edits
13. Export to Photoshop as full size 16-bit PSD master file
14. Perform any new global edits
15. Perform any local corrections
16. Apply Local Contrast Enhancement
17. Finalize master file
18. Flatten layers and enlarge file to print resolution
19. Perform output sharpening
20. Review image for any anomalies before printing
21. Add any desired borders by expanding canvas
22. Print
23. Evaluate print and return to step 14 if further edits are desired
24. Once print approved, save a copy of the print file as a separate file for archives

My Lightroom-Only Workflow

Many people use a Lightroom-only workflow, and here is what I recommend for editing and printing from Lightroom based on my workflow above:

1. Import photo into Lightroom
2. Perform capture sharpening and any other preset adjustments
3. Perform lens correction (if available)
4. Decide on artistic intent for image and final print

5. Crop
6. Correct any defects (dust spots, etc.)
7. Noise reduction (adjusting sharpness as necessary)
8. Adjust white balance
9. Perform global tone corrections (exposure, white point and black point, contrast, highlights, shadows)
10. Perform global color corrections
11. Perform any local edits using selective adjustment tools such as the Adjustment Brush
12. Reassess noise reduction in light of global and selective edits
13. Go to Print Module, and select appropriate print resolution and output sharpening for the print
14. Print
15. Evaluate print and return to step 5 if further edits are desired

Print Interpretation

Print Interpretation is my term for assessing your artistic intent for a particular image and then making the necessary modifications and choices to realize that artistic intent in the final print. We discussed artistic intent in chapter 1 as related to the feeling or thought you hope to evoke in a viewer of your print.

Overview of Image Editing and Print Interpretation Relationship

1: **Image Editing** – Everything you would normally do to make your image look good on the screen
2: **Choose Artistic Intent** – What you'd like for the final print
3: **Print Editing (first part of Print Interpretation)** – Make changes to your image to make the print harmonious with the image on the screen
4: **Artistic Editing (second part of Print Interpretation)** – Make changes to selectively emphasize or deemphasize aspects of your image, or otherwise edit, to make your final print better embody your artistic intent; also consider changes necessary to be consistent with a print statement for a body of work (see chapter 13, "The Next Level")
5: **Print Interpretation Final** – Decide on paper, size, treatment, and the like to best embody your artistic intent

Your artistic intent is entirely up to you. Many photographers simply hope to have a print that matches the scene they photographed as closely as possible. Other photographers hope to convey in their final print the feeling or emotion they felt when photographing. Yet others desire to highlight to the viewer some object or combination of objects they noticed and photographed, such as a beautiful arrangement of objects on the forest floor or an intriguing and telling street scene. All of these are valid artistic intents.

Whatever your artistic intent for an image might be, Print Interpretation is the way that you can take your image and best achieve that intent in your print.

Print Interpretation is a step beyond normal image editing in the digital darkroom, as image editing is instead focused on making the image look good on the screen. Certainly artistic intent can and should play a role in image editing generally, as all of us will make basic decisions about how an image should look while we are editing. Making a physical print is enough of a mental step, though, that we will spend more time thinking about what we artistically intend with an image if we are going to the trouble of printing it. Images intended only for a life on your computer or online often have an ephemerality to them that does not encourage deep thought or careful analysis when compared to embodying that image in a final print (though of course there are surely exceptions to this!).

Print Interpretation encompasses the following two key editing steps (though in practice they may blend together):

- Print Editing
- Artistic Editing

First, Print Interpretation involves additional editing of your final image so that when printed, it matches as best as possible how you've edited the image on the screen, a process I call **Print Editing**. At its core, this Print Editing includes changes you make to the image for print that account for the differences between a print on paper and your image on screen. Very often these Print Edits involve increasing brightness, contrast, or saturation to compensate for the differences between the backlit LCD screen where your image lives and the reflected light of the paper and ink that make up your print.

After Print Editing, the next stage of Print Interpretation is **Artistic Editing**. Artistic Editing is any editing you perform that, in your judgment, makes your final print better realize your artistic intent for that image. This stage may include, say, adding emphasis to one part of your image to make it "pop" more in print. Artistic Editing may include, say, de-emphasizing part of your image that is distracting to your artistic intent, such as downplaying a background figure in a portrait or darkening down or softening a distracting element of a landscape.

Print Interpretation goes beyond basic editing of your image in another way as it relates to *any* decision you make that helps you realize your artistic intent for the image. One common and essential decision in interpreting your print is choosing a paper, as paper choice can have a dramatic effect on the look and feel of your final print. Another fundamental decision is print size, and whether your intent is better realized with an intimate, handheld small print or an immersive large print.

Print Interpretation, in all its aspects, is a vitally important step in creating final, fine art prints that you love and that convey to the viewer your artistic intent for the image and print. We'll keep on coming back to this idea throughout this book and we'll talk about how you can use the tools and information within to create your own fine art prints that you love.

Print Mastery: Harmony Between Image Editing and Print Interpretation

I've separated Image Editing from Print Interpretation as I have found this to be the most effective way of approaching the concepts with both students and clients. If you do consistently use this methodology in your printing practice, you'll likely find that the distinctions between these categories start to collapse.

As your experience and comfort level increase, you'll naturally start incorporating more and more of the ideas in Print Interpretation into your Image Editing so that your "final" image becomes much closer to the edited image you use for your "final" print. I believe this to be a good thing; as very often the types of changes we perform to make a better print just so happen to also make a better and more powerful digital image.

As you gain more experience printing, don't be surprised if you start internalizing how images will be realized in a print and thus your Print Interpretation becomes more embedded in your Image Editing. With a properly calibrated monitor, consistent color management, and experience, you'll likely need to do less and less to ready for print a final image that has been edited for screen.

Editing Your Image

Now that you've chosen your software and thought about your artistic intent for your image and print, it is time to start editing the image. We can use the same tools and methodologies for doing Image Editing as we do for Print Interpretation, so our discussion will be generally applicable to both types of editing.

In this book I am not trying to be exhaustive in covering each type of editing method. Photoshop and Lightroom are immensely complex tools and many books and other resources are dedicated to documenting how every aspect of these programs works. I love those types of resources and encourage you to explore them if you'd like to learn more about how to edit your images and to "get under the hood" in terms of how the programs work.

What I am doing instead is describing the tools that I believe to be the ones most important for editing the vast majority of images for print. My experience with workshop students and my clients tells me that the common changes we need to make for print are the global and selective adjustments to tonality, noise reduction and sharpening, and color, and we'll therefore focus our energies on those topics in this chapter and the next.

As I've emphasized before, there is no one right way of editing an image with respect to either the final result or the path to get there. Consider this discussion to be my own best practices for the editing steps you will most likely need to take to prepare your image for print.

Initial Editing Steps

My initial editing steps use the tools that impact the actual pixels of the image, either by removing them (via cropping) or by actually changing them (lens correction and defect correction). I prefer to perform these steps early in the process since I've found that my later changes to tonality and color are more successful when I'm looking at a more final crop and an image without visible defects. A curved horizon line, for example, is distracting to me, and if it can be easily fixed with lens correction, then I prefer to do that early in the process.

Cropping

My first step in editing is usually to crop the image. Given that my personal work is almost exclusively square format but my camera is not, it is not surprising that I choose to start here. Cropping first does potentially reduce the workload for everyone, though (it does not make sense, for example, to spend time dust spotting a portion of an image that will eventually be cropped out). I also find that I can better edit my image and judge color and tonality when I am looking at something close to the final crop. Those additional areas that will likely be cropped can prevent me from easily judging the balance and feel of my image.

When you do crop, I recommend doing it in a nondestructive fashion. This is automatic in Lightroom and can be handled in two ways in Photoshop. In Photoshop, the classic way was to crop the file using the crop tool and to save this new image as a new file (I would add "-crop" to the filename). This has the downside of creating additional files that take up storage space, but it keeps you from losing your original full image if you later change your mind.

Starting with Photoshop CS6, you can also make sure the box called Delete Cropped Pixels is unchecked (**Figure 5-2**), which means your crop is reversible and you can go back later and change it, eliminating the need for extra files. An advantage of this is that any later edits will be effective for whatever crop you might choose, since all of the edits will be in the same file. If the box is checked, whatever you crop off will be permanently gone after you save your changes, but your file size will be reduced since there is less informa-

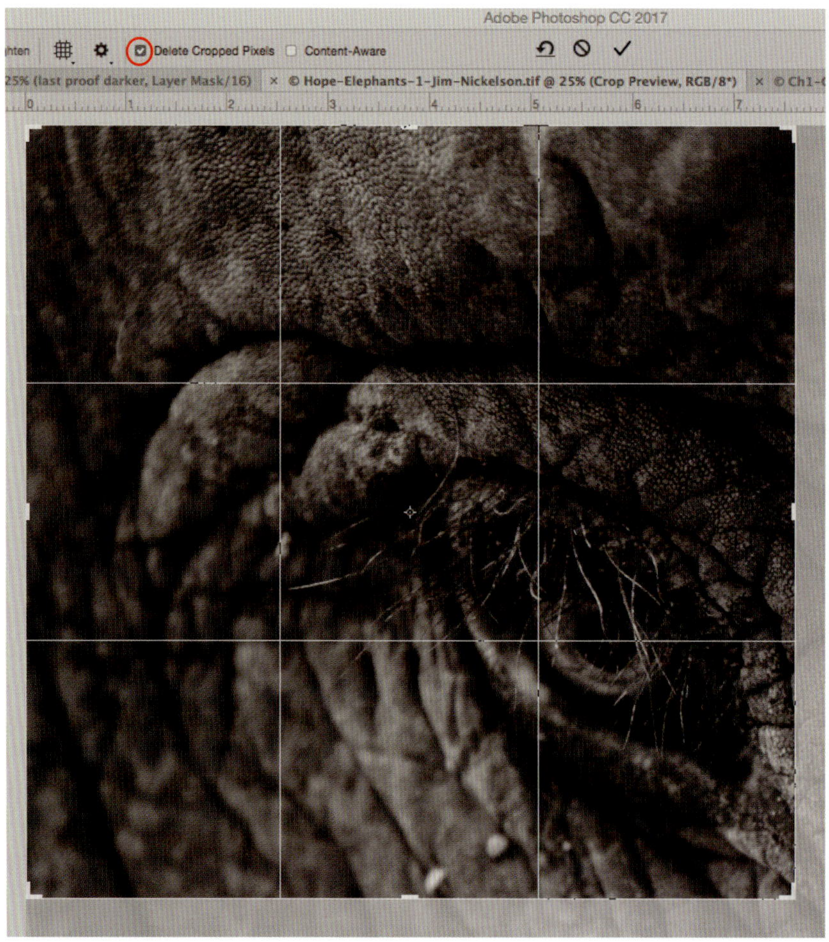

Figure 5-2: Using the Crop tool in Photoshop CS6 or later, you can select the Delete Cropped Pixels box so that your cropping is reversible. One downside is that you retain the original file size, however.

tion to save. If you go forward with editing, your changes will only apply to the newly cropped file, so if you change your mind later you'll have to redo those edits on the file with the original crop.

Lens Corrections

Lens Corrections is a relatively new tool in Lightroom and ACR, and it can be a powerful one. If information regarding your lens is available, the Lens Corrections tool (**Figure 5-3**) will correct for distortion and vignetting based on a profile for your particular type of lens (and based on your aperture settings).

To turn on Lens Corrections, simply click the Enable Profile Corrections box. In most cases the tool will identify your lens and automatically select the correct profile. If your camera has built-in lens profiles (newer Olympus and Fuji cameras, among others, have this), it may appear that no profile is available, but the profiles are being automatically applied without you even checking the box. Some lenses require you to manually select the profile as well.

Lens profiles are basically models of how your lens will distort and vignette at a particular aperture setting, and Lens Corrections works by using that model to essentially "subtract" the typical distortion and vignetting, leaving a distortion-free and vignetting-free image.

That is the theory, at least. I find it usually does a great job, but any flaws in the model, or the variance of your particular lens from the ideal, will provide less than optimal results. Using the sliders, you can vary the amount of the distortion and vignetting correction if you find it goes too far (or not far enough), or if you prefer to leave some or all of the vignetting for creative effect.

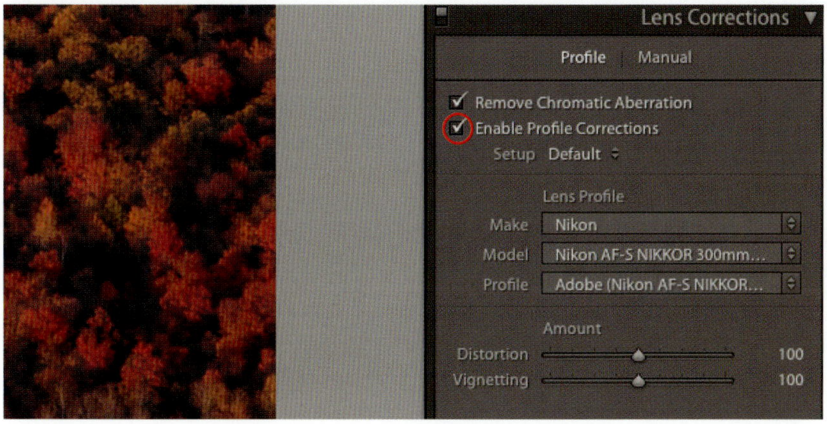

FIGURE 5-3: Once you select Enable Profile Corrections, Lightroom will try to automatically determine your lens and, if it succeeds, it will automatically apply the right profile. Otherwise, you can choose the profile manually.

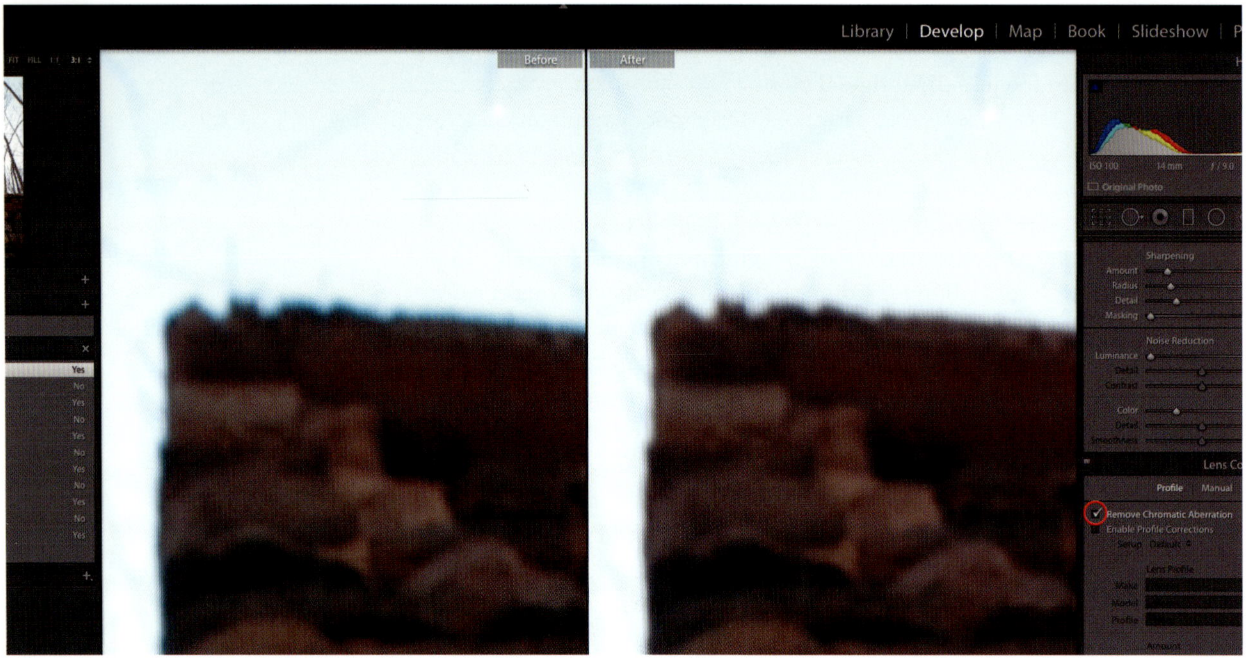

FIGURE 5-4: If you look carefully at the top of the old chimney on the left (in a highly magnified view at 3:1 magnification), you can see a green chromatic aberration along the top edge. In the version on the right, the chromatic aberration has been quickly and easily removed using the Chromatic Aberration tool, and the green line has disappeared.

The ability to use the Remove Chromatic Aberrations tool is another important aspect of Lens Corrections as it can be quite powerful in removing chromatic aberrations. Chromatic aberrations are a characteristic of lens/ body combination in certain shooting situations, and usually manifest as green or magenta areas along the edge of a bright/dark boundary in your image (**Figure 5-4**). In my own shooting, this usually happens when objects are backlit, such as a backlit branch, or near a very bright light source such as a full moon. Generally speaking, I see these chromatic aberrations as an image flaw and prefer to remove them, though I'm sure some can find a creative effect for them.

To activate the tool, simply check the Remove Chromatic Aberration box and automatic removal will take place. Most of the time, I find this to be sufficient, but if you find that the tool is not catching some chromatic aberration you've seen, go to the Defringe section of the Manual tab. Here you can manually adjust the amount of correction using the sliders, but what I normally do is click the Eyedropper tool and then select the area of the image where I'm still seeing chromatic aberration. This will instruct the tool where you are seeing the aberration and it will adjust the correction accordingly. In most cases this should correct the aberration without needing to manually adjust the sliders.

Defect Correction

Defect correction, namely the removal of dust spots or other artifacts that are not part of the scene, is typically my next step. A good argument could be made that you should not spend time on this step until you decide whether or not the image is a "keeper," but I prefer to do at least a first pass at this early in the process so that I'm not distracted by big dust spots or the like.

The defect correction tools are very powerful and their detailed workings are beyond the scope of this book. There are entire books on the subject of doing these edits in Photoshop, but I will instead highlight my basic methodology. I do encourage you to experiment with all of these tools to discover what works and doesn't work for your own images, allowing you to get better at using these tools the more you use them.

The Spot Removal brush in Lightroom/ACR has become significantly better as the program has evolved, and it's a good choice to do as many corrections as possible. I find that for more difficult situations I need to take the image to Photoshop for its more sophisticated defect correction tools, but the Spot Removal tool will work, and work well, for many spots you need to correct.

To use the Spot Removal tool (**Figure 5-5**), select the Spot Removal icon and then proceed with finding the spots in your image, make the circular selection area the correct size using either the bracket keys or the Size slider, and then click. The tool will find what it feels is an appropriate nearby area and intelligently replace the part of the image where you clicked with new and hopefully better information. For a dust spot in a sky, for example, the tool grabs nearby sky and smoothly replaces the dust spot.

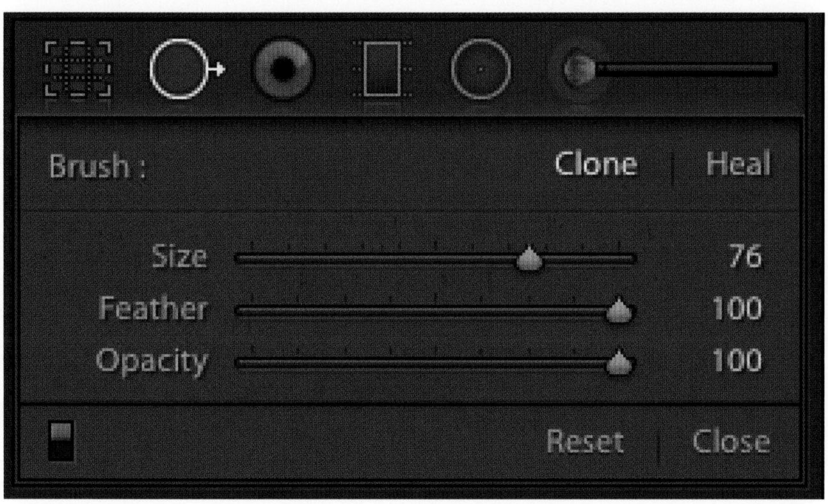

FIGURE 5-5: A close-up of the Spot Removal tool in Lightroom

Lightroom provides an extremely powerful tool to help find spots or other blemishes in your image. When the Spot Removal tool is active, if you click the Visualize Spots box toward the lower-left corner of the screen below your image, the view will change to a special mode that helps you visualize where there might be spots in your image (**Figure 5-6**). In this view (and experiment with moving the slider left and right), you can quickly and easily identify the location of potential trouble areas of your image, particularly if you have large uniform areas of the image like sky, since any blemishes will visually jump out. You can even use this Visualize Spots view to perform the Spot Removal, though I always check the actual view, too, to make sure any changes are acceptable.

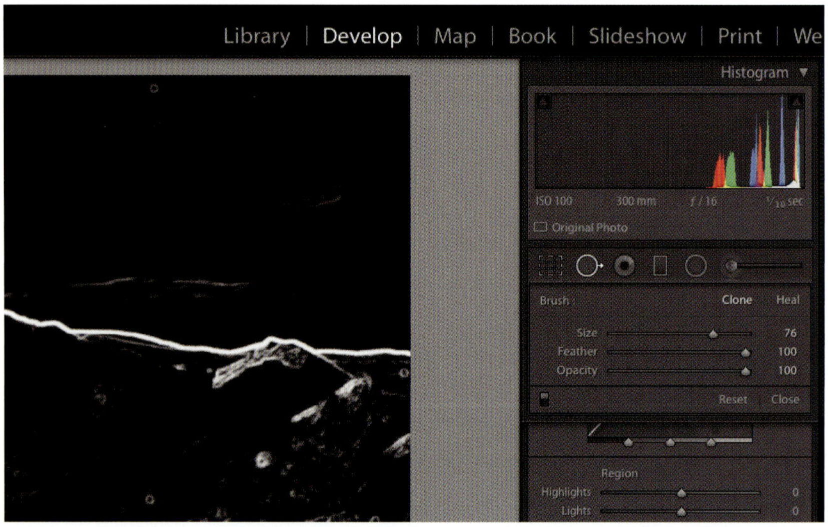

FIGURE 5-6: This view of the Spot Removal tool in Lightroom when Visualize Spots is turned on reveals a number of potential dust spots (identified by the white circles) in the sky and in the mountain area of this photograph. Once identified, these types of spots are easy to remove.

Print Mastery: Defect Correction in Photoshop

For images where I need to go to Photoshop to perform more sophisticated edits, my recommendation is to create a new empty layer as your first step (Layer > New > Layer while you are on the background layer) and then perform your corrections on this layer. This allows for all pixel-level changes to be reversible, as you can delete the entire layer or you can create a mask for the correction layer and paint off areas of your layer mask if you decide that some of your changes were erroneous. For tools, I use a mix of the Spot Healing Brush tool and the Clone Stamp Tool.

Lightroom continues to improve in its ability to perform defect correction, but Photoshop remains more powerful and flexible. The nature of Lightroom as a parametric editor rather than a pixel-level editor like Photoshop makes it very likely that Photoshop will remain superior indefinitely. Continued improvement of Lightroom, though, will make performing defect correction in Photoshop less and less necessary.

Basic Sharpening and Noise Reduction

Overview of Sharpening

Sharpening of digital images is an area that is complex in many ways, but modern tools have greatly improved and streamlined the process, particularly in Lightroom.

It is generally accepted that sharpening of images is best performed in up to three separate stages as follows:

1. **Capture sharpening** provides initial sharpening of the file after digital capture and before other changes are implemented, and also helps to remove the effects of the anti-aliasing filter prevalent on most DSLR sensors.
2. **Creative sharpening** is optionally and selectively applied to any parts of the image that need additional sharpening.
3. **Output sharpening** sharpens the image in ways optimized for whatever output type and size you desire, whether it be screen or print, glossy or matte paper, and so on. Output sharpening need not be applied until a file is used for a particular purpose (e.g., upon making a print).

Overview of Noise Reduction

Even with current technology, noise is often a fact of life with digital images. Noise reduction has dramatically improved with recent software tools, including both from Adobe and third parties. I recommend using the noise reduction available in RAW processors such as Lightroom and Adobe Camera Raw because they use very sophisticated and effective algorithms. They also have the benefit of working with your RAW file to maximize overall image quality and streamline your workflow.

There are two types of noise relevant to digital images; luminance noise and color noise. **Luminance noise** is the type of noise that most resembles film grain as it is random noise and, at least at lower ISOs, it is relatively small (**Figure 5-7**). This type of noise is not as objectionable as color noise but can still be problematic. Luminance noise is closely related to sharpness: increased sharpening will increase the visible luminance noise, and vice versa.

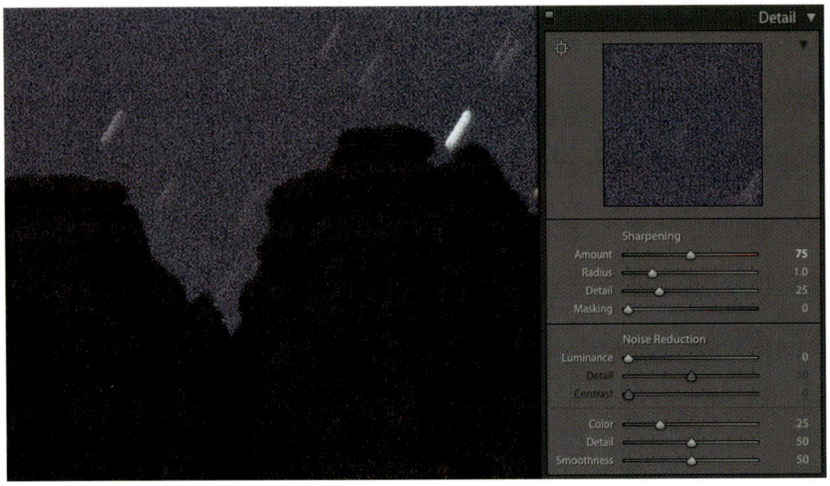

FIGURE 5-7: This is pretty severe luminance noise from an ISO 6400 night photograph. This level of luminance noise will almost certainly result in loss of detail if entirely removed.

Color noise is the result of demosaicing inherent in digital image processing with current technology and it appears as different-colored pixels through noisy areas of an image. While luminance noise can look like grain to some extent, color noise definitely looks "digital" and is thus something that should usually be avoided (**Figure 5-8**).

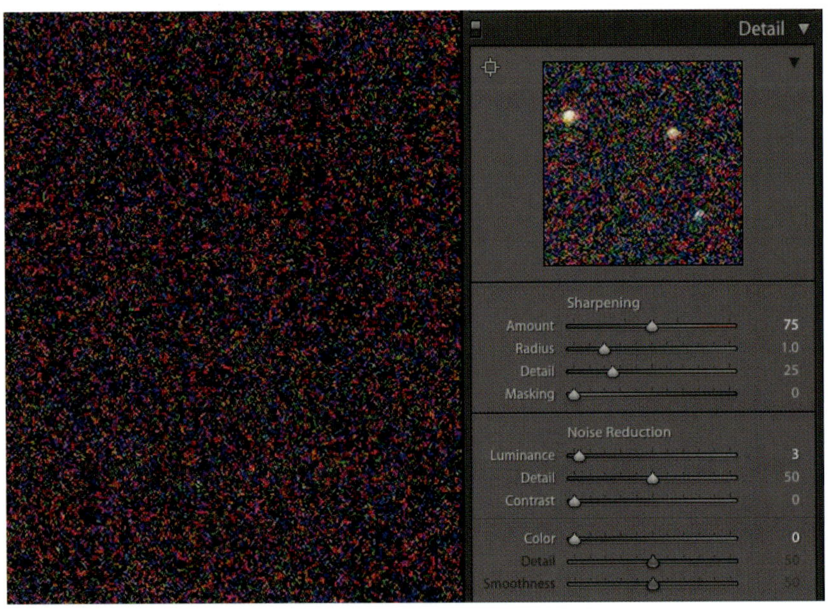

FIGURE 5-8: A particularly dramatic patch of color noise from a night photograph taken at ISO 6400 and with 3 extra stops of Exposure. You'll hopefully never see color noise this bad, but it does give a good idea of what to look for.

Sharpening and Noise Reduction Are Related

Sharpening and noise reduction are related and each should be performed in conjunction with the other. Increasing noise reduction will reduce sharpness, and increasing sharpness will make any evident noise more apparent. Because of their close connection, the process of setting proper values for sharpening and noise reduction is often iterative, and you should tweak both of them until you find the right balance appropriate for your image and your own preferences.

My recommendation for addressing sharpening and noise reduction, and how to fit it into your overall workflow, is as follows:

1. Perform capture sharpening
2. Perform any noise reduction
3. Reassess sharpening to see if it needs to be increased in light of noise reduction
4. Edit image for tonality, color, etc.
5. Perform any creative sharpening

After completing the bulk of image editing, if the image has been heavily manipulated or brightened, reassess noise reduction to see if it needs to be increased in light of the editing.

Performing Capture Sharpening

In this chapter we will focus only on capture sharpening, the first of the three stages of sharpening, and we'll address creative sharpening and output sharpening in later chapters. Capture sharpening is optimally performed in either Lightroom or Adobe Camera Raw directly in the RAW file. RAW captures (usually) have no inherent sharpening, so additional sharpening is necessary to maximize image quality. JPEG files shot in-camera usually have some sort of capture sharpening already applied by the camera, so I recommend refraining from applying additional capture sharpening to JPEG files unless you feel it is necessary.

While in Lightroom or in ACR, capture sharpening of a RAW image is found in the Detail section in the Develop module (**Figure 5-9**). The four image sharpening sliders in Lightroom are designed to allow photographers to sharpen by eye when viewing the image at the 100% or 1:1 pixel view.

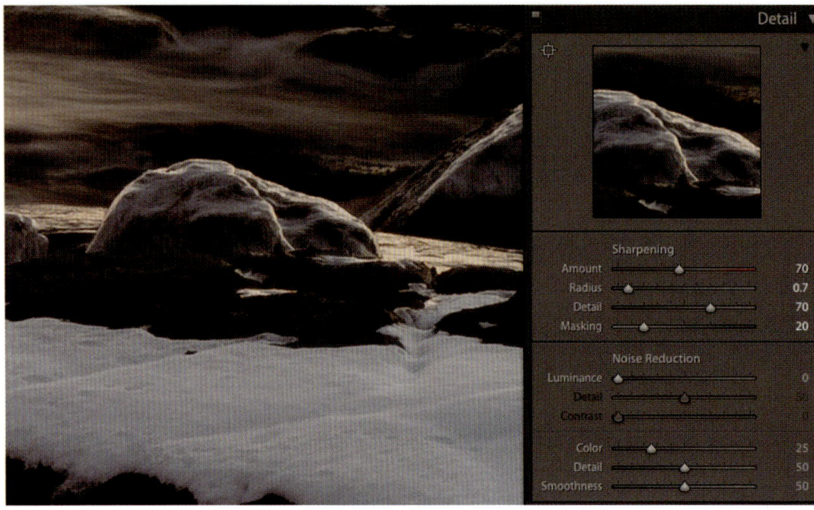

Figure 5-9: Capture sharpening is controlled from the Detail panel in the Develop module of Lightroom. I recommend zooming in to important areas to view the effect of the sharpening on your image.

Viewing at higher or lower resolutions will necessitate the software to upsize or downsize your image for viewing and will thus skew the actual impact of sharpening and potentially give you an inaccurate view of image sharpness.

To perform capture sharpening of an image, the best technique is to start from defaults (standard or otherwise) and adjust to taste. It is better to err on the side of less sharpening as a general rule. The idea of capture sharpening is to make the amount of sharpening look "right" on the screen, and we'll compensate for different types of print media when we perform output sharpening later in the workflow.

Sharpening, in a broad sense, looks for edges and then darkens the dark side and lightens the light side. The Amount slider is a volume control that controls the intensity of the other settings, ranging from 0 and no sharpening to 150 and maximum sharpening (**Figure 5.10**). The Radius slider defines how far the impact of sharpening will extend beyond the detected edge. Higher-frequency edges are best with a lower radius whereas lower-frequency edges are best with a higher radius. A higher radius also avoids attacking and exacerbating noise that is relatively fine-grained.

The Detail slider performs a complicated balance between halo suppression and deconvolution sharpening, with 0 being pure halo suppression and 100 being pure sharpening. Highly detailed images usually benefit from Detail levels above the default, but increased Detail may also result in more required noise reduction. The higher levels of Detail are actually a deconvolution-based sharpening that attempts to fight inherent de-blurring of an image from the time of capture. I would only recommend very high Detail settings for images with virtually no noise and that have very fine details.

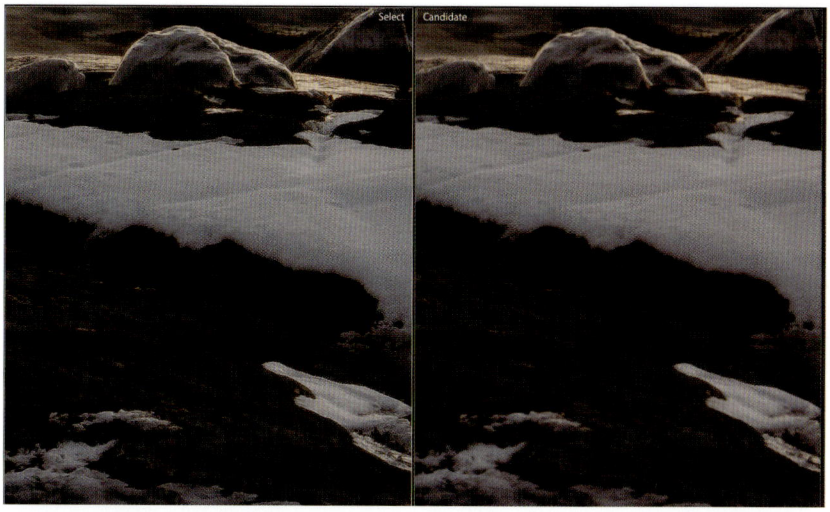

FIGURE 5-10: In this extreme case for display purposes, the version of the photograph on the left has the Amount slider at the maximum of 150 and the version on the right has the Amount slider set at 0 (sharpening turned off). The version on the left is almost "crunchy" as it appears over-sharpened, but you can see how much difference capture sharpening can make.

The Masking slider controls the edge masking and reduces the sharpening of non-edge areas such as surfaces. By holding down the Option key (or Alt key on Windows), you can see a visual representation of the mask as you adjust this slider up or down. Usually some masking is beneficial and often in the range of 5 to 15 for most images. By using this tool, you can apply more sharpening to edges without detriment to surfaces and smooth areas.

I recommend a very general starting point of Amount 60, Radius 0.7, Detail 60, and Masking of 15 for detailed landscape images, but each image, and each type of camera, will of course have its own optimal settings. For other images that are not highly detailed, or images that are noisy, I would lower the Detail slider to 50 or less.

Lightroom comes with two built-in presets, too, found in the Lightroom General Presets section of the left column when in the Develop module. Sharpen-Faces has an Amount of 35, Radius of 1.4, Detail of 15, and Masking of 60. Sharpen-Scenics has an Amount of 40, Radius of 0.8, Detail of 35, and Masking of 0. I consider these reasonable starting points for your own experimentation.

I experimented a bit with capture sharpening settings for my cameras and decided to make capture sharpening a default that is automatically applied to each and every RAW file upon import into Lightroom. I have found that the desired level of capture sharpening is consistent enough to use these defaults as a starting point for every image, and I usually only modify it for images that have a decent amount of noise or are significantly different in terms of detail than my typical photograph.

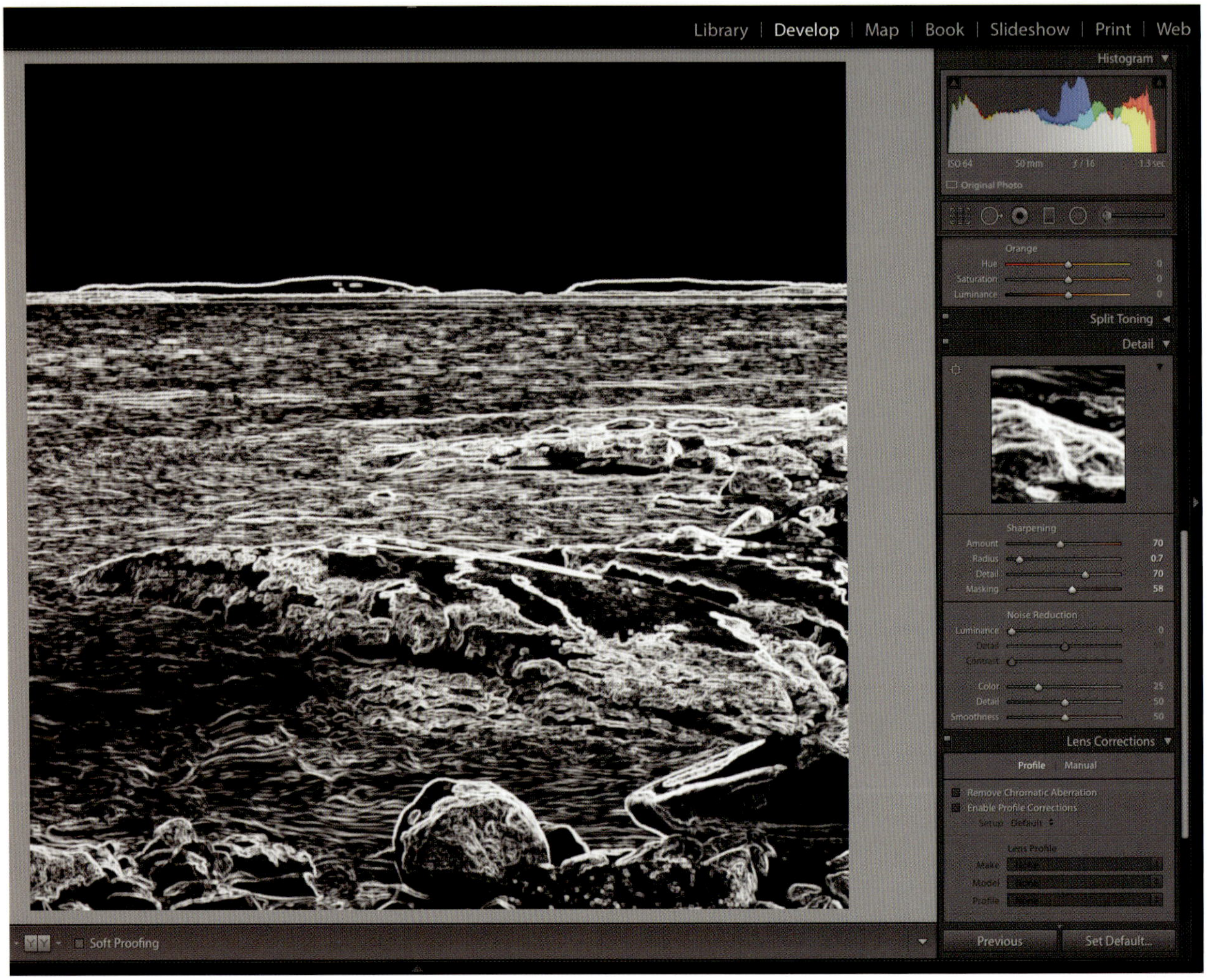

FIGURE 5-11: The visual representation of a mask depicted here shows you can choose to limit sharpening to edges rather than smooth areas, which can help in preventing an increase in noise. The areas in white are where sharpening will be applied at the current Masking setting, and the areas in black are where no sharpening is being applied. This is an important tool in helping to balance noise reduction and sharpening. You can greatly reduce increased noise as a result of sharpening by masking off smoother areas. By moving the slider back and forth in this view, you can find the setting that best balances applying sharpening to edges and avoiding sharpening smooth areas for your particular image.

Performing Noise Reduction

Choosing the appropriate level of noise reduction is a very iterative process. Experiment, see what the controls do, and trust your eyes. Many recommend going beyond 100% view to set noise reduction, but be careful with this, too, especially if you are going back and forth with sharpening adjustments, since that view can be misleading. I recommend just evaluating noise (and sharpness) at the 100% or 1:1 view as that is the only view that is showing the real pixels, rather than an approximation created for display.

The default for luminance noise reduction is set to off but it is often necessary. To find the proper level of noise reduction for an image, I first push up the Luminance (which is basically a control of the amount or volume of luminance noise reduction) to a point where it starts looking objectionable (i.e., overly smooth or processed), and then I pull back.

Next, I consider adjusting the Luminance Detail slider by increasing its value, which biases the noise reduction toward preserving details. The more details you preserve, however, the more likely that pockets of noise will be missed. Reducing details will increase image smoothing and is more likely to incorrectly delete desired details in the image. The Contrast slider restores contrast that is lost in the noise reduction. Increasing Luminance Contrast better preserves image contrast and texture. Contrast is most useful for really high ISO images and restores some of the lost contrast. With low ISO images that do not have a lot of noise, the Detail and Contrast adjustments may not have a lot of impact.

Color noise defaults to a level of 25 and that default level is usually sufficient to deal with any color noise issues. As you increase it for noisy images, you run the risk of losing color edge detail. Color Noise Detail should probably only be used on very noisy images that are full of speckles of color, though low levels of it seem to have no apparent negative effect on the image.

Principles of Printing #7:
You Have to Go Too Far to Know That You've Gone Far Enough

As an editing philosophy, the photographer and publisher Brooks Jensen said it best:

> *You don't know if you've gone far enough unless you've gone too far, and then come slightly back.*
>
> —Brooks Jensen

Experimentation in the digital darkroom is essential in learning how the software works and in finding what settings will work best for a particular image. This can apply not only to noise reduction but also to every step of the editing process.

Assessing Noise Reduction and Sharpening in Combination

Assessing the end result of noise reduction and sharpening can be difficult. You have to evaluate how the image looks on the screen and extrapolate to how it will look in print, particularly if the print is going to be large. I recommend undershooting a bit on sharpness, as I find a little bit of softness to be better than any signs of over-sharpening such as halos or weird edge effects. I will often undershoot a little bit on noise reduction, too, so that my photographs do not look over-processed (but see the next section regarding adding grain). As with so many things, experience in making prints of your own images will help you find your own taste as to the appropriate levels of each adjustment tool.

Adding Grain

If you do find that, after noise reduction, your image feels a little over-processed or "too digital" or "too clinical," one solution is to add a bit of grain to it. It seems counterintuitive to add grain back in after removing it during noise reduction, but it can be very effective in improving your image.

This tool is especially useful in cases where you performed significant noise reduction, as the addition of grain to add a bit of texture can improve how the image looks. In some cases, the addition of a slight bit of grain can improve the image quality by increasing the perceived sharpness and acutance, particularly in situations where there was significant noise reduction. This effect is often described as the image appearing more photographic/less plastic, more film-like, etc. For some photographers, higher levels of grain may be desirable for aesthetic reasons to replicate a film look, but I prefer a much more subtle rendition to counterbalance the smoothing of noise reduction.

To add a small amount of grain in Lightroom, a good starting point for settings would be as follows:

- A very small grain (4–6)
- Increase roughness above 50
- Add just enough grain (10 or less) to add a tight bit of texture

Many people prefer this sort of light grain look on all images because of the increased appearance of sharpness and acutance and that is a valid approach—I normally do not, but I recommend trying prints both ways to see what you prefer. Assessing the level of grain is one of those cases where the appearance on screen can be deceiving.

These suggested settings will add a fine layer of grain over the entire image, which can add a little "tooth" to the entire image and overcome the effects of too much noise reduction. Noise reduction has the effect of smoothing the image and removing micro-detail, and adding grain afterword can add the perception of micro-detail. Similarly, for those who don't like large, very smooth areas such as a blue sky, it can add a little detail to those areas.

My recommendation is to go carefully in adding grain and not to overdo the effect, but small amounts can be very beneficial in terms of print quality, even if the effect is small enough to be nearly imperceptible to viewers. Subtlety is key.

Print Mastery: Adding Grain in Photoshop

To add grain in Photoshop, I recommend making a duplicate background layer and then use Photoshop's Noise Filter (Filter > Noise > Add Noise), select Uniform and Monochromatic, and then apply gently to taste (usually just a few percentage points). If performing this in Photoshop, I also recommend performing this step after enlargement to print size so that you don't enlarge the grain. PhotoKit Sharpener and other plug-ins can also add grain emulation from within Photoshop.

Global and Selective Adjustments

6

Global image adjustments are edits to the image that are applied to the entire image. Global image adjustments are the foundation of editing an image and are essential to determining the overall look and feel of the print.

Selective image adjustments are edits that are not applied to the entire image but instead are applied to only some localized portion of the image. Selective image adjustments are equally essential as global ones in taking an image to the next level, particularly for print.

Countless types of edits can be performed in Lightroom and Photoshop, and we will not even attempt to cover all of them. Instead, we'll focus on the types of edits that we need to address most frequently in the context of making prints. In chapter 10, we'll also apply many of these global and selective image adjustments to images as part of our discussion of Print Interpretation.

This is not intended to be a basic primer for Lightroom and Photoshop beginners. We will proceed with the assumption that you have some knowledge of how to use these tools, and I will explain how I apply them to my images.

> *And only the photographer himself knows the effect he wants.*
> *He should know by instinct, grounded in experience, what subjects*
> *are enhanced by hard or soft, light or dark treatment.*
> —Bill Brandt

Global Image Adjustments

There are many different types of global image adjustments, and we'll address the three most commonly used for preparing images for print here:

- Tonality
- Local Contrast Enhancement and Clarity
- Color

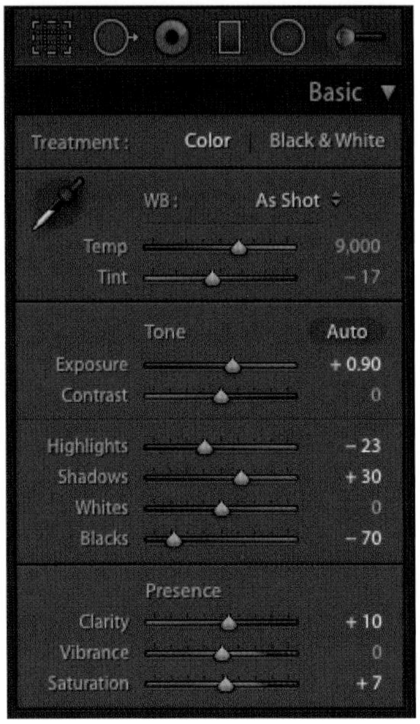

FIGURE 6-1: In the Basic panel in Lightroom's Develop module, in the Tone section, you will find various tonality adjustment sliders, including Exposure, Contrast, Highlights, Shadows, Whites, and Blacks

Tonality

Tonality in a photographic image references the overall quality and distribution of tones in an image. Tonality includes the overall brightness or exposure, contrast, and distribution of tones in the shadows, midtones, and highlights.

Adjusting Basic Tonality in Lightroom/ACR

Exposure and tonal relationships should usually be performed near the beginning of your global image adjustments, and they are positioned accordingly just below white balance in the LR and ACR Basic panels (**Figure 6-1**). Good RAW captures will often be flat and lacking in contrast at first, leaving you to decide how much tonality adjustment to apply.

I recommend modifying **Exposure** first as the other tonal modifications flow from that basic exposure. Increases in exposure can have very large impacts on the image, so be careful not to go too far. You can also see whether (and where) you might be blowing out highlights or pushing shadows to black by holding down the Command (Mac)/Ctrl (PC) key while moving the exposure, which will give you a visual representation of what parts of the image are being pushed beyond the limits (the white areas that appear on the otherwise black representation), so you can decide whether those areas are critical and then pull the modification back accordingly.

One additional consideration is that brightening the exposure (or any other modification that brightens the image, such as the Shadows slider) can dramatically exacerbate any noise in the image, particularly in the shadow areas. The increased noise can often be at least partially overcome, but one will quickly learn that additional exposure in the field that allows for a brighter exposure will result in a better image. Brightening the image during processing might be a necessary evil sometimes, but the increased noise that results is a definite trade-off.

Contrast adjusts the overall contrast of the image and is next in my preferred workflow. Using both the Exposure and Contrast tools, you should be able to be able to achieve a reasonable overall tonal range even for difficult images, and this should provide a good starting point for the fine-tuning available with the next four adjustment sliders.

Highlights, Shadows, Whites, and **Blacks** are the other four tonal adjustments and they essentially modify the general adjustment achieved through exposure and contrast. Pulling the Highlights to the left will decrease the highlights, often restoring details from the RAW file that seemed forever lost.

Pulling the Highlights up (to the right) will brighten your existing highlights. I find this tool very useful in creating a gentler highlight curve and a more natural look (more "film-like," to use that loaded term).

Opening the shadows by pulling the Shadow slider to the right will perform an improved version of the old fill light adjustment by spreading out and increasing the value of tones in the shadows, effectively adding light to the shadows of your image.

Figure 6-2 shows a relatively flat RAW image file before applying the Whites and Blacks adjustment sliders as shown in **Figure 6-3**. Adjusting the whites and blacks in this fashion will distribute the tones of your image across your entire dynamic range, will increase contrast, and will often result in an aesthetically pleasing image when applied to a relatively flat RAW file.

The Whites and Blacks sliders will adjust the white point and black point of your image, respectively, and have the effect of moving the end points (and thus also brightening/darkening and changing contrast in those areas). If you are looking for a tonal range that is as large as possible between your deepest shadow and brightest highlight, you can pull the Blacks to the left until just before the histogram shows pure black being achieved and pull the Whites to the right until just before the histogram shows the whites being blown out (**Figure 6-3**).

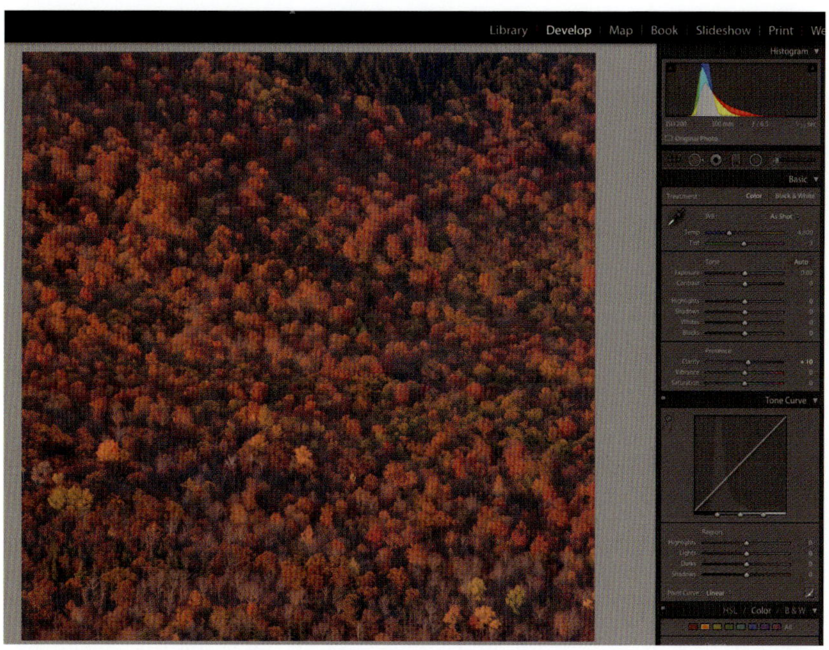

FIGURE 6-2: In this photograph from Maine's Borestone Mountain, the well-exposed RAW file looks flat. Note that the data in the histogram is not spread out very far and is not near the edges on either side.

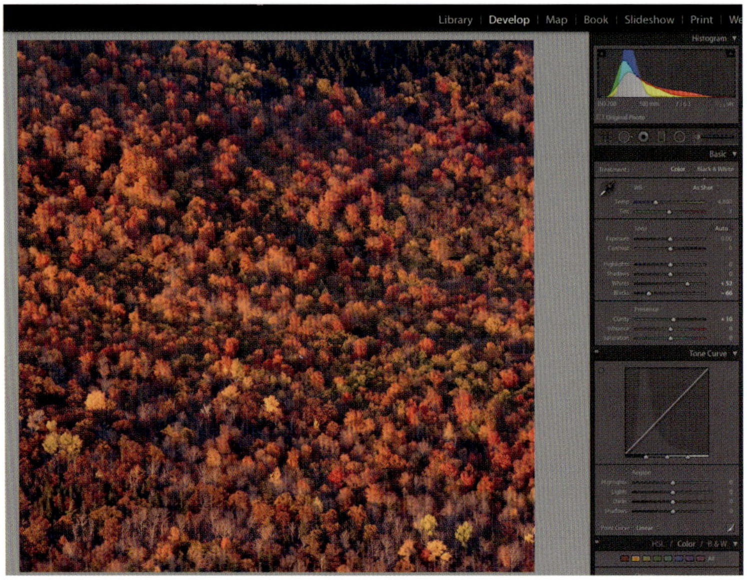

Figure 6-3: I made an initial adjustment of Whites and Blacks to open up the histogram and spread the tones of the image over the entire range. This change has the effect of increasing contrast, too. Simple tonality changes can change the look and feel of an image quite a bit.

Even though we've discussed the basic tonality adjustments in a particular order, very often you will want to experiment and iterate with the adjustments to achieve the tonal appearance you like. I make my first pass in this order, but then will go back and tweak one or more of them so as to achieve my final result. Each adjustment can and will have an impact on others, so further refinement might be necessary or desirable. Pulling highlights down may, for example, let you bring the exposure up more than you had previously.

Adjusting Tonality in Photoshop

If you are no longer working on your RAW file and are instead in Photoshop, my tool of choice for adjusting tonality is the Curves adjustment layer. If you prefer, the Brightness/Contrast, Levels, and Exposure adjustment layers will also work fine for adjusting tonality. I prefer using the Curves adjustment layer as I find I can perform almost any tonal adjustment using it (everything except Exposure, and that I generally take care of in my RAW processor) and because, after using it for many years, I find it very intuitive and powerful.

Let's look at an example of using a Curves adjustment layer to increase brightness and contrast in an image (**Figure 6-4**). My first step is usually to move the white points and black points to increase contrast in the image, similarly as to we did in the previous section in adjusting the Blacks and Whites in Lightroom/ACR.

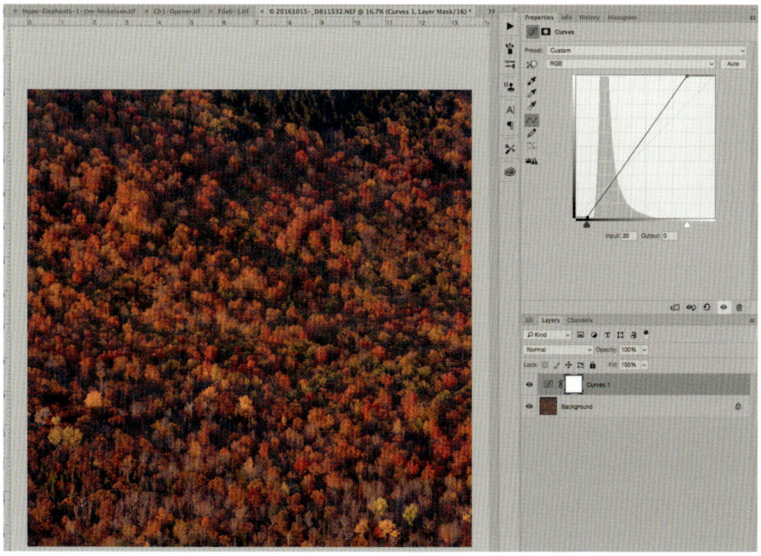

Figure 6-4: Pulling in the black point and white point in the Curve of a Photoshop Adjustment Layer increases the contrast of the RAW image from Figure 6-2. The black and white triangles in the Curves Histogram can be pulled to the left and right to adjust the black and white points, respectively.

After adjusting the white and black points, I typically add a point in the center of the curve and adjust the brightness higher or lower by moving the point up or down. I then add two more points, one halfway toward the highlights and one halfway toward the shadows, and then adjust contrast. This type of edit using the Curves adjustment layer can quickly and efficiently change a flat RAW capture to a pleasingly bright and contrasty image (**Figure 6-5**).

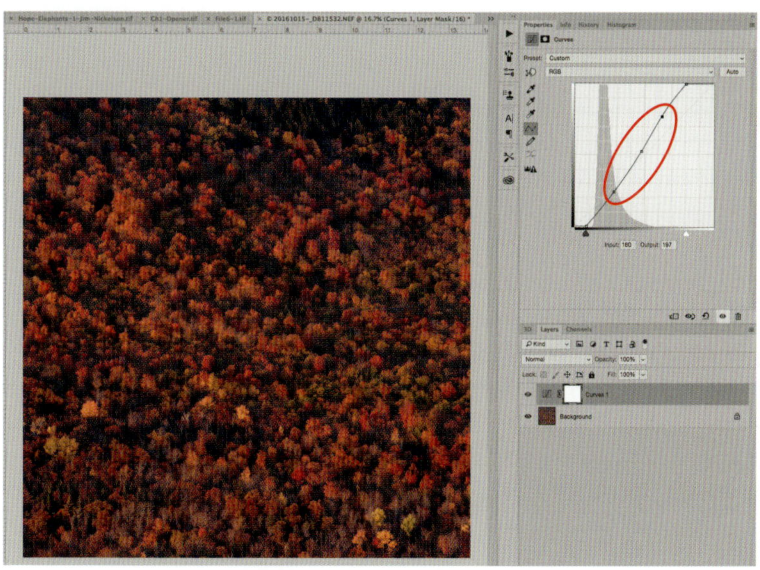

Figure 6-5: Three control points on the curve of Figure 6-4 allow you to control brightness and contrast more precisely. This is a very shallow S-curve, associated with increased contrast, as the first point toward the shadows is pulled down and the third point toward the highlights is pulled up.

To increase contrast using this curve, you pull up the point in the highlights and pull down the points in the shadows to create what is called an "S-curve." To reduce contrast you would do the opposite, pulling down the highlights and pulling up the shadows.

There are many images that require more sophisticated adjustments than these, but for the majority of the prints I make these types of basic adjustments are sufficient for global edits.

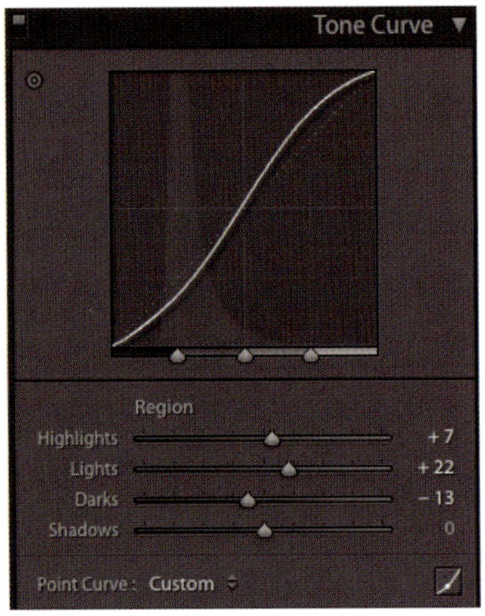

FIGURE 6-6: An "S-curve" applied using the parametric tone curve. Note that the Highlights, Lights, Darks, and Shadows sliders all changed values, too. You can edit this curve using either the sliders or the curve itself.

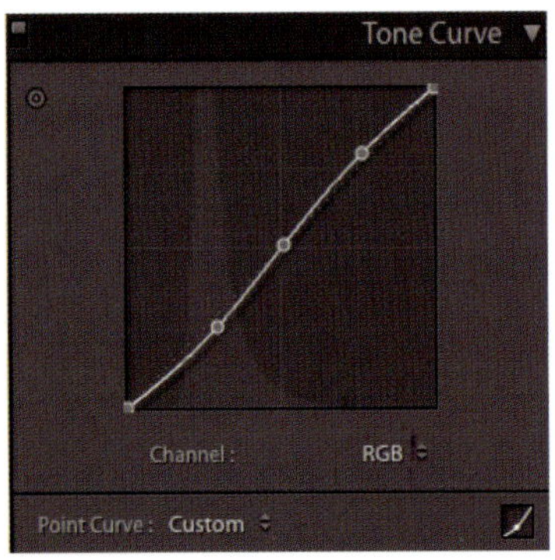

FIGURE 6-7: An S-curve applied to the point tone curve, similar to how such a curve could be done in Photoshop

Adjusting the Tone Curve in Lightroom/ACR

Lightroom and ACR maintain two different curve editors that provide additional opportunities for tonality adjustment: one a parametric tone curve editor for quick adjustments and the other the point curve editor for more precise adjustments. These tone curve adjustments can be performed in addition to, or instead of, the basic tonality adjustments.

Tone curves are a tool for adjusting tonal relationships using a curve-based approach rather than the slider-based approach in a fashion more like Photoshop than the basic Lightroom/ACR tools. Using tone curves, you can replicate the Photoshop method of controlling tonal relationships by applying points to a curve and adjusting to taste.

For many users and many images, tone curve adjustments won't be needed as the standard tonal relationship tools will be sufficient, but for fine control, the addition of tone curves gives a powerful new tool for photographers. If you do modify the tone curves, I recommend iterating any modifications with those to standard tonal relationship tools as you may need to modify your Highlights or Shadows, for example, after adjusting the tone curve.

The parametric tone curve editor is available when you first access the Tone Curve tool in the Develop module (**Figure 6-6**). Instead of adding points to the curve, here you use the Highlights, Lights, Darks, and Shadows sliders to control tonality. The tone curve will move as you adjust the sliders, or you can grab the curve itself and move it. Some find this set of tools more intuitive than the basic ones, and it is worth trying these to see if you find them useful to you. I rarely use them myself and instead rely on the other tools, but others love them.

To access the point curve editor, click the graphic icon in the lower right of the Tone Curve module (**Figure 6-7**). You can use this very similarly to the Curve Adjustment layer of Photoshop (as described previously) by adding points to the tone curve to increase or decrease brightness and contrast.

Local Contrast Enhancement and Clarity

Because of the nature of digital capture and the compression of data into the dynamic range of a camera, the contrast in the midtones of an image is often relatively flat. One common technique to boost the contrast in these midtones is called **Local Contrast Enhancement** (or simply midtone contrast). It is something worth trying on every image as it very often has a subtle but noticeable effect of adding more presence or punch (or clarity, or pop) to an image.

Clarity in Lightroom

Lightroom and ACR have a version of local contrast enhancement called Clarity (**Figure 6-8**) located in the Basic panel of the Develop module. Clarity is an effective tool for increasing or decreasing midtone contrast and I recommend using it, but it lacks control beyond simply an amount of Clarity to be applied. It is an effect that, in small doses, usually improves the look of a digital image, but it can also be easily overdone. Interestingly, Clarity can be set to a negative value for a glowing effect, too.

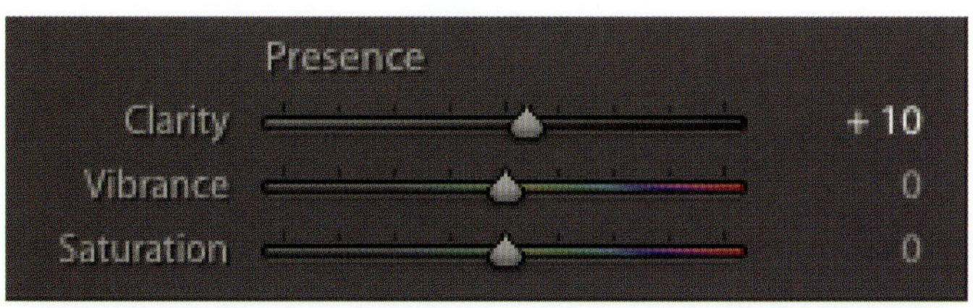

Figure 6-8: The Clarity slider defaults to 0, and for most images I'll pull it up just a bit to somewhere between +5 and +15. I'd use that range just as a starting point and adjust to taste, but be careful not to go too far.

Local Contrast Enhancement in Photoshop

Like most things in Photoshop, there are many ways of accomplishing local contrast enhancement. I usually use the Midtone Contrast tool in the PhotoKit Sharpener plug-in when I do apply midtone contrast in Photoshop, but it is also relatively easy to perform this manually. For whatever method you choose, I recommend working with a duplicate background layer rather than your background layer so that you can easily remove the layer or reduce its opacity without impacting your background layer.

My preferred method to manually add local contrast enhancement to an image in Photoshop is as follows:

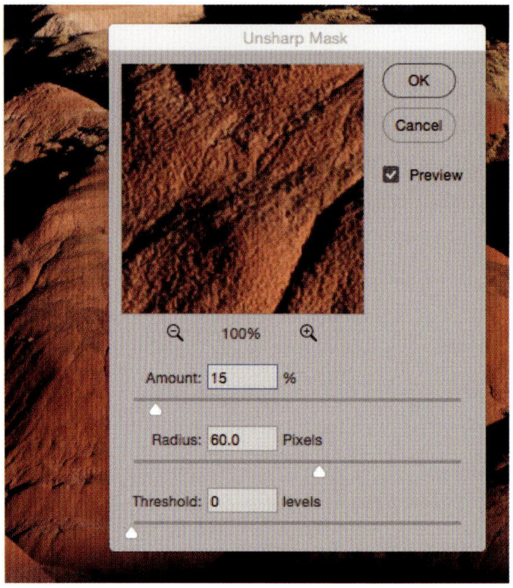

FIGURE 6-9: Typical settings for the Unsharp Mask filter in Photoshop to perform Local Contrast Enhancement

1. Create a duplicate background layer
2. On the duplicate background layer, pull up unsharp masking (Filter > Sharpen > Unsharp Mask) (**Figure 6-9**)
3. Set the Radius for 50 or 60 pixels or so (between 30 and 100 can work) and the Threshold to 0
4. Set the Amount to around 15%, or perhaps a bit less

For simplicity you can leave the Radius alone and just vary the Amount to help get a feel for what is happening (this is closer to Lightroom/ACR's Clarity tool). With these sorts of settings the Unsharp Mask looks at tonality over a broad area and increases each pixel's variation from the local average, effectively enhancing subtle variations in tone and texture, especially in the midtones.

Other Methods to Add Local Contrast Enhancement

Another simple way of applying local contrast enhancement is to copy the Background layer, change the blend mode to Overlay, apply the High Pass Filter (Filter > Other > High Pass), and use a Radius of around 10. You can also desaturate this sharpening layer by selecting Image > Adjust > Desaturate to prevent any change in saturation of the overall image.

There are third-party plug-ins that can also add Local Contrast Enhancement. In PhotoKit Sharpener, for example, you can select Automate > PhotoKit Creative Sharpener > Special Effects > Midtone Contrast, and then adjust the opacity to your desired level. PhotoKit Sharpener also offers a Negative Midtone Contrast much like Lightroom with its negative Clarity.

One caution with this technique is that it can reduce the smoothness of tones within in an image, so consider using sparingly or in a localized fashion for portraits or other images that value smoothness, landscape images with continuous-tone skies, and the like. If you use a duplicate background layer, you can mask off any areas where you'd like to eliminate the local contrast enhancement effect.

Color

The adjustment of color is extremely important in processing your image, both for creative control of the final look as well as correcting for any undesirable colors shifts. A myriad of tools are available to achieve whatever look you'd like.

Adjusting Color in Lightroom/ACR

When processing a RAW file, typically, the first thing to look at editing with respect to color is the white balance of the image. The white balance represents the color temperature of the light striking the subject. Modern cameras have a white balance sensor that detects the white balance of the scene as best as it is able, and that recorded white balance stored in the RAW file will be the default white balance applied to the image unless you have chosen to override this.

The **White Balance** tool in Lightroom/ACR (**Figure 6-10**) allows you to control the color temperature (Temp) and tint of the image and is the primary control of the global color of your image. I recommend moving the Temp setting up and down to warm (make more yellow) or cool (make more blue) your image. I tend to use the captured default white balance as my starting point and often my ending point, but I like to experiment to see how the

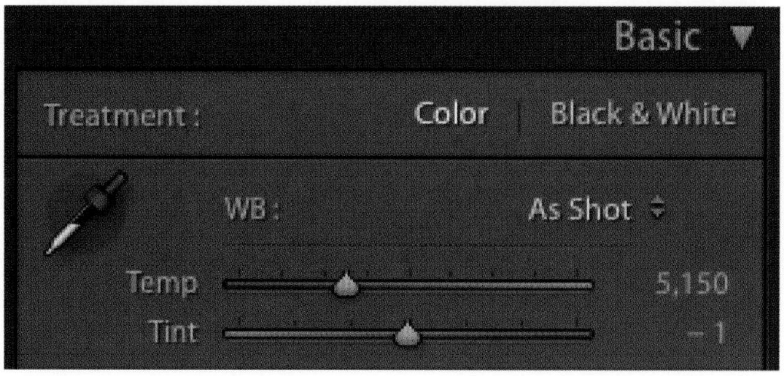

FIGURE 6-10: The very simple White Balance tool in Lightroom/ACR is extremely powerful. As one of my first edits, I usually experiment by moving the Temp slider left and right (cooler and warmer) to see the effect on my image. The Eyedropper on the left allows you to specify a neutral point and adjust the overall white balance in response.

image will look when made warmer or cooler. I find the Tint control to be less useful creatively, as even small changes in the setting can dramatically change your image, but it is wonderful for removing small green or magenta tints.

One aspect of the White Balance tool I use frequently is the eyedropper, with which you can select an area of the image you think should be neutral, and then adjust the white balance of the whole image accordingly to bring that particular location to neutral. When white balance appears off, this is the first tool I use to try to correct it. Even if I think that it goes too far, it can at least give me an idea of the direction I should go in temperature or tint.

The next color controls in the Presence section of the Basic panel are **Vibrance** and **Saturation** (**Figure 6-11**). **Saturation** controls the overall saturation of the image, changing the saturation of each color simultaneously. **Vibrance** is a nonlinear control of saturation and impacts less saturated areas of the image more than heavily saturated areas, making it less likely to create extreme effects. Vibrance also typically does a better job with skin tones than normal Saturation, as it seems to protect red colors from becoming too saturated. In most cases, I recommend adjusting Vibrance instead of Saturation when making any global changes to your image.

The **Hue/Saturation/Luminosity (HSL)** tool (**Figure 6-12**) allows users to control the hue, saturation, and luminosity of the colors of an image individually. Instead of, say, a global adjustment of saturation, you can choose to just modify the saturation of blues using the HSL tool. The color palette is divided into eight channels of color, so experimentation as to which color to change is always in order (random hint: to adjust green saturation, try adjusting the yellow slider). The Targeted Adjustment tool (the little icon in the upper left of the HSL tool) allows you to click on an image and adjust the HSL setting by dragging, providing a simpler way of identifying the colors comprising any particular part of the image.

The **Tone Curve** tool in Lightroom/ACR can also be used to adjust color globally. Instead of adjusting the entire RGB curve as we do for tonality, we can instead adjust each of the Red, Green, and Blue channels individually (**Figure 6-13**). By selecting Red, Green, or Blue in the lower portion of the Tone Curve tool, you can switch to any of three individual color channels.

The key to using the curves is to remember that each color has an opposite: red is opposite cyan, green is opposite magenta, and blue is opposite yellow. So, if red is removed from the image there is also the effect of adding cyan, and the inverse is also true. Similarly, decreasing green results in adding magenta, increasing green subtracts magenta, adding blue removes yellow, and removing blue adds yellow. By adding points to the curve, you can apply any of these color tweaks to different parts of the image, such as by adding red and yellow to the highlights, removing blue from just the shadows, or other selective adjustments.

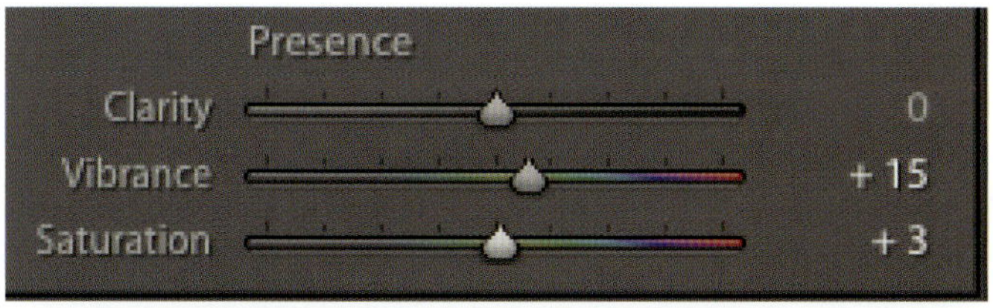

Figure 6-11: Saturation and Vibrance are controlled in the Presence section of the Basic panel in Lightroom's Develop module

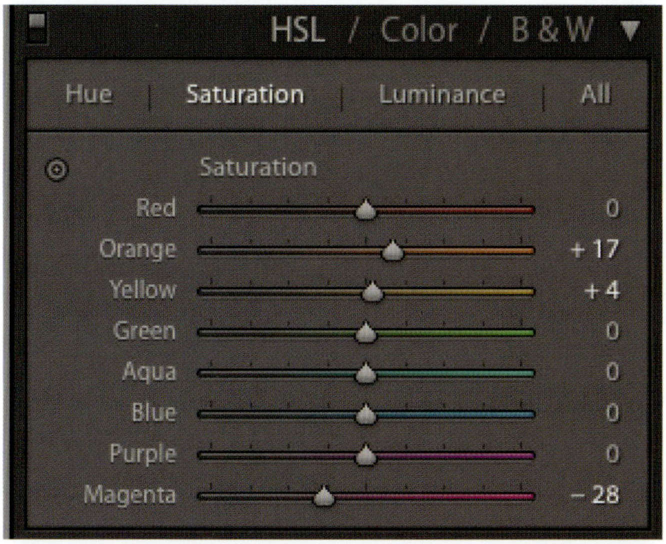

Figure 6-12: The HSL tool in Lightroom gives you excellent control over individual colors, allowing you to individually control Hue, Saturation, and Luminance for eight distinct colors. Using this tool, you can shift or intensify (or de-intensify) specific colors throughout your image.

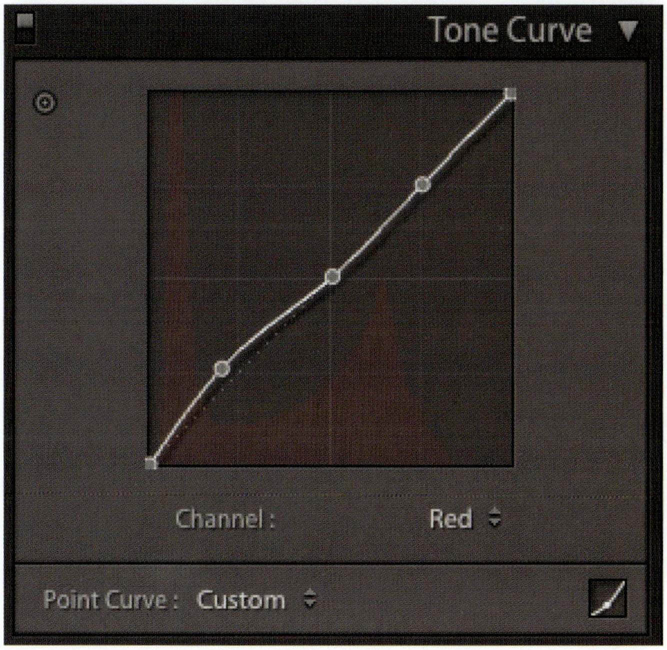

Figure 6-13: You can control color more precisely using the Point Tone Curve in Lightroom by selecting a channel (Red here) and then use points on the curve to give either an overall shift or adjust highlights, midtones, and shadows separately. Here, I've added red (and thus removed cyan) in the shadow area but minimized the effect in the midtones and highlights by locking down the curve with more points.

Principles of Printing #8: Problems Are Opportunities

Encountering a problem provides an opportunity to learn a new technique. Most things I've learned about image editing have been the result of researching and trying out different things when faced with problems on particular images. In a simple example early on, I increased saturation in an image and was frustrated that all of the colors were increasing in saturation when I just wanted to increase the greens. Learning how to increase the saturation in only the Green channel taught me about channels, an idea I then could apply to other problems.

Learning how to make an HDR image to deal with a large dynamic range can, for example, open up the ability to use HDR techniques to solve other problems or can give you ideas on whole new bodies of work. Problems can be frustrating at times, but remember that all of those frustrations are making you better at performing processing and realizing your vision.

The Tone Curve tool is thus immensely powerful for adjusting color, but, more so than almost any other tool, this is one where your technique will improve with experience. If you felt that your image was too cyan, for example, you would go to the Red channel, pull the Red curve up, and thus make the image simultaneously more red and less cyan (**Figure 6-14**). This sequence of steps will become more intuitive with experience.

Importantly, more precise adjustments to the Red/Green/Blue channels are also possible to greatly increase the power of the tool. You can, for exam-

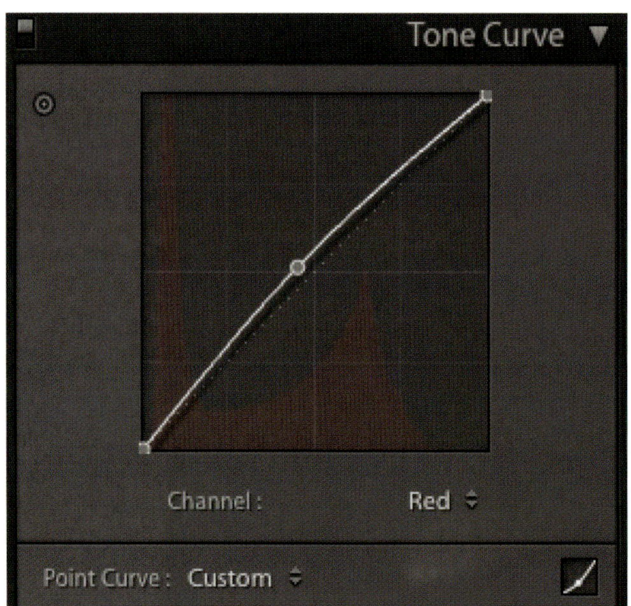

FIGURE 6-14: By pulling up the Red channel in the middle, you can impose an overall red shift (this also removes cyan) that impacts the midtones primarily and then blends in the effect into the shadows and highlights

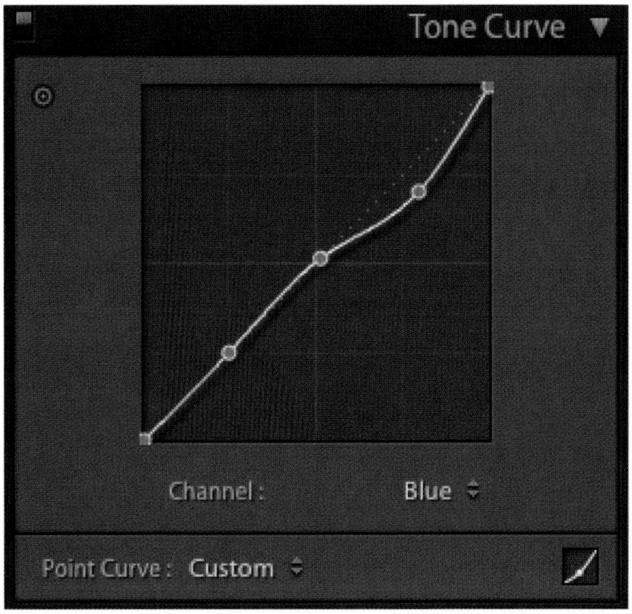

Figure 6-15: By pulling down the highlights of the Blue channel and locking down the rest of the curve, you can warm the highlights with yellow (and remove blue)

ple, warm the highlights in an image by limiting an increase in yellow to just the highlights area by locking down the midtones and shadows with points on the Blue tone curve (**Figure 6-15**).

Adjusting Color in Photoshop

If you complete processing your RAW file and desire to make further modifications to color, Photoshop has an incredible array of choices to do so. Except in a few rare cases, I am able to accomplish any color modifications that I need using just two of the many available tools, as I'll describe below. I'd like to emphasize that many of the other tools are just as viable and effective as the ones I use, so please don't interpret my focus on these two tools as a prohibition on using others.

The first Photoshop tool I use regularly is our trusty Curves adjustment layer. To modify the color balance, the individual red, blue, and green channels can be used to adjust the colors throughout an image, including by impacting the shadows, midtones, and highlights separately, just as described above in reference to the Tone Curve tool in Lightroom/ACR (**Figure 6-16**).

Through skillful application of these Red, Green, and Blue curves almost any sort of color shift can be obtained in Photoshop using a Curves

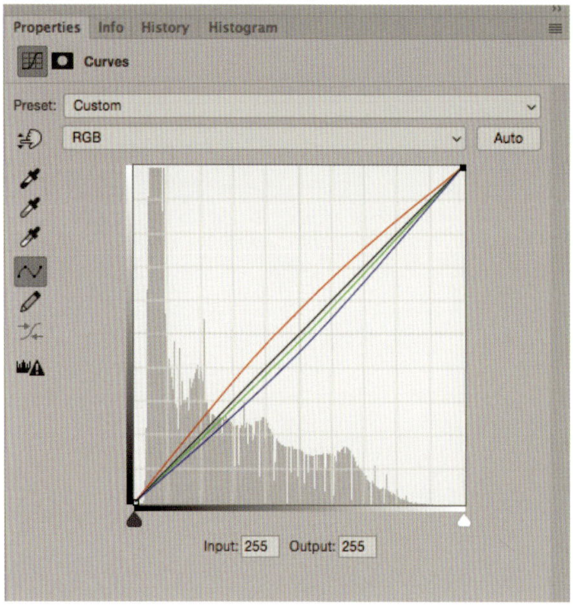

Figure 6-16: You can control all three channels of color in one adjustment layer—when in the RGB mode you can see your RGB curve (the black line) as well as any color curves (the colored lines)

adjustment layer. I do recommend performing color correction using a separate Curve adjustment layer from any tonality Curve adjustment layers (**Figure 6-17**), each with a different name, so that you can easily control each curve and its effect for ease of editing. However, you could also perform both tonality and color corrections in the same Curve layer.

The second Photoshop tool I use regularly to control color is the Hue/Saturation adjustment layer (**Figure 6-18**). The Hue/Saturation adjustment layer is incredibly useful in that it allows you to control the hue, saturation, and

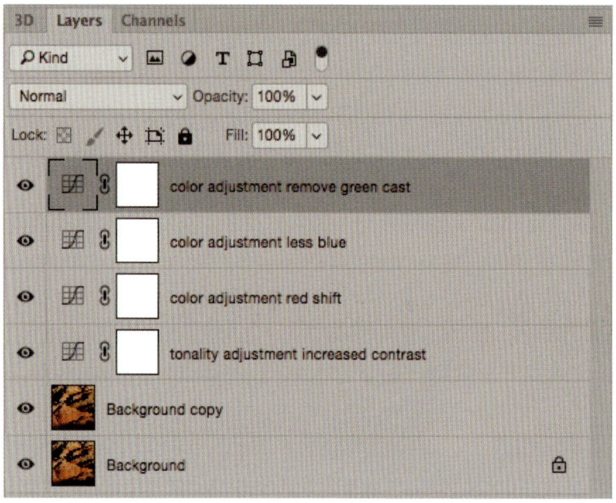

Figure 6-17: An example set of adjustment layers in Photoshop, with each color shift and tonality modification residing in a different layer for maximum control

lightness of each individual color channel, just as it does in Lightroom/ACR.

Since these two tools are available during RAW processing via Lightroom and ACR, why would they be necessary to use in Photoshop? Because our ability to selectively apply these particular tools, rather than apply them globally, is much more powerful in Photoshop, as described in the next section.

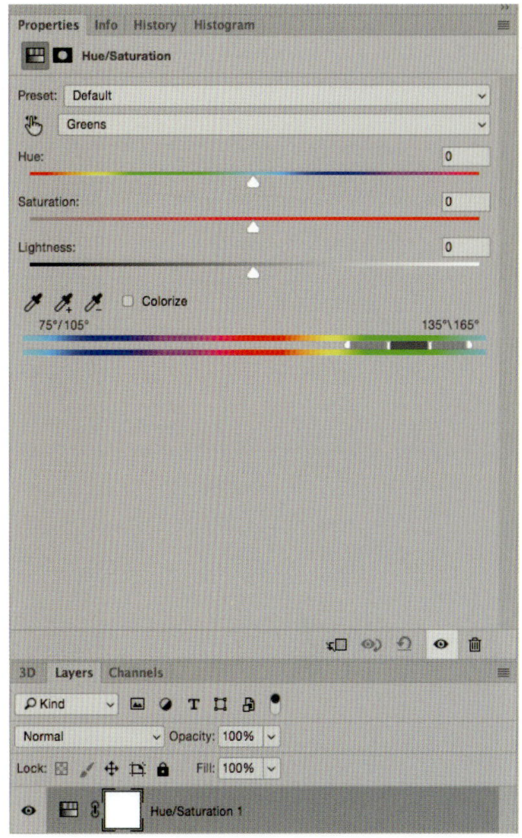

Figure 6-18: In the Hue/Saturation adjustment layer you can individually change the Hue, Saturation, and Lightness of six different colors. Note that you can treat Lightness the same as Luminance in Lightroom/ACR and that Photoshop has a slightly different set of colors available.

Selective Image Adjustments

Almost any of the *global changes* to an image identified in the Global Image Adjustment section can also be applied to only a selected local portion of the image. **Selective image adjustments** are those edits that are applied to only a localized portion of the image rather than to the entire image. Selective adjustments are a powerful and essential tool for Print Interpretation and making your final print realize your artistic intent.

While every adjustment can be selectively applied in Photoshop, only a limited group of adjustments can be selectively applied in Lightroom/ACR. For this reason, I often perform basic edits in Lightroom and then export the image to Photoshop for final selective tuning.

Next, I'll describe the tools I typically use to make selective adjustments in both Lightroom/ACR and Photoshop. The tools we'll cover are as follows:

Lightroom Tools	Photoshop Tools
Graduated Filter	Masks
Radial Filter	Brush
Adjustment Brush	Gradient Tool

In chapter 10 on Print Interpretation, I'll demonstrate how I apply these tools to specific images.

Selective Adjustments in Lightroom

Selective adjustments in Lightroom are performed in the Develop module by using the Graduated Filter tool, the Radial Filter tool, or the Adjustment Brush tool. As of the time of this writing, there are 15 Lightroom/ACR tools that can

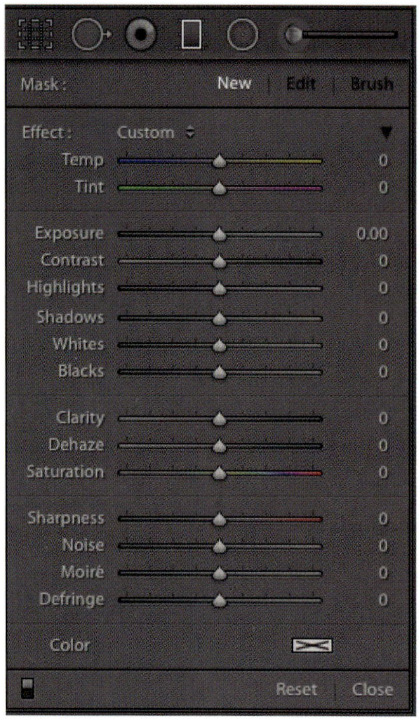

FIGURE 6-19: Tools in Lightroom/ACR that are available for selective adjustment using the Graduated Filter, Radial Filter, and Adjustment Brush tools

be selectively applied using one of these three tools (**Figure 6-19**). This list has expanded as Lightroom/ ACR have developed, and a significant portion of the types of edits commonly performed in preparation for print can be accomplished with these. There are still a few notable omissions for those who print, though, including the ability to selectively apply Hue/Saturation/ Luminance adjustments by color channel, Vibrance, and tonality adjustments using the Tone Curve.

With any of the tools, press the letter "O" on your keyboard to toggle the visible mask you are applying to assist you in its application (**Figure 6-20**). The mask is an indication of where your change will be applied in the image (and where it won't be). The default color of the mask is red, and the intensity of the red indicates a partial application of the mask. In other words, where the mask is fully red

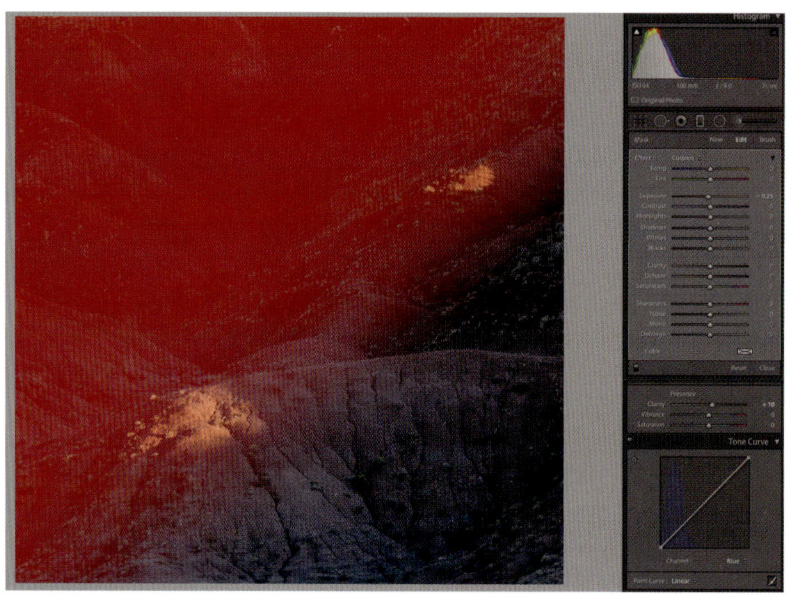

FIGURE 6-20: An example of the Graduated Filter tool being applied to an image in Lightroom in an effort to darken the left upper part of the image to make the central diagonal shape more prominent. The red overlay indicates where the change (a –0.25 Exposure) is fully applied, which is in the upper-left part of the image. The effect gradually dissipates over the center of the image until the effect is gone on the lower-right corner of the image (as indicated by the lack of a red overlay).

the edit is applied fully, where the mask is not visible no edit is being applied, and where the mask is a transparent red the edit is only partially applied.

The first of the tools is the **Graduated Filter** tool (as shown in **Figure 6-20**), which applies adjustments in a gradient pattern extending from a full application of the adjustment and fading to no application of the adjustment. The gradient pattern can be modified by changing its midpoint, starting point, and end point, and it can also be rotated. As with all of the tools, you can make more than one adjustment, too, on the same gradient, and you can also make more than one gradient by selecting New and proceeding with a new one.

The **Radial Filter** tool is a relatively new addition to the toolset of Lightroom/ACR and is quite powerful. It is similar in concept to the Graduated Filter tool but with a circular or elliptical application rather than one based on a straight line. Using the tool to make a circular or elliptical shape, your adjustment will be applied either within the shape (if Invert Mask is checked) or outside the shape (if Invert Mask is not checked) (**Figure 6-21**). The Feather adjustment controls how gradual the transition is between impacted areas and non-impacted areas.

The third adjustment tool is the **Adjustment Brush** tool, which lets you "paint" on an effect anywhere in your image, making it immensely flexible (**Figure 6-22**). I usually recommend selecting Auto Mask (for areas that have relatively well-defined edges) and having a Density of around 20 so that you

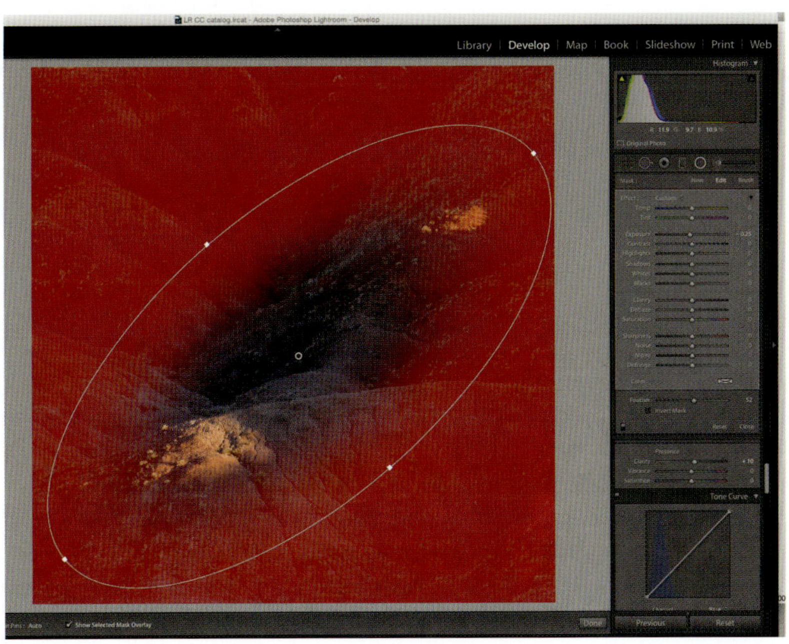

FIGURE 6-21: Here is an example of using the Radial Filter to limit the area of application of a change. In this case I wanted to darken the area beyond an ellipse running from the lower left to the upper right to help emphasize the area within the ellipse by darkening the area outside of it. Adjusting the points of the ellipse and rotating it, as well as controlling the feather, can give you precise control of its application.

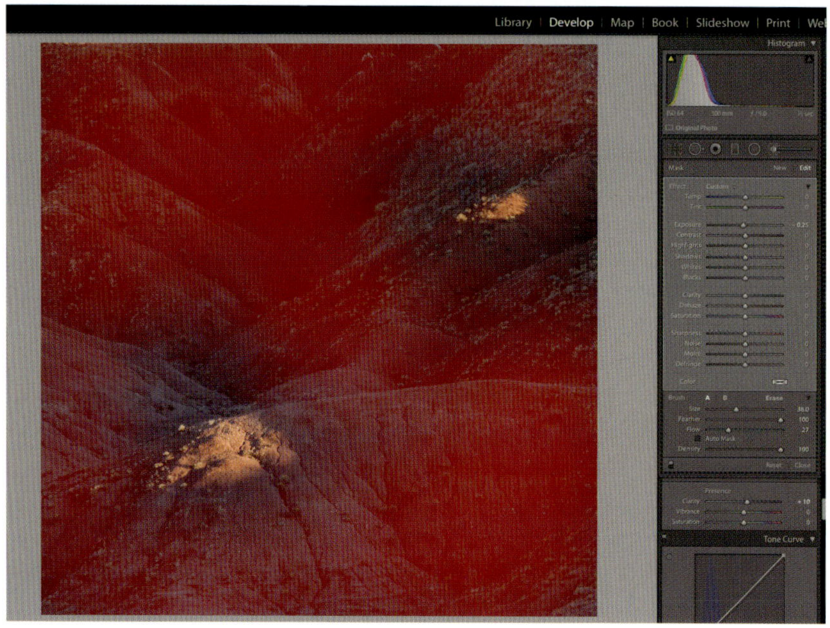

FIGURE 6-22: An application of an Adjustment Brush mask to the same image as Figures 6-20 and 6-22. The Adjustment Brush, here applied without an Auto Mask, allows me to apply the mask more flexibly than the other tools, as evidenced by my ability to paint in a change between the two brighter areas near the center of the image.

can slowly paint on changes. You can also modify the size and feather of your brush for additional control.

Once you select one of these tools, you can then see what types of adjustments are possible for that tool, make an adjustment, and then selectively apply the adjustment. You can, for example, burn an image (as in "burning" and "dodging" in the film darkroom) by selecting the Adjustment Brush tool, applying a slight decrease in exposure, and then brush on that decreased exposure wherever you'd like to burn. I find that it takes quite a bit of practice to become proficient at these tools, but they are powerful additions to the Lightroom/ACR arsenal.

Selective Adjustments in Photoshop

Any global image adjustments you make using a duplicate or adjustment layer in Photoshop can also be selectively applied by making a layer mask for that particular layer. **Masks** are the key to this power, and there are many different ways to go about creating and using masks. Indeed, there are entire books about this subject. Photoshop has many powerful and complex tools designed to create and modify selections and masks.

I make the majority of my layer masks using just the **Brush** tool. Here's how I recommend using this tool for Adjustment Layers:

1. Create your adjustment layer of whatever edit you'd like to selectively apply, such as a Curves Layer or Hue/Saturation Layer. A pure white layer mask will automatically be created as well (**Figure 6-23**).
2. Make changes to your adjustment layer so that you are close to the edit you'd like to apply, even though your change will be temporarily applied to the entire image, including areas where you don't want it to be.
3. Select the layer mask (the white square) and then invert it to remove its effect (Command/Ctrl+I while you have it selected), making it pure black (**Figure 6-24**). Whatever edits you made with the adjustment layer will no longer be visible.
4. Using the Brush tool, slowly paint over the areas where you'd like to have the effect visible by choosing a low opacity for the Brush tool (20% or so). Multiple passes of the Brush tool will gradually apply the edit more and more strongly to those areas (and make the mask whiter). At any point you can Alt+Option-click on the Mac on the tiny

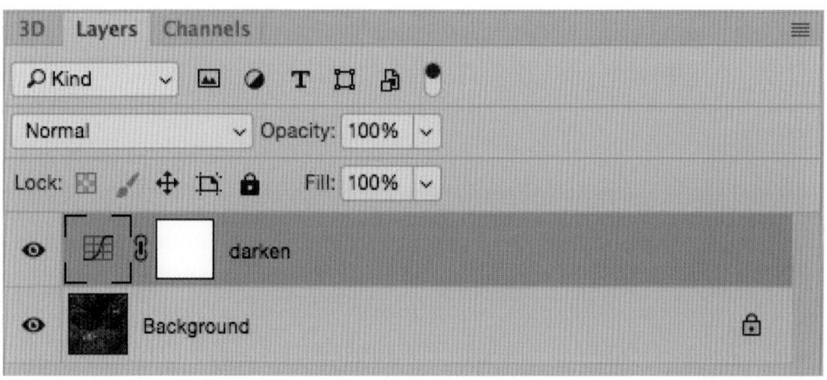

FIGURE 6-23: Your editing adjustment layer with a pure white mask (the white square next to the word "darken")

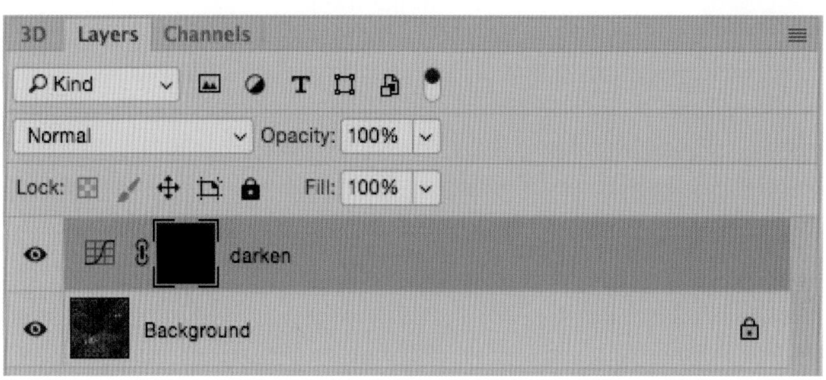

FIGURE 6-24: Your editing adjustment layer inverting the mask. The mask is now shown as a pure black square.

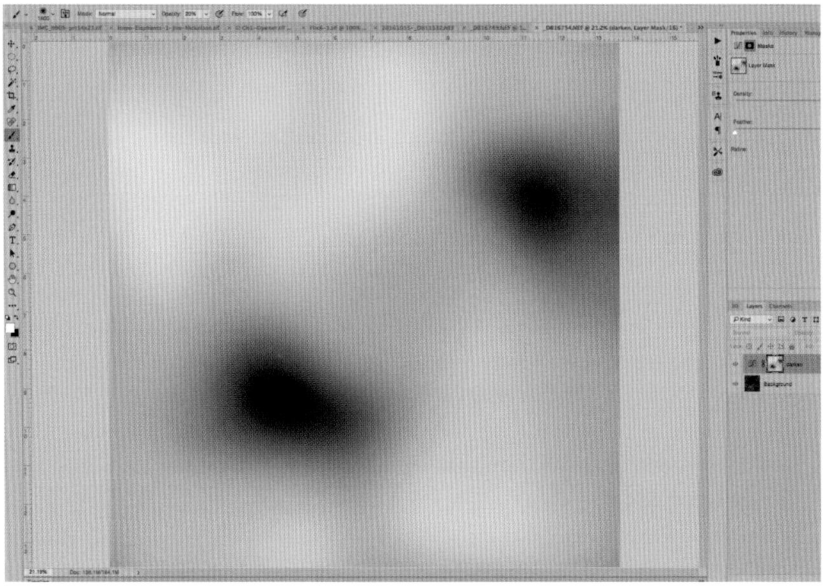

FIGURE 6-25: The mask I created using the Brush tool to paint on white. I love using a soft brush like this for editing as the gentle masks (without hard lines) are much less likely to be visible in the final print. They don't work for every image, but they work well for many.

version of your mask to see how the mask now looks on a large scale, with white being where the edit has been applied, black being where no edit has been applied, and grays being in between (**Figure 6-25**).

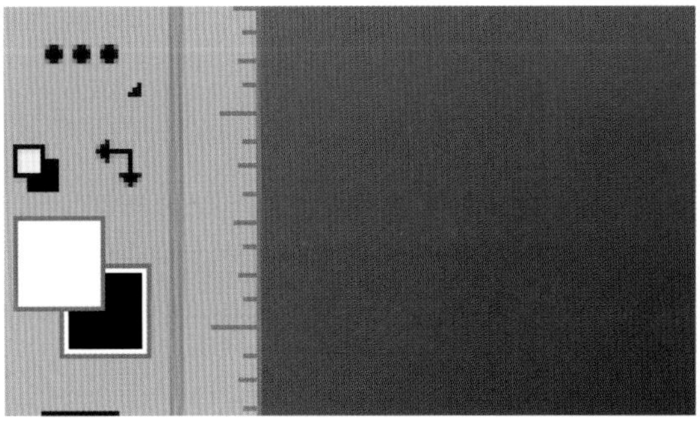

FIGURE 6-26: This small selection tool lets you toggle back and forth between the foreground and background colors being active. I like having white as the foreground and black as the background, and you can add to a mask, and remove from a mask, by selecting the appropriate color to paint with the Brush tool.

The reason I prefer this method of modifying my layer mask is that, by gradually building the changes up using a soft brush with a low opacity, I am less likely to have any visible evidence on the final print that I've used a mask. Subtlety and gradualness are vital in successfully creating masks. I also rather enjoy the process of painting on the adjustments rather than trying to create a perfectly precise selection.

If you find that your brush is not having an impact on the mask when you are trying to paint white on a black mask, double-check to make sure you have the white foreground selected in the foreground and background tool (**Figure 6-26**).

If your layer doesn't already have a layer mask, such as when you have a duplicate layer rather than an adjustment layer, you can highlight your layer and select the Add Layer Mask button at the bottom of the Layers panel to add a layer mask in between steps 1 and 2 above.

The **Gradient Tool** is another tool I commonly use in Photoshop to selectively edit my image. The Gradient Tool can modify your layer mask in a similar fashion to the Paint Brush described previously. It is conceptually like the Graduated Filter tool in Lightroom/ACR but can be used on any layer-based edit in Photoshop, making it very powerful.

To use the Gradient Tool with a layer mask:

1. Create your adjustment layer for whatever edit you'd like to selectively apply, such as a Curves Layer or Hue/Saturation Layer. A pure white layer mask will automatically be created as well.
2. Make changes to your adjustment layer so that you are close to the edit you'd like to apply, even though your change will be temporarily applied to the entire image, including areas where you don't want it to be.
3. Select the layer mask (the white rectangle) and then invert it to remove its effect (Command/Ctrl+I), making it pure black. Whatever edit you made with the adjustment layer will no longer be visible.
4. Select the Gradient Tool and make sure the foreground color is white.
5. Click where you'd like your gradient to be fully applied, hold the mouse button down and drag the cursor to where you'd like the gradient to no longer be applied, and a smooth transition between the two spots will be created in your layer mask (**Figure 6-27**).

Using the Gradient Tool and Paint Brush, you can create very precise and sophisticated edits to your layer mask, allowing equally precise and sophisticated selective adjustments to anything you can do in a layer in Photoshop, whether it be tonality or color adjustments, sharpening, noise reduction, or anything else.

FIGURE 6-27: For this mask, I first clicked near the upper-left corner and then dragged the mouse down and right, releasing just before the center. This gave me a gradient with full application in the upper left and fading to no application near the center. If you don't like your first application of it, just do it again and your old gradient will be replaced by the new one.

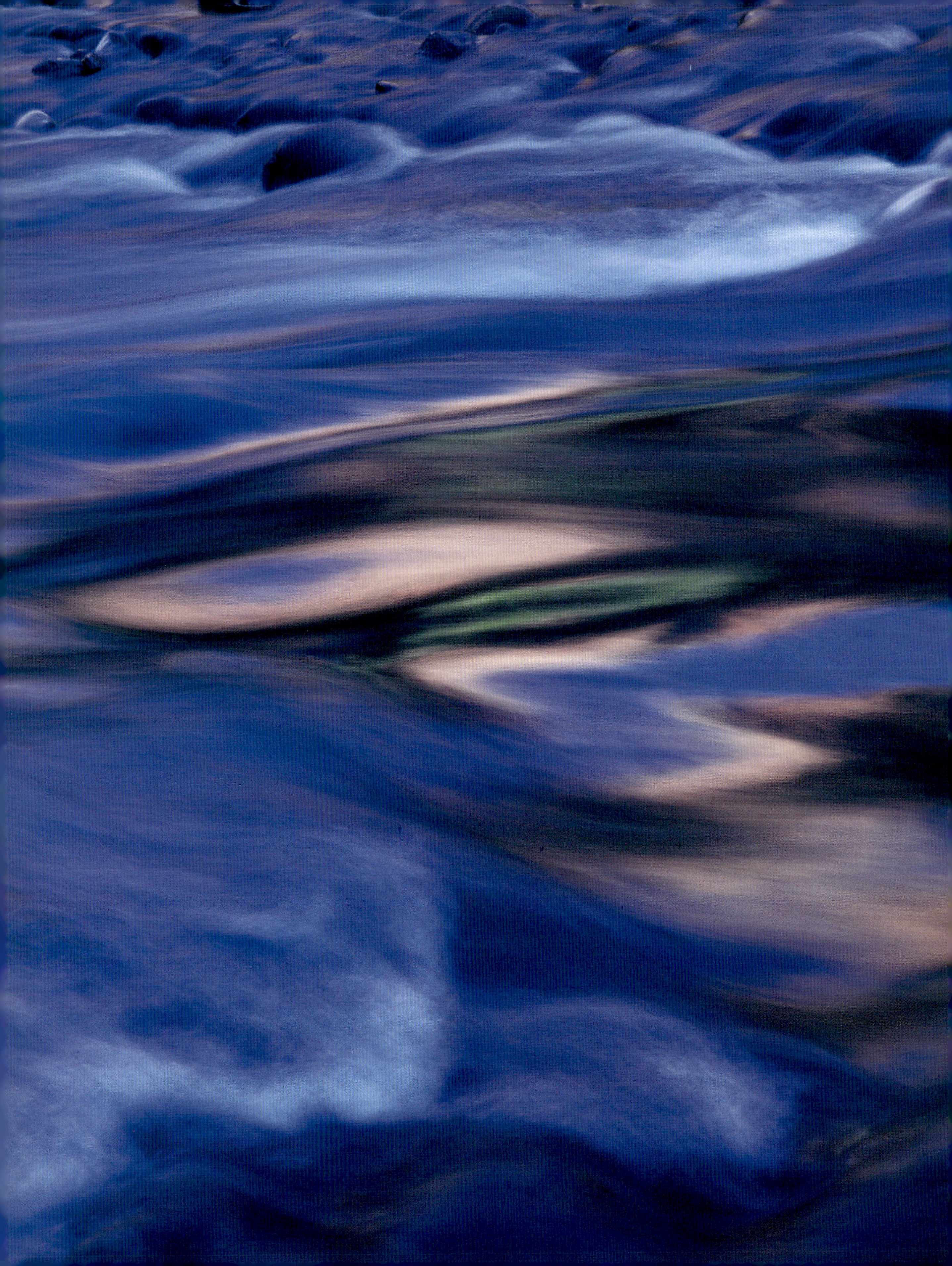

Making the Print

7

Once you've completed editing your image, it's time to actually make your print. In this chapter we'll go over a basic workflow of steps to perform both in software and in handling your paper.

> *For me the printing process is part of the magic of photography. It's that magic that can be exciting, disappointing, rewarding, and frustrating, all in the same few moments in the darkroom.*
> —John Sexton

Basic Printing Workflow

My basic printing workflow is as follows:

1. Complete editing of your image and save all changes (automatic in Lightroom, or as a master file in Photoshop)
2. Optionally, soft proof the image based on your printer-paper profile, choose a rendering intent, and possibly edit your image before printing in light of the soft proofing
3. If printing from Photoshop, resize the image for print based on your desired print size and the target PPI (if you have a layered file in Photoshop, I recommend flattening the layers first)
4. If printing from Photoshop, perform output sharpening on the resized image
5. Perform a final review for any defects such as spots
6. Load your selected paper in the printer (gently bend down the corners if necessary because of curl or thick paper)
7. Choose the appropriate settings and print the image
8. Evaluate the image, and if changes are desired, make necessary modifications and reprint
9. Once the print is completed, optionally save a copy of your print file if using Photoshop

This is my recommended order of steps, but certainly, you can make variations to this based on your preferred working style. Steps 3 and 4 drop out as separate steps when printing from Lightroom, for example. Soft proofing in Step 2 is often optional and some do not find it useful.

Let's talk about each step in more detail.

Soft Proofing

Soft proofing is a technique used to model or simulate how an image will appear in **print** while using your **display**. Soft proofing is a solution to a very difficult challenge—how to emulate a print made of inks on paper (with light reflected off its surface) on an electronic, backlit LCD. Generally speaking, soft proofing will illustrate the loss in saturation and contrast you'll get in the translation between mediums by presenting on your display an image that has less contrast and saturation. Soft proofing emulates the lesser dynamic range of ink and paper compared to the screen as well.

Soft proofing can also reveal how any out-of-gamut colors will be treated in print, and can thus help you choose how to best manage that situation by choosing the appropriate rendering intent for printing.

Soft proofing is a source of consternation for many photographers because of its complexity, but it has become much easier to do in later versions of Photoshop and Lightroom. In this section, we'll discuss how to perform and utilize soft proofing in both Photoshop and Lightroom.

While I feel that a soft proof is important to try, I am also a firm believer in the hard proof and how the actual print looks. I am less concerned with whether my print has as much contrast as does the screen image; rather, I care whether the print looks good on its own and whether it would benefit from more contrast. Print and screen are different mediums and different characteristics look better on each.

I am not saying that you shouldn't soft proof—you should. What I am saying is that soft proofing is no substitute for a hard proof, in my opinion, and that you should use your judgment in trying to make changes in light of the soft proof. The soft proof can indeed be invaluable in determining rendering intent and for diagnosing problems before you put ink to paper, but you should consider analysis of the actual physical print itself to be the ultimate arbiter of whether you have achieved what you'd like with your print. At some point in your process you need to look away from the screen and judge your physical print on its own merits.

Soft Proofing in Lightroom

To soft proof in Lightroom, select Soft Proofing in the lower-left corner while in the Develop module. The background will change to an almost-white paper emulation to help you imagine what the image will look like on paper (it uses the base color of the currently selected profile). A Soft Proofing panel will open in the upper-right corner that includes a histogram as well as a few options to control the soft proofing (**Figure 7-1**).

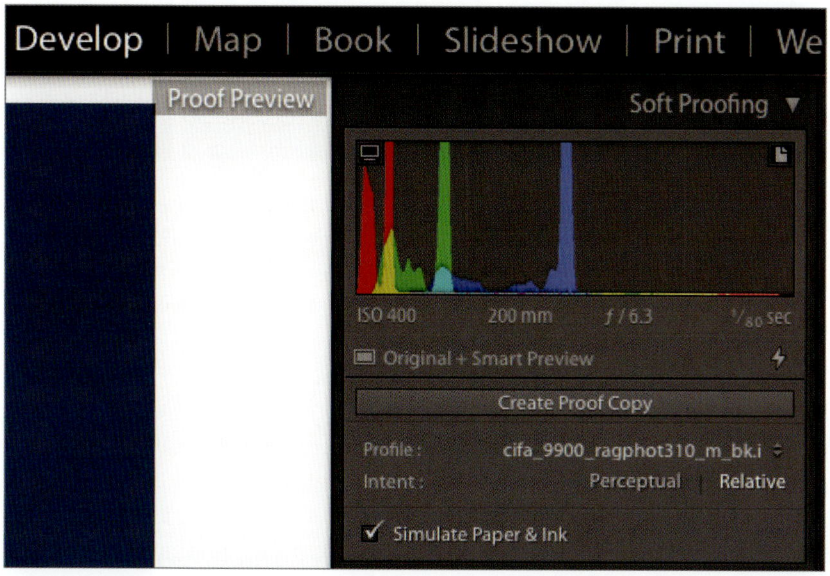

Figure 7-1: The Soft Proofing panel in Lightroom, set to simulate printing the image using the printer-paper profile for Canson Rag Photographique 310 for the Epson 9900 printer using the Relative Rendering Intent

To create an accurate soft proof, make sure the proper print-paper profile is selected by clicking on Profile, and choosing the appropriate profile for your printer and the paper you have chosen. As the screen changes, what will now be shown is a first approximation of how your print will actually look based on the paper white of the selected printer-profile. The view shows the white border around your image to emulate the paper border, and the shade of white is based on the actual paper you will be using.

You can toggle back and forth between the Perceptual and Relative Colorimetric Intents by simply clicking on the appropriate button to see how each will handle any out-of-gamut colors and to determine which you like better. I do this first with the Simulate Paper & Ink button unchecked to check colors. If no colors are out-of-gamut, then there will not be a difference between the rendering intents. If there are any colors out-of-gamut, you can choose which rendering intent gives you a more satisfactory soft proof so that you know which to choose at the time of printing.

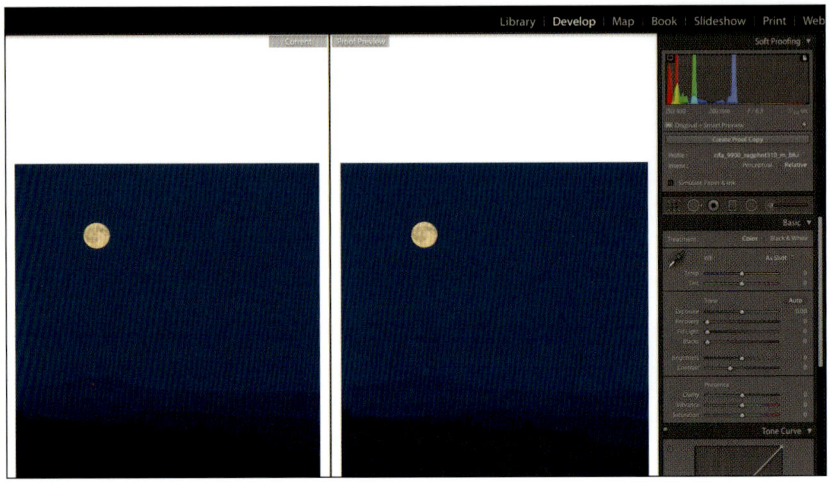

FIGURE 7-2: With the Relative rendering intent selected and Simulate Paper & Ink turned off, the soft proof version on the right is relatively close to the original image on the left. The blue in this image is out-of-gamut for the selected paper, and toggling the rendering intent back and forth led me to choose Relative rendering intent as a better match for what I wanted out of my print. In this case, Relative Colorimetric gave me a deeper blue at the expense of some loss of gradation—but since this is an image with little gradation, I decided that the deeper blue was more important for this specific photograph.

Next, push the before/after button just to the left of the Soft Proofing button in the lower-left corner of the screen (the icon looks like two Y's side-by-side) so that you can see the impact of the rendering intent changes compared to your original image (**Figure 7-2**). You'll see your edited image on the left and the soft proof on the right.

Next, select the Simulate Paper & Ink button in the Soft Proofing panel to see the soft proof based on your chosen profile (**Figure 7-3**). You will likely see an image that looks noticeably worse than the original (usually more dull or less contrasty), and that is to be expected with this option.

The idea behind Simulate Paper & Ink is that it is trying to simulate the loss of contrast and punch going from screen to print, and that you can then modify the soft proof to bring it in line with the original image. The theory

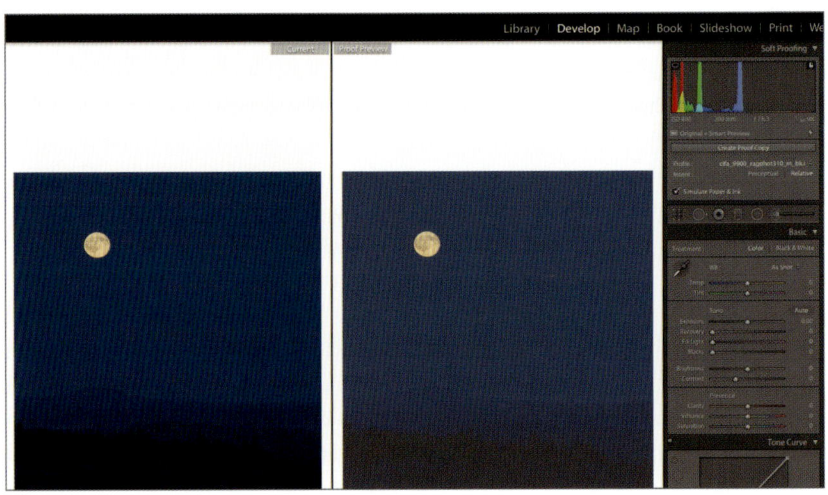

FIGURE 7-3: With the Relative rendering intent selected and Simulate Paper & Ink turned on, the soft proof version on the right is much duller compared to the original image on the left (compare with Figure 7-2). I find that the Simulate Paper & Ink option often over-exaggerates the drop-off in print.

is a good one, but I find from my subjective experience that it often exaggerates the effect so much that I don't find it useful. Therefore, I typically don't use this option. I encourage you to try it yourself to see if it matches your perception of the drop-off between screen and print, as others disagree with me. Even if you treat it with caution like myself, it still can provide valuable information about the sorts of challenges you'll face when making your print as well as the types of edits you can do to conquer those challenges.

While still in the Soft Proofing mode, you can now make edits to try to bring the soft proof in line with your original. The kinds of things you will likely consider changing are increasing contrast, increasing Exposure or Clarity, adjusting hue and saturation, and bringing up the shadows. You can adjust all of these things while viewing the before-and-after images together. One nice feature of Lightroom, if you make any edits, is that it will automatically create a virtual copy for you specifically for your print modifications (and the printer-profile name will helpfully be in the name of the virtual copy). You can have copies for any papers that you use.

Soft Proofing in Photoshop

Soft proofing in Photoshop is very effective but not quite as easy to use as Lightroom's implementation. To soft proof an image, chose View > Proof Setup > Custom to open the Customize Proof Condition box and then, in the Device to Simulate dropdown, choose your printer-paper profile (**Figure 7-4**). You can also change the rendering intent to view the impact of the different intents so that you can choose the appropriate one for your image. I recommend only choosing between Relative Colorimetric and Perceptual for printing photographic images despite the two other options being available.

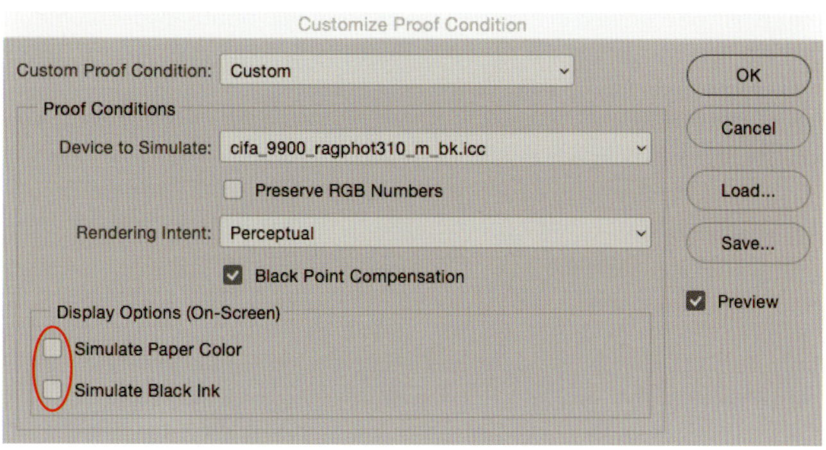

Figure 7-4: View of the Customize Proof Condition menu. I normally do not check either box in Display Options. I choose the printer-paper profile for the Device to Simulate and toggle the Rendering Intent between Perceptual and Relative Colorimetric to evaluate that setting.

To view the soft proof in Photoshop, make sure the Preview box is checked and then you can check and uncheck the Simulate Paper Color box to see the soft proof turned on and off. You can also save a proof condition (i.e., the combination of your printer-paper profile and rendering intent) for easy access later by clicking Save in the Customize Proof Condition dialog box.

If you decide you would like to modify the image for proof, I recommend creating a duplicate image (you can add soft proofing for your particular paper in the name, too). Then you can view the original and soft proofed versions side-by-side by selecting Window > Arrange > Tile All Vertically to view them simultaneously (**Figure 7-5**). The next step would be to make your soft proof image active and make any adjustments to make it look more like the original.

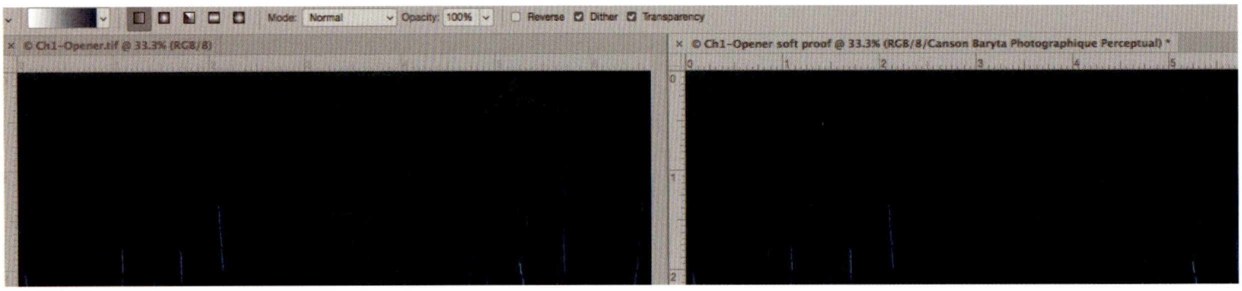

FIGURE 7-5: Two images viewed side-by-side, the original image on the left and a soft proof version on the right. When the soft proof version one is active, you can make edits to it as desired to bring it closer to the original image.

Selecting Your Rendering Intent for Print

I've talked about choosing between Relative Colorimetric and Perceptual rendering intents. As we discussed in chapter 3, your choice of rendering intent will dictate how an image that is out-of-gamut for a particular print-paper profile will be modified to fit within the space of that printer-paper profile. In other words, we need to tell the computer how to modify the image to make it fit. Remember, this only applies to images where there is data beyond the range of the destination printer-paper profile. For images that are in-gamut, rendering intent does not matter.

To make your out-of-gamut image become in-gamut, the Relative Colorimetric rendering intent will convert everything that is beyond gamut to the maximum value that is within gamut (**Figure 7-6**). The advantage of this is that anything that was already in-gamut is not impacted. The disadvantage of this method is that everything that was already out-of-gamut is truncated and treated the same—so if you have important parts of your image in the out-of-gamut range, you could lose gradations and detail.

Perceptual rendering intent will take your maximum value that is out-of-gamut and move it just enough to bring it in-gamut. Everything else that has the same color will be "squished" down. The advantage of this is that relative relationships between colors are retained and you don't lose gradations and detail. The downside is that colors that were in-gamut and safe are actually modified—so you might diminish or modify colors that started off in-gamut. If, say, your reds are compressed because the brightest red was out-of-gamut, you might shift colors in purples. Since purple includes blue and red, if the red is lessened, the purple could shift in hue toward blue.

Neither rendering intent is "the best" and the one you should use depends on your image. Generally speaking I've found Relative Colorimetric more often the best choice for nature images and Perceptual more often the best choice for intense urban scenes containing lots of color, but it really is a case-by-case determination. Luckily, our software tools let us evaluate this before printing (though like everything, a hard proof is the only way to know with absolute certainty which is best for your image).

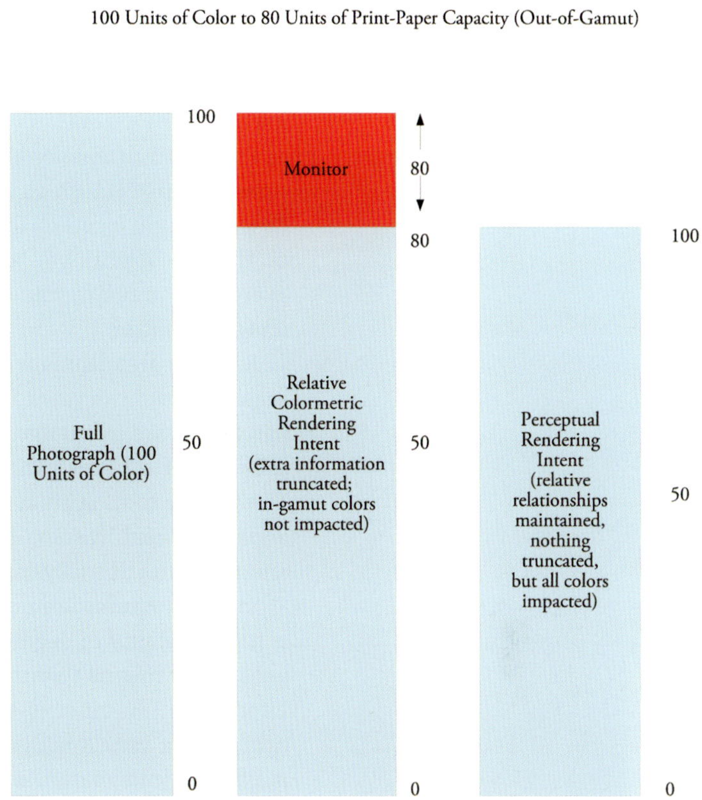

Figure 7-6: In this highly simplified version of the rendering intents, we assume that our photograph has 100 units of some color and the printer-paper can only handle 80 units of that color. Relative Colorimetric will treat everything from 80 through 100 as 80, the maximum it can handle; everything below 80 is untouched. Perceptual will take that 100 and put it at the maximum 80 level, and then everything else is proportionally spread between 0 and the former 80. With Perceptual, every value of that out-of-gamut color is changed to some extent, but the relationships between values are maintained.

Resizing for Print

Once you have finalized your image and wish to make a print, the next step is to resize your image for print. To do so, you must determine your desired print size and a target pixels-per-inch (PPI) based on your printer. Why do this? Because your printer wants to see your image at a particular PPI setting, and if you don't provide it what it wants, it will resize your image itself to the right size. Given that the enlarging algorithms on your computer are

Print Mastery: PPI vs. DPI

The difference between pixels-per-inch (PPI) and dots-per-inch (DPI) is a source of endless confusion for photographers. PPI is typically a measurement of image resolution—in other words, a reflection of how many pixels high and wide are in your image. An image that has been resized for print to 10" × 15" at 360 PPI will have a size in pixels of 3600 × 5400. PPI is about your image and the density of your pixels.

DPI is about how your *printer* works and the density of droplets of ink that it lays down. Epson printers, for example, usually lay down ink at either 1440 dpi or 2880 dpi. It is a measurement of how many dots are spread out over the space of one linear inch.

almost certainly better than those inside your printer, we should avoid that situation. Moreover, proper output sharpening should be performed on a properly resized image, and that is impossible to do if enlarging is happening inside the printer.

For Epson professional printers the target resolution is 360 PPI or multiples of 360 PPI (such as 720 PPI), and for Canon and HP printers (and some Epson desktop printers) the target is 300 PPI or multiples thereof. Depending on the size of print you are making and the size of your image, you'll very likely have to resize your image to a larger or smaller size to get to the best image resolution.

Resizing algorithms within Photoshop and Lightroom have significantly improved over the years and now do an admirable job, so the need for third-party software to enlarge images has been greatly reduced. Many of the old tricks, such as increasing size in 10% increments, are no longer relevant. Third-party tools such as Perfect Resize (formerly Genuine Fractals) also do a great job and in some cases can even be better, particularly for extreme enlargements or tricky cases.

These programs are not magic, however. When doing any resizing, there is the possibility of degradation of the image. Resizing an image up in size necessarily means that the algorithm has to interpolate data (i.e., make up information) in order to fill the new space in the file. While modern algorithms do a very intelligent job of creating this information, they are still making up information and you will eventually reach a limit where the degradation becomes too much for an acceptable print (something we'll address in the next section).

Lightroom will resize your file at the time of print, whether enlarging or downsizing, so choosing the right image resolution is a matter of choosing the right settings. In the Print Job panel of the Print module, you can ensure proper resolution simply by clicking the box next to Print Resolution and then choosing the appropriate PPI number (360 PPI for most Epson printers, 300 PPI for others) (**Figure 7-7**). Lightroom will automatically resize for you when it generates the file to send to the printer.

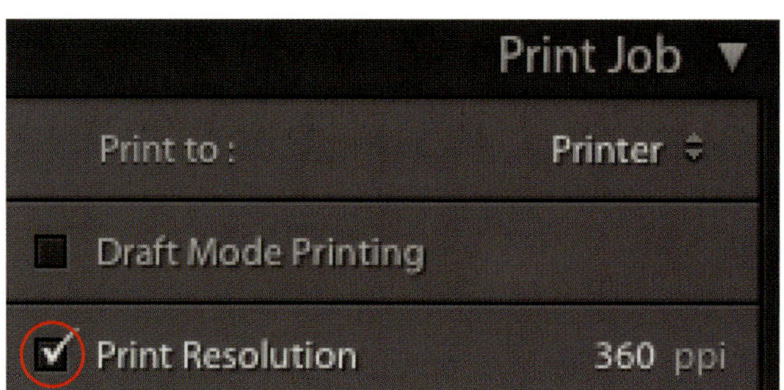

FIGURE 7-7: By checking the Print Resolution box in the Print Job panel of Lightroom's Print module, you can have Lightroom automatically resize your image for print.

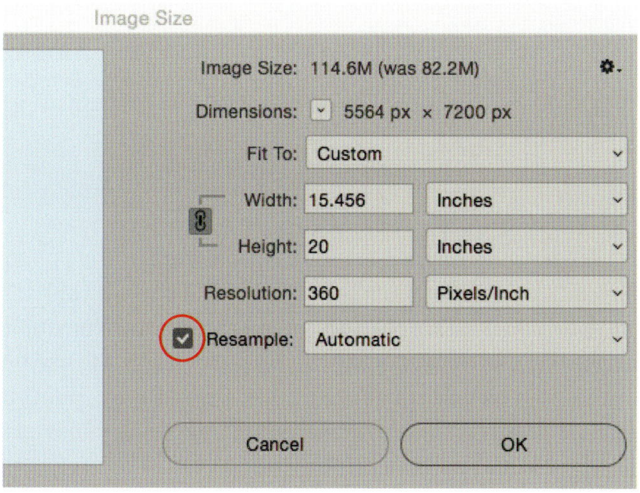

FIGURE 7-8: In the Image Size dialog in Photoshop, select the Resample Image button, input your target Resolution in PPI, and select your Width and Height for print. Once you click OK, Photoshop will resize your image to your print size.

In Photoshop, you need to resize the image manually. To do so, go to Image > Image Size on the menu to open the Image Size dialog box (**Figure 7-8**). Choose the size of your print for Width and Height, enter the appropriate Resolution, and make sure that the Resample Box is checked. Under current versions of Photoshop, I recommend leaving the resampling method on Automatic. Once you hit the OK button, Photoshop will use its algorithms to resize the image to the new size.

I still suggest going through an enlarged file to make sure that there are no aberrations, but unless you are making a significant enlargement such a situation is unlikely. If you are having trouble with a particular enlargement, trying another method or program sometimes eliminates any issues. Other times, you can deal with any issues by pixel-level tools in Photoshop (clone stamp, healing brush) or smoothing-type routines. Lightroom does not allow you to see the results of an enlargement before printing, so my recommendation is to simply review the print for the rare issues for reasonable enlargements.

Print Mastery: Finest Detail Printing

If your image file and print size requires you to downsize your image for print, you may benefit from Epson's Finest Detail Printing. To use this you would enlarge to 720 PPI (double the normal 360 PPI) and then select Finest Detail Printing in the Print Settings dialog, discussed subsequently, or your efforts will be in vain. In these cases where your image file is high enough resolution that it is above 360 PPI without interpolation, it is sometimes possible to extract more detail from the file and have it resolve in print. My experience is that this is only of benefit for files that are capable of holding a high level of sharpness, such as a glossy or luster-type baryta paper.

How Big Can You Go?

> *With virtuoso technique, large prints can look almost as good as small ones.*
>
> —Attributed to John Szarkowski talking about Ansel Adams

The most common question I receive from fine art photographers is "How big can I print?" As you might expect, the answer to that question is rather complicated. Factors such as the type of printer, the quality and size of the image file, the subject matter of the photograph, the texture of the paper, the anticipated viewing distance of the finished print, photographer and/or client preferences, and other factors all can come into play in determining acceptable and optimal printing sizes.

Print Mastery: How Big *Should* You Go?

Whether or not your image will be a successful big print, you need to decide if you should try to make it a big print. Artistic intent plays a role in your anticipated size for prints of your image. Printing large can be beneficial if you want your viewer to be immersed in your image or to be overwhelmed with grandeur; a small print can be more intimate and can invite a different kind of immersive study.

Many photographers desire to print large, many photographers desire to print small, some look at it on an image-by-image basis or by body of work, and still others are not sure but want to leave their options open. If you desire to print large, your anticipated print size can impact the entire image editing process as you will need to be more careful and work harder to preserve image quality.

Subject matter is one of the more important factors in determining how large you should print. Images that rely on intricate detail are more difficult to enlarge and thus have smaller acceptable print sizes. Images that do not rely as heavily on detail and instead rely more on color, shape, or other aspects of design can often be successfully enlarged to a greater degree, allowing larger acceptable print sizes. Viewers don't have the same expectation of perfection for images that are clearly from an iPhone as they would from an Ansel Adams-esque landscape.

Lower quality files are more difficult to enlarge, as any image flaws like noise, fuzziness, or lack of detail, will be magnified as you enlarge. If you are printing on a watercolor paper or other heavily textured paper, the paper texture itself can help hide slight image flaws.

One other factor that is hard to quantify is your tolerance for imperfection. Does it have to be perfect with no enlargement artifacts? If so, you cannot be as aggressive in enlarging.

For most subject matter and images, however, the size of your file (in pixels) from your digital camera or film scan will tell you roughly how large you can successfully print. You can determine the size print you can make from a file without any resizing simply by dividing the number of pixels by 360 (or whatever your printer prefers). If, for example, you have an image with 3600 pixels in one dimension (e.g., height) and 2400 pixels in the other (e.g., width) and you want to print at 360 PPI, it would result in an image that is approximately 10" × 6.7". This means that from that original file you can make a "perfect" 10" × 6.7" print without any resizing. For a larger print, you'll have to interpolate your image up in size.

Print Mastery: Estimating Print Size on Screen

As a rough approximation on screen in Photoshop, I'll use the rulers to approximate how an enlarged image will look in print. To turn on the rulers, simply go to the View menu and select Rulers. If the image is enlarged to print size, I zoom in or out so that 1" of the ruler equals about 1" on the screen (in real life). Once you get the zoom roughly correct, the level of enlargement on screen should approximate how it will look in print. It isn't perfect, but I use this as an extra check.

From my experience and with current technology and careful effort, I believe that for most files you can successfully enlarge a file to twice its size, and with a high-quality file and forgiving subject matter you can sometimes even go up to four times the calculated size. For the above example, that would mean I'd be reasonably safe at 20" × 13.4", with larger sizes possible in the right situation.

None of these rules are absolute, and the degradation of the print as you print larger is gradual. It is not the case that a print is completely fine at 30" across but unacceptable at 31". Enlarging to big print sizes means finding an enlargement level that gives you an acceptable level of degradation.

Of course, many images and situations will prove to be exceptions to this rule of thumb, but image size is a good indicator of acceptable print sizes. If the optimal viewing distance for your final print is a few feet or more away (which often happens with larger prints), you can certainly push the print size up as the increased distance will help hide any problems in the print. Many viewers will engage with your print closer, though, if at all possible, so I try to avoid relying on this factor.

Despite these rules of thumb, sometimes it makes sense just to print your image at the size you want and see how it looks. I've been surprised many times at how good prints can look even when the original image was "too small." Experimentation with your own work and printing solution will help you decide what print sizes work best for you.

Output Sharpening for Print

Output sharpening, the third type of sharpening we use after capture and creative sharpening, should always be performed and should be customized for your actual usage, whether it be print or the web, glossy paper or lustre paper, and so on. Proper output sharpening is performed after resizing to your print size as described in the previous section.

What we are trying to accomplish with output sharpening is to oversharpen the image just enough to compensate for the loss in sharpening we'll get when we put our image to ink and paper. Because matte papers and lustre/glossy papers retain sharpness differently, there are different output sharpening algorithms for those two types of papers. Output sharpening is not just for inkjet prints, either; there are output sharpening routines for web use, CMYK printing, and so on.

In contrast to capture sharpening, it is very difficult to accurately judge output sharpening on the screen. I generally recommend to apply a preset amount of output sharpening for the particular medium rather than to try to edit it by eye. I personally rely on automated routines to do so.

Lightroom makes this process easy as output sharpening is built right in. To perform output sharpening for printing in Lightroom, simply select Print Sharpening in the Print Job panel of the Print module and then choose the Media Type for printing to Matte or Glossy paper (**Figure 7-9**). I usually choose the Standard sharpening setting, but higher and lower options are also available. Lightroom will automatically apply output sharpening after the image is enlarged to the image resolution for print. The only downside to Lightroom's method of output sharpening is that you cannot see its effects before you print, so you must instead rely on searching for the rare issues on the print itself.

FIGURE 7-9: To turn on output sharpening in Lightroom, click the Print Sharpening box and choose your level of sharpening and type of paper (Matte for matte papers, Glossy for lustre or glossy papers).

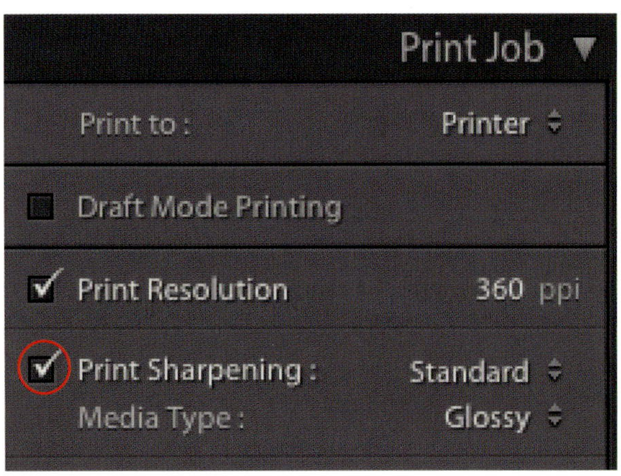

If you are printing from Photoshop, output sharpening is not quite so simple. My recommendation is to use a third-party sharpening plug-in, such as that by PhotoKit Sharpener (**Figure 7-10**), which is what I use, and it is very similar to what is built into Lightroom. Alternatively, I suggest downloading the free Nik Sharpener Pro. Either will do a great job of providing output sharpening for a wide range of output media and target PPI. Simply resize your image to print size, apply the output sharpening, and proceed with printing.

You should be careful judging output sharpening from your screen as proper output sharpening for print often

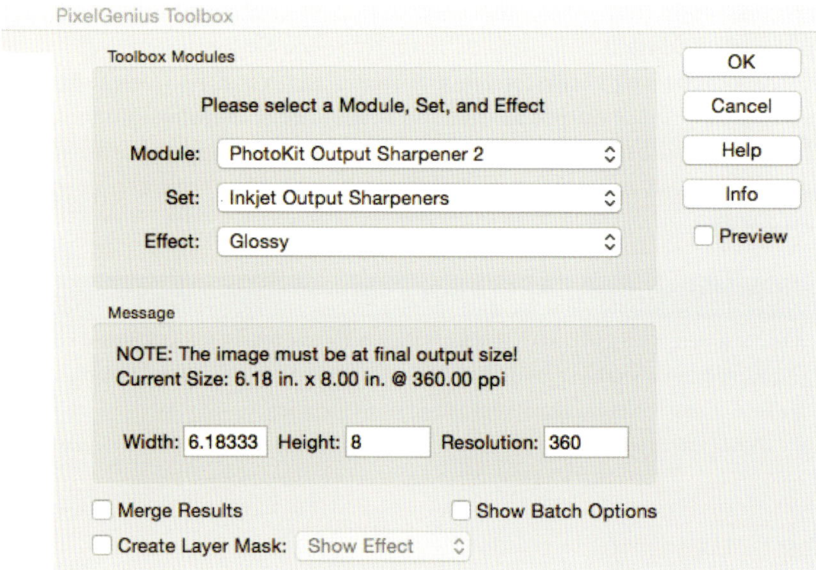

FIGURE 7-10: The Output Sharpening panel of PhotoKit Sharpener Pro 2. Select your type of media (here, Inkjet) and the Effect (which is the type of paper) and then click OK. Note that you need to be at your output size; this is performed after resizing for print.

looks over-sharpened on the screen, but if you see potential issues you can either reduce the effect of output sharpening performed on a layer by decreasing the opacity of the layer, or mask out troublesome areas using a layer mask. This is an advantage of using Photoshop for output sharpening as you can actually view the results of output sharpening before print, and you can selectively mask out areas that might prove troublesome. The Lightroom output sharpening is applied uniformly across the image (and invisibly to the user) at the time of print, so no control is possible beyond turning it off or increasing or decreasing the intensity. The selective adjustment of sharpening in Lightroom is limited to controlling capture sharpening rather than output sharpening.

Final Review for Defects

Before printing—and especially if I am making a large print—I like to make a final on-screen check of my image at its final print size. What I do in this stage is to scan through the entire image at a 100% view looking for any problems, like dust spots in the sky or other things I didn't notice previously. It is much better to catch these problems at this stage when they are easily fixable than to see a blemish on your print that ruins it and wastes your paper, ink, and time.

The other thing I look for are any issues that resulted from either the resizing for print or output sharpening. It could be something that looks too sharp, it could be an enlarging artifact that I didn't notice previously, or something even more unusual, but catching it before print allows you to avoid waste.

Print Mastery: Correcting the Edge of Your Image

A tip for finding small things near the edge of your image is to change the background color to gray or white rather than black as this will allow you to more easily see small artifacts near the edge of your image. Another way of doing this in Photoshop is to add a white canvas to the edge of your image, look for problems and fix if necessary, and then remove the canvas.

Paper Handling

The ability to properly handle paper is a skill you'll develop as you gain experience in printing, but I'd like to share a few tips I've learned the hard way.

Determining the Printable Side

FIGURE 7-11: Using your thumb and finger, both slightly wet, to determine the printable side of the paper. The stickier side is the coated side used for printing.

Most inkjet papers are only suitable for printing on one particular side (and prints accidentally made on the nonprintable side are usually very obviously wrong!). With cut sheet paper, manufacturers store the paper in the box so that the printable side is facing up with respect to how you open the box (and the bag usually has some sort of label indicating this, too), so try to keep the paper stored this way within the box. Occasionally, however, you'll find that you are confused as to the printable side, so a way of determining this on a loose piece of paper can be helpful.

Here's my test: the coated side of the paper is the stickier side, so I lightly wet my thumb and first finger and touch the corner of the paper (**Figure 7-11**). Whichever side sticks more is the coated side, and I then proceed to print on that side. Another test is to look to see if the paper is curling at the corners—if so, it is most likely curving upward toward the coated side.

There are some inkjet papers that are coated for printing on both sides so these techniques will not work—but they are not necessary, either, as you can print on both sides.

Paper Curl

Paper curl is inevitable with digital printing (at least with papers that are only coated on one side), and too much curl can result in lost prints and can even damage to the printer as the printer head strikes an upraised corner. Since the paper tends to curl up on the corners (toward the printable side), what I normally do is gently bend down the leading edge corners of my paper to try to minimize or eliminate the curl. You must be careful not to actually bend the corner so much that you form a crease, but if you are careful, you can dramatically reduce the cases where your print gets damaged from the head striking one of those leading edge corners.

I also recommend storing your boxed, cut-sheet paper both flat and upside down (so that the labels are upside down when you view it from the side (**Figure 7-12**). This allows gravity to help you out in trying to keep the paper from curling toward the printable side. I also recommend keeping your paper in plastic bags to help reduce the impact of moisture—the plastic bags that most papers come in are sufficient for this.

For paper with severe curl, it may be necessary to pre-flatten the paper using a D-Roller or other device that is designed to impart a reverse curl before printing, as will be described in more detail in chapter 12.

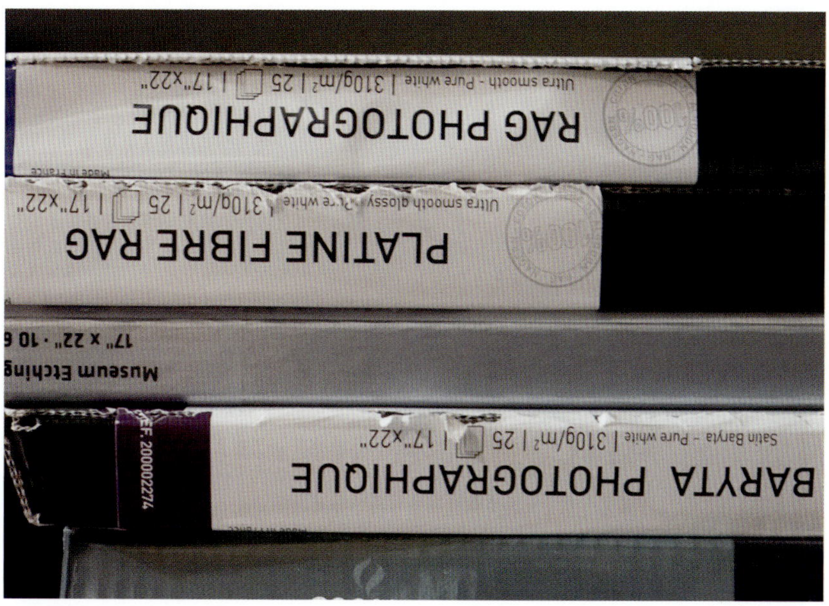

FIGURE 7-12: Cut-sheet paper stored upside down to help combat curling

Print Settings and Making the Print

Now that we've prepped the image for print and loaded our paper, let's discuss how we actually send the image file to the printer.

Printing with Photoshop

After you've resized your print and performed output sharpening, it is time to move to the **Photoshop Print Settings** dialog box and make your print. To access this, go to File > Print, and Photoshop Print Settings will open (**Figure 7-13**). This box will show your image positioned on the paper on the left-hand side, and the various settings on the right-hand side. In the **Printer Setup** panel, you choose your printer, the number of copies you'd like, and whether your layout is landscape or portrait (click either to see how the image will be positioned on the page). The Print Settings box goes to the Epson Print Driver, which we'll discuss in a little bit.

The **Color Management** panel is the other most important panel besides the Printer Setup panel. Here, you first choose your Color Handling option, which means whether Photoshop is in charge of color, or whether color should be handled by the printer. For color prints, I recommend selecting **Photoshop Manages Colors** here. By selecting this, the printer will take

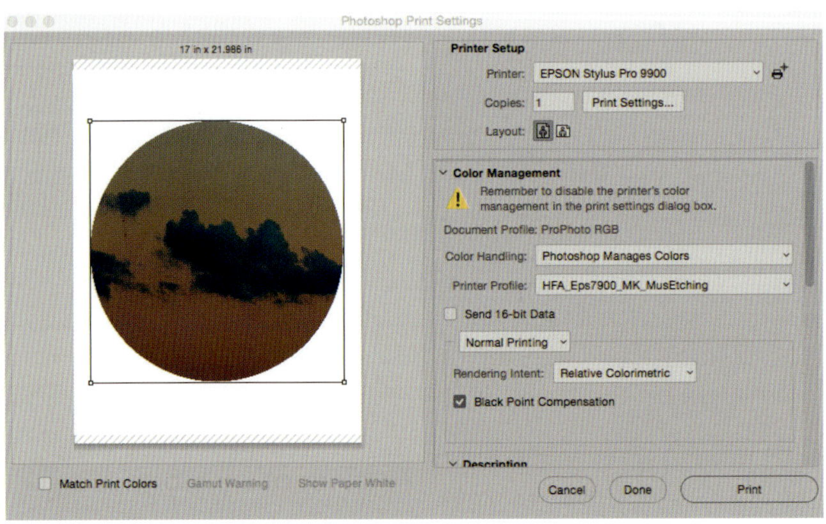

FIGURE 7-13: The Photoshop Print Settings dialog box set up for color printing

advantage of printer-paper specific profiles. Once you've selected Photoshop Manages Colors, you can then specify your **Printer Profile** (which is your printer-paper profile).

If your file is in **16-bit** (and you are not using a PC with an Epson printer), you can choose to send 16-bit data to the printer—unless you are having trouble with very large file sizes, I'd recommend doing this. I have not seen any convincing evidence that it makes a difference at all in real-world prints, but I still select it if I am printing a 16-bit image in case it does.

Lastly, you choose your **Rendering Intent** (choose either Relative Colorimetric or Perceptual, as discussed previously) and then check the Black Point Compensation box. I recommend always selecting **Black Point Compensation** as it maps your images black point to the paper black, helping image quality in the blacks.

After you've set up here, click on the Print Settings box to make changes to the Epson print driver. You can print either from there or return here to start the printing process.

Printing with Lightroom

Printing in Lightroom is managed in the Print module. Once you've chosen an image to print, simply click on the Print module and a vertical set of panels will appear with various options for print. There are many options available but I will focus on the functionality most relevant for fine art printing.

While in the Print module, I first set up my page by clicking Page Setup in the lower left-corner. This opens the Page Setup box (**Figure 7-14**), and this is where you choose your printer as well as the Paper Size (from the pull-down list, or by entering a custom size).

Print Mastery: Multiple Prints in Lightroom

One of the powers of Lightroom is to do tasks like printing in a mass-production fashion. If you have a group of photographs selected, you can go the Print module, set up your print, and Lightroom will automatically generate the print files for each and send them to your printer. I take advantage of this quite a bit, as I love to make small proofs of my images as an early editing step. Using this feature of Lightroom, it takes the same amount of time on the computer to make 20 or 30 prints as it does to make one.

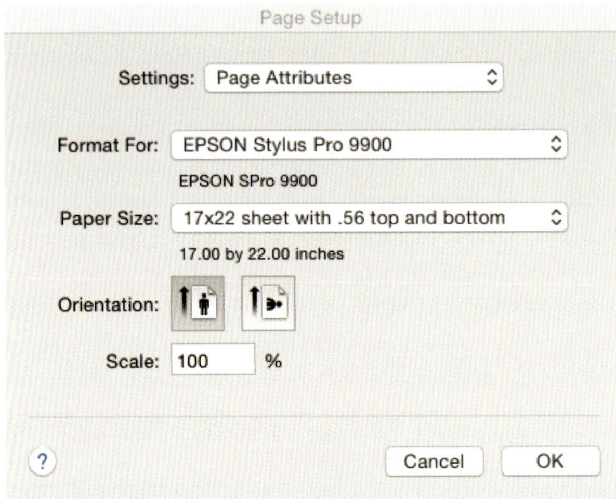

FIGURE 7-14: Lightroom's Page Settings panel, reached by clicking the button in the lower left of the screen while in the Print module

In the Layout Style panel on the upper-right column of the Print module, I recommend selecting Single Image/Contact Sheet for printing fine art prints. Picture Package and Custom Package provide great tools for making casual prints, but we'll focus on the more precise control of the Single Image/Contact Sheet layouts here.

Once you've selected Single Image/Contact Sheet, the Layout panel in Lightroom (**Figure 7-15**) is where you control the size of the image on the paper and where the image is positioned on the paper. This is a powerful tool but most people find it a bit frustrating when first using it.

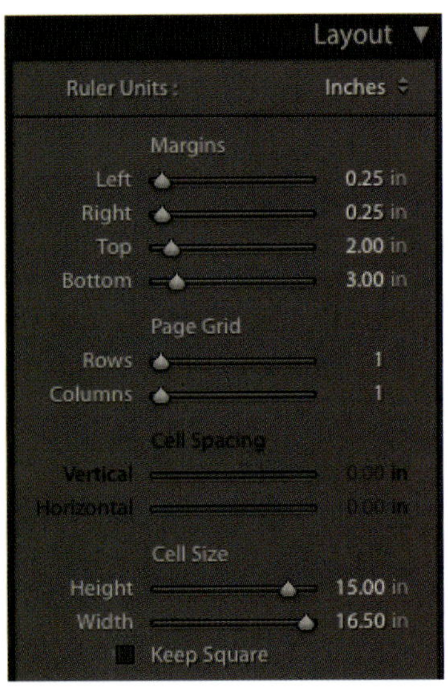

FIGURE 7-15: Lightroom's Layout panel as part of the Print module

Basically you set your margins for all four sides of the paper, and the result will be a Cell Size. Lightroom will automatically fill the Cell Size with your image made as large as possible within the Cell Size. What is confusing for people is that the Cell Size and Margins are interconnected—if you would like to make your Cell Size (and thus image) bigger than it currently allows, you have to make the margins narrow enough to accommodate. You can, however, make your Cell Size (and thus image) smaller without having to modify the margins. With a little experience, this process will become more intuitive.

Print Mastery: Image Settings Panel

The Image Settings panel in Lightroom's Print module has a tool called the Stroke Border, which allows you to add a solid line around the edge of your image for print.

One dangerous setting is Zoom to Fill. What this does is, if your Cell Size is a different aspect ratio than your image, it will zoom into your image to fill the Cell and crop off anything that doesn't fit. There are times when this is something you might like to do, but if you are having weird cropping issues, this could be the culprit.

The **Print Job** panel of the Print module is the last of the most important modules for fine art printing (**Figure 7-16**). Here, make sure to select enlarging to your target PPI (Print Resolution on and target PPI selected) as well as output sharpening (Print Sharpening turned on, and paper type chosen), as discussed previously. You can select 16-bit if your file is 16-bit and your printer driver supports it.

For **Color Management**, choose your appropriate printer-paper profile under Profile and select your desired rendering intent, as also discussed previously. For specialized purposes, you might choose Managed by Printer for Color Management, such as if you are printing using Epson Advanced Black & White mode—otherwise make sure this setting has your appropriate printer-paper profile.

Lightroom offers a **Print Adjustment** option where you can adjust Brightness and add Contrast at the time of print. I recommend not using this functionality but rather taking care of those sorts of mismatch issues in other ways, such as with your monitor brightness setting.

As your last step before printing, I recommend selecting the Printer button just below the Print Job panel, which will take you to your printer driver for final settings. I like to print from the printer driver, but if you prefer not to do so, you can return here and print from the Print Job panel instead.

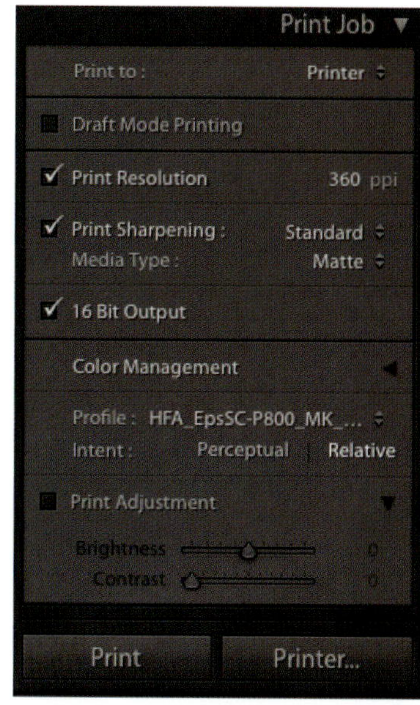

FIGURE 7-16: Lightroom's Print Job panel as well as the Print and Printer buttons as part of the Print module

Printing with Epson Print Driver

Once you've set up your print in either Photoshop or Lightroom, you then go to the printer driver to set up the printer itself. I'm going to discuss here using the Epson printer driver. If you are a user of the Canon printers, this section will not apply to you in its specifics.

When I first go into the Printer Driver (**Figure 7-17**), I make sure I have the correct printer chosen (in the Printer pull down) and then select Printer Settings in the Layout pull-down menu. Once you choose Printer Settings, you'll be able to configure details about your paper of choice. Note that if you are using Photoshop, this is when you would set your

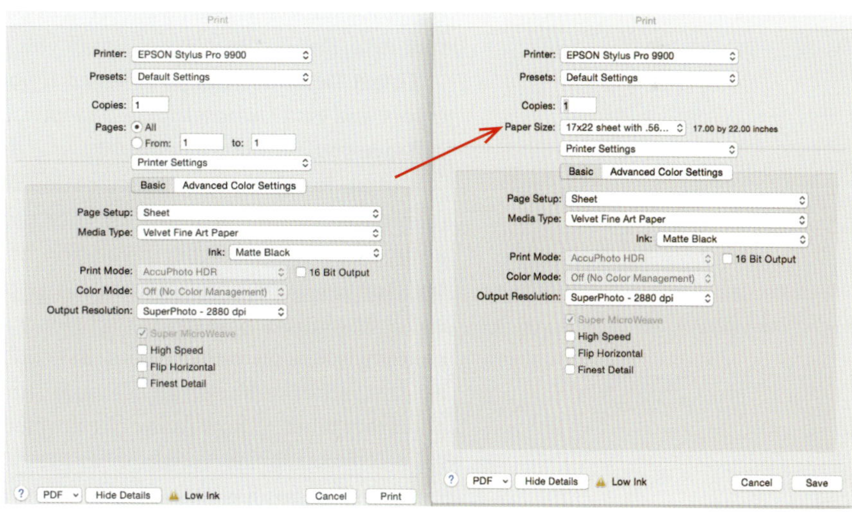

FIGURE 7-17: The Epson print driver accessed from Lightroom on the left and from Photoshop on the right. They are almost identical, but Photoshop has the extra option of Paper Size, as you do not set that from within Photoshop.

Paper Size, too (in Lightroom we did it as part of Page Setup, but in Photoshop it is handled in the driver).

Going through the menus in the Printer Settings panel, first you set **Page Setup**, where you specify sheet paper or roll paper according to your printer's capability. For papers with multiple feeds this is where you would choose the feed path.

Next, you choose **Media Type**. Media Type will, in response to you selecting a media, make other changes, including paper thickness, platen gap, and ink load that are based on your selected media. As a starting point, use the media type recommended by the manufacturer of your paper. Usually this information is provided in the documentation that either comes with the paper or is available on the manufacturer's website. If this information is not available, as a starting point, choose the existing media type that seems closest to your paper. Once you choose Media Type, your available options in some of the other menus may change also.

Once you've selected Media Type, it will essentially dictate your **Ink** choice. Matte papers require Matte Black ink and glossy/lustre papers require Photo Black ink. If you are using a third-party paper, the manufacturer's specifications should address this issue as well.

If you've selected a printer-paper profile before coming to the driver so that Lightroom or Photoshop manages colors, the **Print Mode** and **Color Mode** will be grayed out (as it is in my examples), which is a good thing, as you don't want both the printer and the software to manage colors simultaneously.

High Speed Option allows the printhead to print bidirectionally rather than just in one direction, doubling the speed. Theoretically, if there was some sort of misalignment, bidirectional printing could cause trouble. I have never actually seen any downside to printing bidirectionally, but encountering problems are at least a theoretical possibility, so if I have time I deselect this. Also, if you select Finest Detail you should deselect this.

Finest Detail should be selected if you are printing to a glossy or lustre media and your un-interpolated resolution is above 360 ppi, as this selection can give you a bit more detail.

Output Resolution is a specification of the inkjet droplet density and the manufacturer specifications for your paper will likely specify this. I almost always choose the higher resolution of 2880 dpi for printing available on my printers. With more textured matte papers, this is probably unnecessary and a resolution of 1440 dpi will give you the same results, but I have had banding issues on matte papers that could only be resolved by choosing 2880 dpi instead of 1440 dpi. Please note that these numbers are dots-per-inch and are related to how many ink droplets are laid down—this setting is not related to your print resolution you set in pixels-per-inch.

Once changes have been made to the Printer Settings, I then choose to go to **Advanced Media Control** (**Figure 7-18**). Your choice of Media Type will define the defaults of these settings, but you can override them if you'd like.

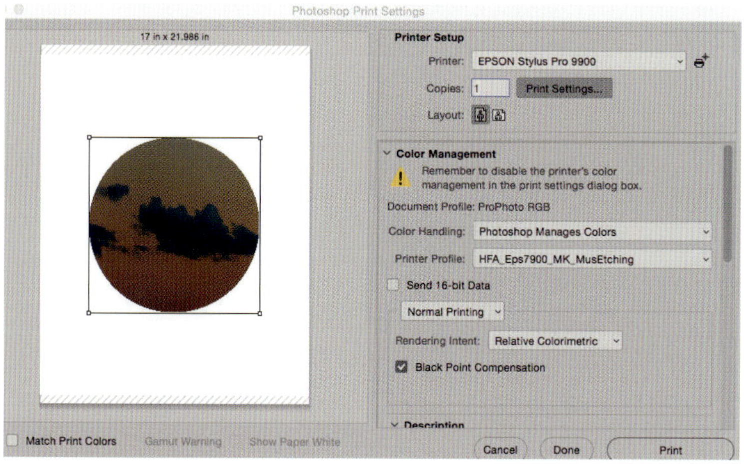

FIGURE 7-18: The Advanced Media Control page for the Epson print driver and Epson 9900 printer (this page will vary based on your printer). I often choose a wider platen gap and larger paper thickness when I'm printing with third-party papers.

I very often do, particularly with Paper Thickness and Platen Gap, because with thicker papers both of those settings can help prevent your printhead from striking the paper.

The Platen Gap (for Canon this is Head Height) is the distance between the ink nozzles at the bottom of the printhead and the surface of the paper. If your paper is thicker than the printer is expecting, the printhead may pass too close and even hit the paper. Paper thickness is a setting that impacts the internal printer feed and transport mechanism.

After configuring your various settings, you can move on to actually make the print. In Lightroom you can select Print right in the printer driver; with Photoshop, you save the settings and go back to the Photoshop menu and choose Print from there.

RIPs

Many people use dedicated printing software called raster image processors (RIPs) to print their images, and specific details of their operation are beyond the scope of this book. RIPs such as ImagePrint (a popular one) bypass the manufacturer's printer driver with the intent of providing improved printing.

ImagePrint promises reduced ink usage through more efficient screening, improved print quality, better layout ability, and hundreds of available custom profiles. ImagePrint is priced according to the size of your printer and is very expensive (near to the cost of the printer itself in many cases). The layout tools and profiles are certainly worthwhile, and there is some dispute as to improvement in image quality as compared to the latest manufacturer printer drivers. I have not seen convincing evidence that it provides improved image quality over current drivers for color printing, but I recommend you try it out if it sounds like something that would interest you.

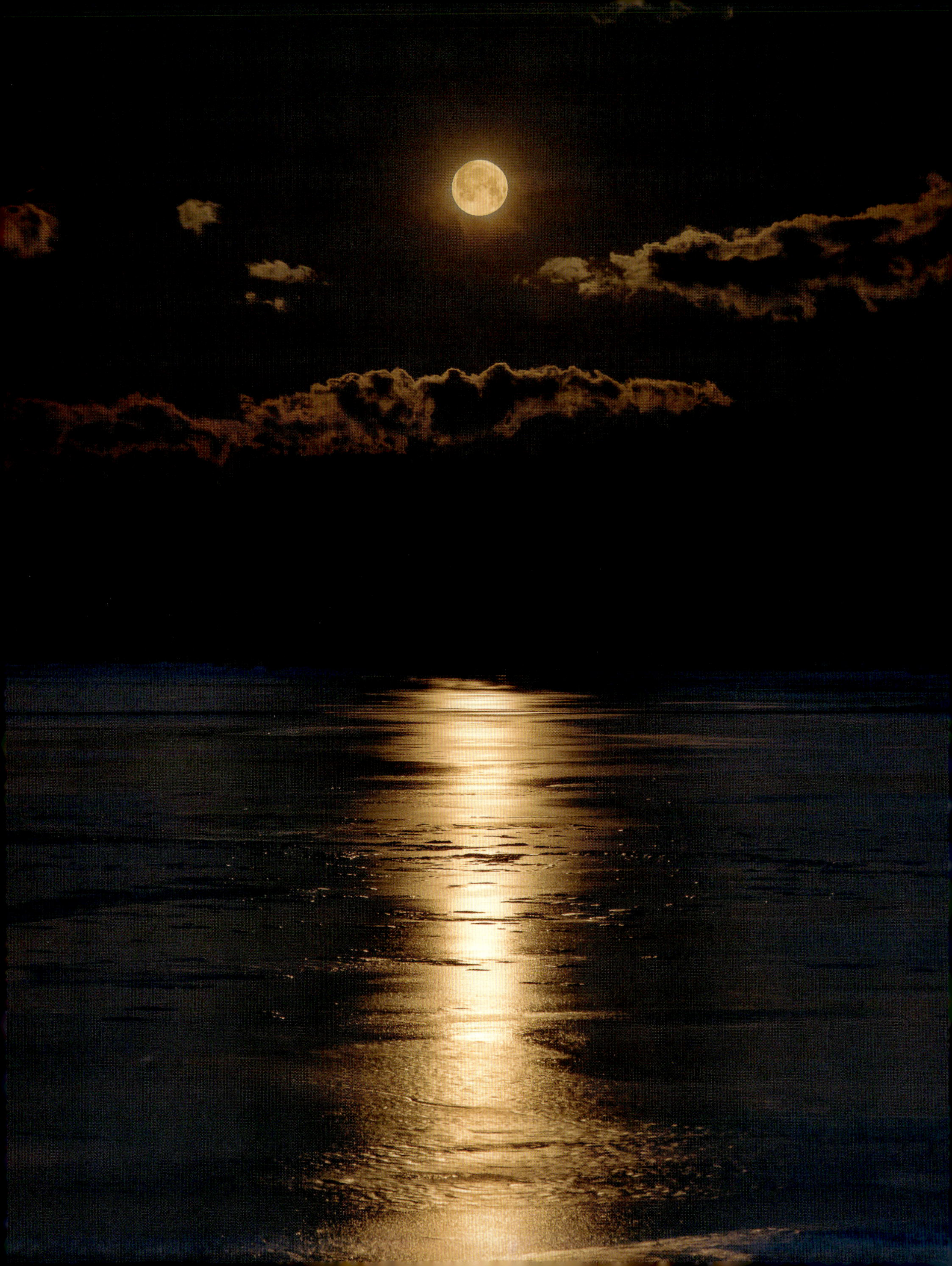

8

Evaluating and Correcting the Print

Once you've made your print, it's time to take a look at it and to decide what to do next. It is a rare print that is perfect in every way the first time you print it. Are there any flaws? Is there anything you can do to make it better match your artistic intent, or just to make it better? And what sort of light should you use to actually look at it to answer these questions?

> *Quality doesn't mean deep blacks or whatever tonal range. That's not quality, that's a kind of quality.... But the quality of Robert Frank is a quality that has something to do with what he's doing, what his mind is. It's not balancing out the sky to the sand and so forth. It's got to do with intention.*
>
> —Elliott Erwitt

Environment for Print Evaluation

When critically reviewing prints, I prefer to review them using a daylight-type bulb, usually around 4700K–5000K (D50), such as those made by Solux (**Figure 8-1**). Since we rarely know where a print is going to end up, I also like to evaluate it under various light sources, particularly warmer ones as are more typical in both galleries and homes nowadays. I recommend being *consistent* in always using the same lights to review images but also *flexible* in not being limited to just one light source.

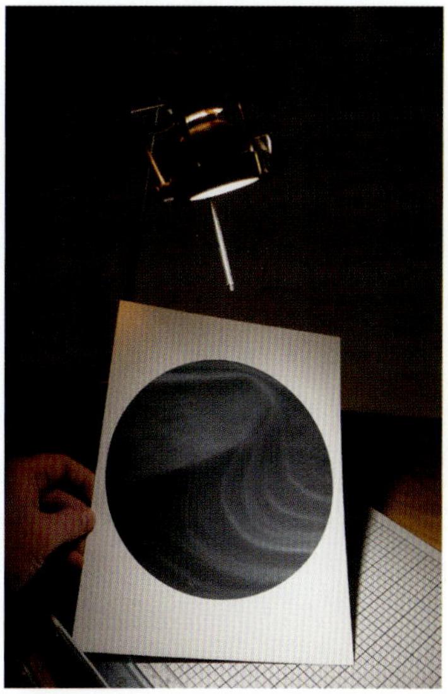

Figure 8-1: This small Solux light with a 4700K bulb provides a great viewing environment for a small print

There are many viewing lights available that are suitable for print evaluation. Light boxes such as those from GTI are amazing but they are very expensive—they provide an excellent quality light along with a reasonably controlled environment that shields a print in the box from other lights, too. You can replicate these boxes to some extent with a high-quality bulb (Solux 4700K bulbs are my recommendation) and a reasonably controlled environment in your print studio. Bulbs are rated by a Color Rendering Index (CRI), with scores of 100 matching daylight perfectly and scores of 97 or more being considered very good. If you look around, you can find fluorescent bulbs with high CRI scores even at hardware stores—the rating can be a little misleading, and they won't be as good as a Solux bulb, but they can do a pretty solid job.

Consistency in viewing conditions is as important as the quality of your light. Make sure the area where you are viewing the prints does not vary throughout the day with sunlight, and that stray lower-quality light isn't hitting the print as well.

Evaluation of the Print

Once you've completed a print and you have a good viewing environment, it's time to evaluate the print for image flaws, print flaws, and ways of improving it.

Image Flaws

Once you make the first print of an image, check for any technical flaws in the image you printed that you didn't notice earlier, either because of a mistake or because they weren't noticeable on the screen. Examples image flaws include dust spots, sharpening artifacts, objectionable noise, chromatic aberration, softness due to depth of field or lens issues, weird enlarging effects, and the like.

Print Flaws

Simultaneously with looking for technical flaws (and for every print), I also look for things that are better characterized as print flaws such as the following:

- Flaking of ink (white specks of paper showing through)
- Indentations or lines that are perpendicular to the direction of travel of the printhead
- Colored dots near the corners or edges
- Horizontal banding (lines in the direction of printhead movement)
- Paper blemishes
- Color or density of blacks being off
- Color shifts

Later in this chapter we'll talk about how best to deal with some of these prints flaws. In most cases, if these flaws are discovered, the particular print will be a reject, but we can solve the problem for future prints.

Improvements and Print Interpretation

After completing my search for image flaws and print flaws, I evaluate the print for things I can do it improve it. Should it be brighter or darker? Is there anything distracting that should be minimized? Is there something important to the image that needs additional emphasis? If there is anything I think can be improved, I go back into my editing workflow, make the appropriate changes, and then print and evaluate again. We'll discuss making changes in light of Print Interpretation in more detail in chapter 10.

Once I have something close to a final print, I then try to live with the image for a while. I hang it up in my studio and see what I think after hours or days or weeks (**Figure 8-2**). Sometimes I show the print to other people to see what they think of the image, and that often gives me clues as to things I've done wrong. Sometimes, after this period of time, I make additional changes, and other times I decide the print is fine just the way it is.

Print Mastery: Dry-Down

Pigment inkjet prints dry remarkably quickly, but some dry-down is still beneficial for accurate evaluation, just as in other types of traditional printing methods. Precise and confirmed accurate information on this issue is hard to find, but many recommend waiting 24 to 48 hours to let the ink become fully absorbed by the paper before assessment of color, shadow detail, and the like, particularly for matte papers.

My experience is that you don't have to wait that long—the dry-down effect seems to mostly occur in the first few minutes after the print comes off the printer. For best results I recommend waiting at least a few minutes before making decisions about your prints based on a hard proof. For matte prints, for example, before deciding that you don't have enough detail in your shadows, wait 15 minutes or more to see if the shadows open up.

Waiting for dry-down also allows the printed surface to fully harden. You can usually handle an inkjet print straight out of the printer without any issue, but allowing it to harden overnight can be helpful.

Dry-down is the name for this drying effect from the silver gelatin days, but with inkjet printing it really seems to be more of a "dry up"—the relatively minor effect that exists results in the print becoming a little brighter rather than darker.

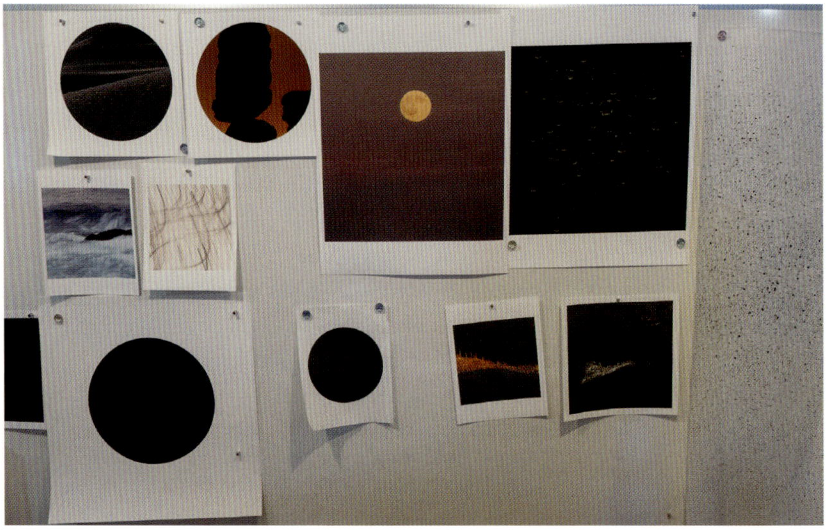

Figure 8-2: I hung this giant metallic whiteboard in my studio and it is one of the best investments I've ever made. I love being able to easily put prints up and move them around using ridiculously strong rare earth magnets.

Principles of Printing #9: Live with Your Prints

One of the best pieces of advice I received (and I wish I could remember the source) was to live with my prints for a while before making any final decisions. Print your work and then hang your print somewhere you can see it, and aspects of the print that can be improved will very likely become evident. Similarly, putting a bit of time between making a print and evaluating it can help you look at the print more objectively.

When evaluating a print, something to keep in mind is that you will never get an exact match with a monitor or other electronic medium. The print on paper and the image on your monitor are fundamentally different mediums—one being backlit and glowing and the other being reflective—and inks sitting on paper cannot match light pouring through a screen. We should try to make our displays match our prints as much as possible through monitor calibration, controlling brightness, and Print Editing, but we are limited from a perfect match by the differences in the media.

I think a better goal is to just work on making the print itself as good as possible, regardless of how closely it matches the appearance of the image on the screen. After all, it is the print itself that matters in the end.

Principles of Printing #10: The Print Is What Matters

You are the artist and it is up to you—you must be the final arbiter of your own print. Don't worry about what is on the monitor, and don't worry about what others say. All the decisions you make during the printing process lead to the actual physical object of the print.

Correction of the Print

Now that we have identified some flaws in our print, let's discuss how best to resolve them. Corrections that are in the category of Artistic Editing—where we hope to improve an otherwise fine print—will be discussed in chapter 10.

Principles of Printing #11: It's Only Paper

It's only paper. While there is nothing in photography I like better than a fine print, don't worry about when one is lost or when you end up making a small change and getting rid of an earlier version. Ink and paper aren't free, but a fine print will last and be appreciated for a lifetime and is thus worth the extra effort and possible wastage. Get your final image to where you like, but don't be afraid of making further modifications to improve it after you've had a chance to live with your print for a while.

Correcting Flaws

Image flaws that become evident on print are solved by going back into the editing process and fixing the flaws, whether it be by adjusting sharpening, applying more noise reduction, cleaning up dust spots, or any other fix.

The solution for **print flaws** will vary case-by-case and I'll address a number of them here.

Problem: Flaking of ink (white paper showing through). This occurs when there is some sort of particle on top of the paper when the printer lays down ink, or more likely when part of the coating layer flakes off with the wet ink (**Figure 8-3**). When this happens, the area beneath the particle or layer is revealed (and it is paper white since the ink didn't hit it). If it is going to happen, it will usually happen shortly after printing from my experience.

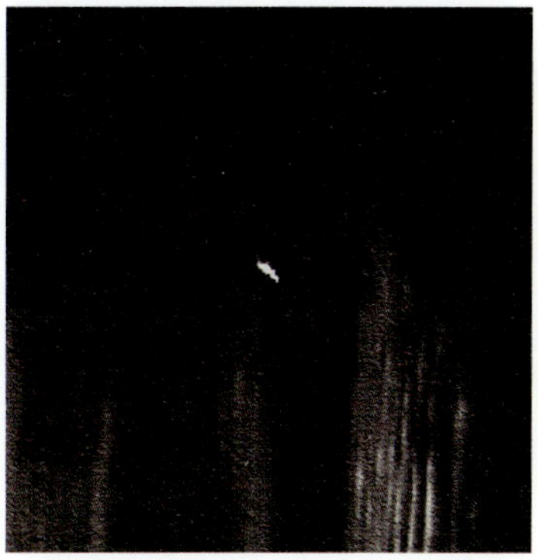

Figure 8-3: An example of part of the ink flaking off (right in the center), whether it be part of the paper coating or a particle on top that falls off

Solution: Most of the time, you will have to redo the print, but you can try to correct the spot with an archival pen such as the Sakura Pigma Micron pigment pens. If this happens on a final print, I'll almost certainly reprint. To prevent it from happening, you can brush your paper with a soft brush to get rid of existing flakes before it reaches the printhead, but be careful not to brush dust into your printer. You can also try swiping the edge (especially the leading edge) of your paper before printing to try to eliminate any particles from entering your printer to help prevent future issues.

Problem: Indentations or lines perpendicular to the direction of travel of the printhead. When you have subtle lines in your print perpendicular to the direction of travel of the printhead, it is likely pressure marks from the edge of rollers that advance the paper through the printer. You can't fix the problem print, but there are ways to help prevent it in the future.

Solution:

- Use a wider platen gap
- Make sure the correct media type has been selected in software and at the printer
- Add a delay time for ink drying between each head pass
- Try to clean the rollers with a cotton swab and water
- Try a different paper with a less sensitive surface

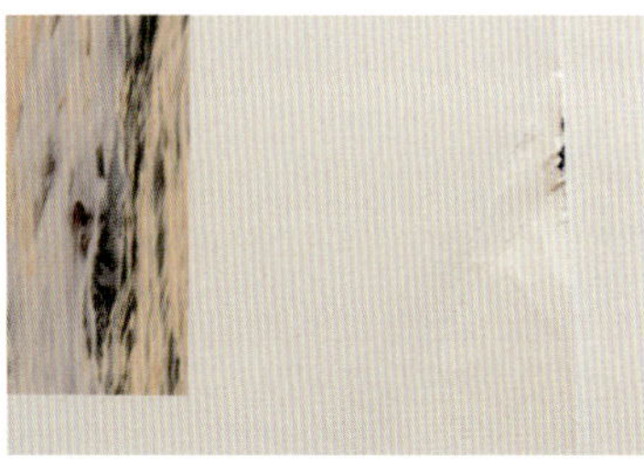

Figure 8-4: Example of head strikes. In this case there are some ink marks, and the head hit the paper so hard it ripped the paper, too.

Problem: Colored dots near the corners or edges (Figure 8-4). This is almost certainly caused by head strikes, where the printhead contacts the edge of the paper. If the paper is curling at all, I recommend trying to flatten the paper or reverse the curl so that the corner doesn't stick up anymore, allowing the printhead to pass over it. The other solution is to change the Platen Gap to a wider setting to move the printhead further away from the paper and hopefully over the corners. Sometimes you'll have to do both.

Figure 8-5: Example of horizontal banding. This is a pretty egregious example of the Cyan nozzle dropping in the middle of a print. Very often banding will be more subtle than this and harder to catch.

Problem: Horizontal banding (lines in the direction of printhead movement) (Figure 8-5). The most likely cause is a clog of nozzles in one of the ink channels, but the printhead could be out of alignment or the paper feed speed could need adjusting.

Solution: Run a nozzle check, and if breaks appear in the test pattern, run one or more head cleanings until the clog is cleared. If the lines on the print are solid, try running a printhead alignment. Your printer may be either too fast or to slow in advancing the paper. Adjusting the paper feed speed may also help here. Make sure you are using the correct Media Type Settings, as they can impact ink load and possibly cause this error. Make sure the banding is not in your file, too—I've had this happen before.

Problem: Paper Blemishes. Occasionally you'll find a blemish in the surface of the print such as a scratch or a small piece of brownish fiber embedded in the paper's surface (**Figure 8-6**).

Solution: If there is some sort of visible blemish after you make your print, there is likely nothing you can do about it besides reprinting. To help prevent such a problem, make sure to check your paper before printing. If I notice a blemish before printing, I sometimes can orient the paper so that the blemish is under a dark area of the image and can be hidden, rather than in a lighter area where it is visible.

Figure 8-6: Example of a stray piece of brown fiber in a cotton rag paper. Quality control by the paper manufacturer usually catches these but they do occasionally slip through. They can be hidden with a darker inked area but will be visible in lighter inked areas or in the border.

Problem: Color or density of blacks is way off (**Figure 8-7**). If your print looks way off (and especially if you've been successful printing recently), the most likely explanation is a clogged nozzle. A clogged cyan nozzle gives a magenta cast, a clogged black can reduce your dynamic range, and so on.

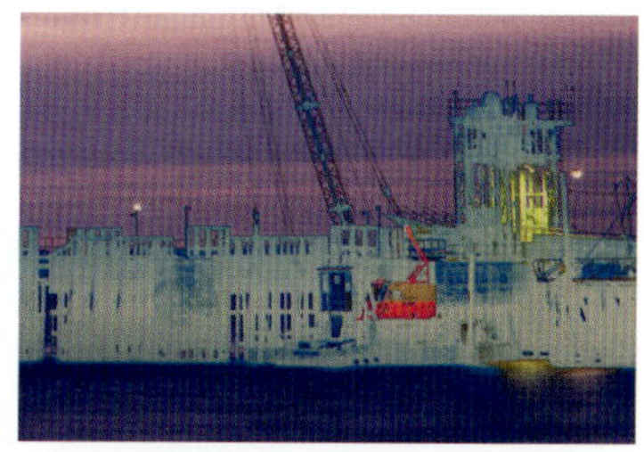

Figure 8-7: Example of a nozzle clog. In this case one of the blacks completely dropped out, leaving a very striking result as the remainder of the image looks fine.

Solution: The first thing I do when I have a bad result is run a nozzle check and then I'll do a head cleaning if necessary. If the nozzles are fine, check your print settings to make sure you've set everything correctly, and that you are using the right printer-paper profile, and the correct black ink setting. Another thing to check when a print is way off is whether you are printing on the correct side of the paper. Prints on the uncoated side are often quite poor looking.

Principles of Printing #12:
If You Think You've Seen Every Printing Problem Occur, You Are Wrong

I print almost every day and I see many of the same problems occur over and over with paper, printers, or files. And yet, I'm continually surprised when there is a new situation where a print has gone wrong in a way I hadn't seen before. When these sorts of situations inevitably occur, it helps to logically work through the problem, eliminate variables, and hopefully find a solution.

Print Editing

In the Print Editing stage, we'll try to make changes to our image so that our final print looks more like the image on screen.

Prints Too Dark

By far, the most common issue I hear about from people printing their own work is that the prints are coming out too dark. In most cases, this issue can be solved by reducing the brightness of your monitor while you are editing your images. When your monitor is set too bright, it will give you a falsely bright view of your image, and you will edit accordingly and make your image darker (**Figure 8-8**).

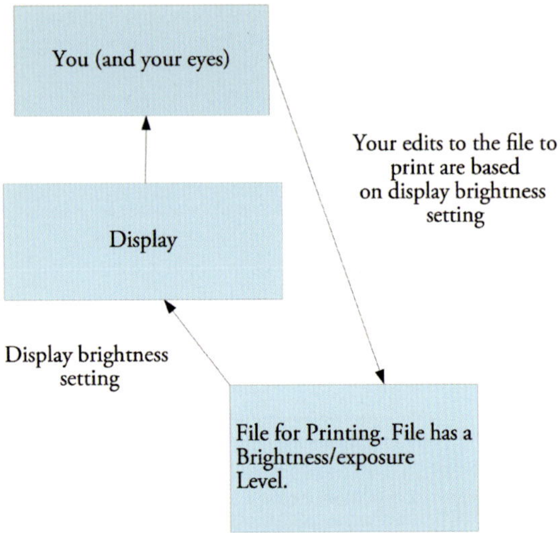

FIGURE 8-8: This stylized schematic illustrates the interrelationship between display brightness and file brightness. If your file has the "right" level of brightness, a display brightness that is too high will give you a falsely bright view of your file. Then you'll edit the brightness down to make it look right on the display, but that will make the file too dark for printing (but just right for viewing on your monitor at that setting). If your monitor is set at a brightness reflective of the print, your edits to brightness will be consistent with the brightness that will come out in print.

To solve this problem, I recommend:

- Try setting your monitor to a lower brightness setting. If you monitor is set to a very bright level, pull it down to 30–40% of the maximum brightness and then re-edit your image with the new brightness level. When you reprint, the print will come out brighter, and you can iterate your brightness level until you have a reasonable match.
- An even simpler solution is, upon making a print that is too dark, hold your print in your evaluation light and then adjust your monitor brightness until it is a reasonable match to your print. Then re-edit your image to make it look right again with your monitor set to the new brightness level, and you should have a much closer match.
- Are you sure that your print is too dark? Make sure you are using a light to evaluate the print that is sufficiently bright—it can make a big difference in how your print looks.
- To confirm the problem is in your print workflow, give your file to a friend (who is successfully printing) or send it to a lab to print for you. If the other print is equally dark, the problem is in your file and how you have edited it, so changing monitor brightness is a likely solution.

Lowering the brightness of your monitor solves the most common problem I hear from clients and students regarding prints—that their prints are too dark. When you edit an image on a properly dimmed monitor, you will naturally brighten it so that it looks correct to your eye, and this brightening will translate to a brighter print. The exact setting will depend on your hardware, but the important thing is that your monitor brightness be in line with your printing.

Most monitors "out of the box" are set to their maximum brightness, and such an intensity will almost certainly result in prints that are darker than you expect. When you first reduce the brightness of your monitor, it may see quite dim at first, but I expect your eyes will quickly adapt to the new level. This is one reason to have less ambient lighting in your print studio, as lower monitor brightnesses are visually acceptable.

Prints Without Pop

Another common complaint from new printmakers is that their images don't have the "pop" of what they see on screen. Part of this issue is likely the monitor giving you a false view of your image as we just talked about, but the other part is likely the result of the differences between screen and print.

If you've set your brightness level correctly and still don't think your print matches your display, that is not unusual. What you usually need to do is add a little Exposure, Contrast, and/or Saturation/Vibrance for printing. It will look like a little too much on the screen as we are overshooting those settings, but it should bring your printer closer to your intent.

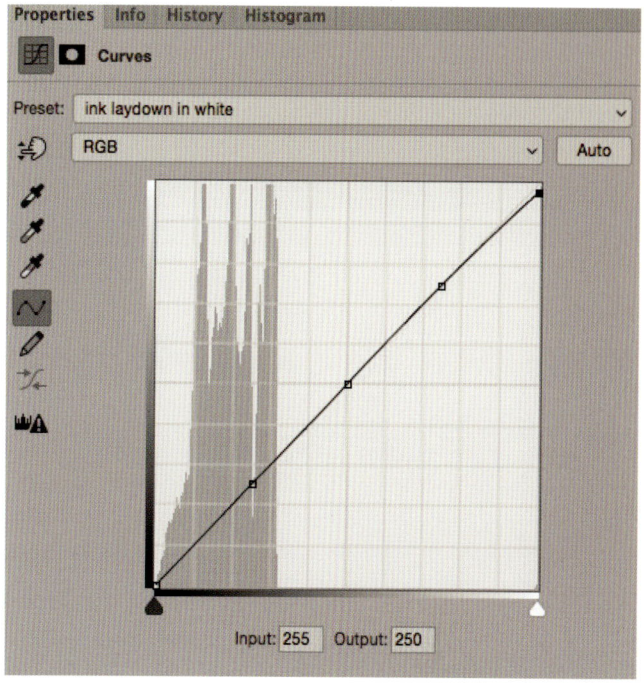

FIGURE 8-9: In this ink laydown curve (which I've saved as a preset for easy access later), I've locked down the bulk of the image. For the point at the end representing the highlights in the upper right, I manually plugged in an Input of 255 and an Output of 250.

The Problem of Pure White Areas

Modern inkjet printers do not have a white ink and therefore cannot print a pure white. If you have an image that has pure white values (such as a blown-out highlight that looks good on your monitor), inkjet printers will not lay down ink at that location and you will instead have just the paper white. Depending on the image, this can result in prints that have a distracting transition from areas with ink and those without. This problem is exacerbated when the highlight touches the edge, as the edge of the print will effectively no longer be straight. So what to do when you have an image with this problem (and assuming you can't go back to your RAW file to save those highlights)?

The solution is actually pretty straightforward. If you are using Photoshop, you can simply make a curve that slightly turns white into light gray. Basically, you need to lock down the bulk of the curve and then just slightly pull down the white point (the upper-right corner). The curve will start out at a value of 255 and you may have to experiment to see what you need for your print (**Figure 8-9**). Usually pulling down the 255 value to somewhere around 250 will add just enough gray to your pure whites so that enough ink is laid down to differentiate those areas from the unprinted parts of the paper. I often run a test print or two to make sure I get to the right balance for a particular paper.

You can do the same thing in Lightroom/ACR using the tone curve, but usually you can best deal with this issue by recovering those highlights from the RAW file using the Highlight tool.

9

Choosing a Paper

If you are interested in digital inkjet printing, whether it is printing for yourself or having a professional printer handle your work, the choice of paper for the task is an important one. We truly live in a golden age for papers—there are literally hundreds of available papers suitable for fine art digital printing. I believe the breadth and quality of available papers is one of the strengths of inkjet printing as an art form, as every artist should be able to find a paper that matches their artistic intent for their print.

This wealth of choices does come with a price, as it has become increasingly difficult to choose the appropriate paper for our work. In this chapter I will outline some of the crucial decisions you will need to make in selecting a paper for fine art digital printing.

> *No amount of toying with shades of print or with printing papers will transform a commonplace photograph into anything other than a commonplace photograph.*
>
> —Bill Brandt

Overview of Inkjet Papers

Papers suitable for digital inkjet printing typically have a **substrate** (such as a cotton rag) upon which an ink-receptive **coating** is applied (**Figure 9-1**). You print on the coated side of the inkjet paper. Without this special coating, image quality, particularly sharpness, can suffer, as the precise dots laid down by your inkjet printer can bleed and spread out on the paper.

Real-world papers may actually have more than one layer of coating applied to the base substrate (which itself may have more than one layer). The coating may include, for example, a first layer to prevent ink from reaching the substrate, a second layer to absorb ink, and a third that fixes the ink pigment that passes through to the second layer so that it does not bleed. Some papers even have another coating on the back to help balance the paper and prevent curl.

The wide varieties of available inkjet paper stem from different approaches to the substrate and the coating—the two core components of inkjet paper.

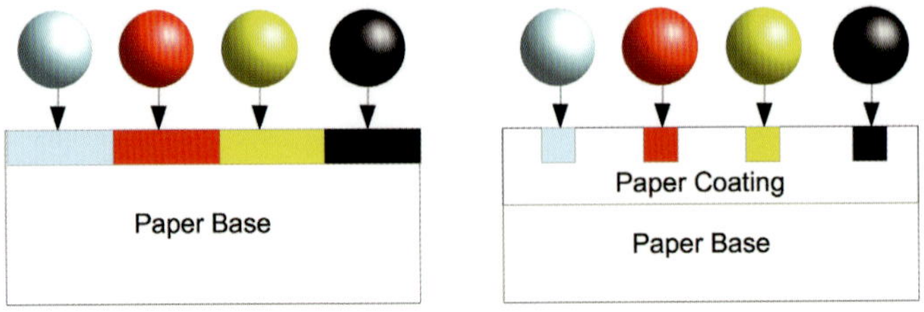

FIGURE 9-1: In this schematic of a cross-section of an uncoated paper (on the left) and a coated paper (on the right), ink droplets fall down on to the paper surface from the inkjet heads. With the uncoated paper, the ink drops spread and do not maintain their dot shape on the paper. With a coated paper, the dot shape is maintained as the receptive coating minimizes any spread of the ink droplets.

Paper Coatings

Paper manufacturers coat their inkjet papers so that the papers can handle ink without the ink bleeding, which would result in a loss of sharpness and a loss of color and saturation capability. For papers made for pigment inks, coatings are micro-porous. Micro-porous coatings have tiny holes in them, allowing the inks to penetrate the coated surface to some extent. These micro-porous coatings allow the inks to dry very quickly as well.

With the current technology of papers, the first question you must answer is what type of coating you prefer: do you prefer **matte papers** or **photo papers** (which include lustre and glossy, among other treatments)? The two types of papers are aesthetically very different, and I strongly recommend photographers try both, as many people express an immediate preference for one or the other.

Besides the difference in aesthetics, matte papers and photo papers differ in another important respect—the black ink you should use in your printer to print on these two types of coatings is different. This is why inkjet printers have Matte Black (MK) and Photo Black ink (PK) inks: Matte Black ink is used on papers with matte coatings, and Photo Black ink is used on papers with photo (or glossy) coatings.

Matte coatings are designed to scatter light, which results in less color and saturation capability but also less glare and fewer reflections. Photo coatings (lustre and gloss) are very efficient light reflectors, giving great color capability but also the potential for glare.

The choice between matte and photo papers is a very personal choice and there certainly are no right or wrong answers, but I will highlight some of the general advantages of each below.

Advantages of Matte Papers

- Potential for more satisfying feel in hand (though some of the newer fiber-based lustre papers are in the same ballpark)
- Minimal reflections from inconsistent lighting

- No gloss differential (areas on a glossy print where it appears a different amount of ink has been applied than in other parts of the image)
- Reduced sharpness as compared to photo papers, which can help hide problems in an image
- Handling of large prints is easier; less likely to get dimples

Advantages of Photo Papers

- Potential for deeper blacks/more dynamic range, larger color gamut (i.e., has more color capability), and increased sharpness
- Lustre papers are less likely than matte paper to suffer damage from paper handling via scratches or surface marks (though they are certainly not immune to it)
- Lustre papers have more sparkle or shine because of their more reflective nature

If your photo has high contrast, deep blacks, or very vibrant colors and you want to maximize those, I recommend a photo paper rather than matte. But everything is relative and I've seen many high-contrast images with deep blacks look great on matte paper (**Figure 9-2**). The print on matte paper might be contrasty enough for what you'd like. Once the print is

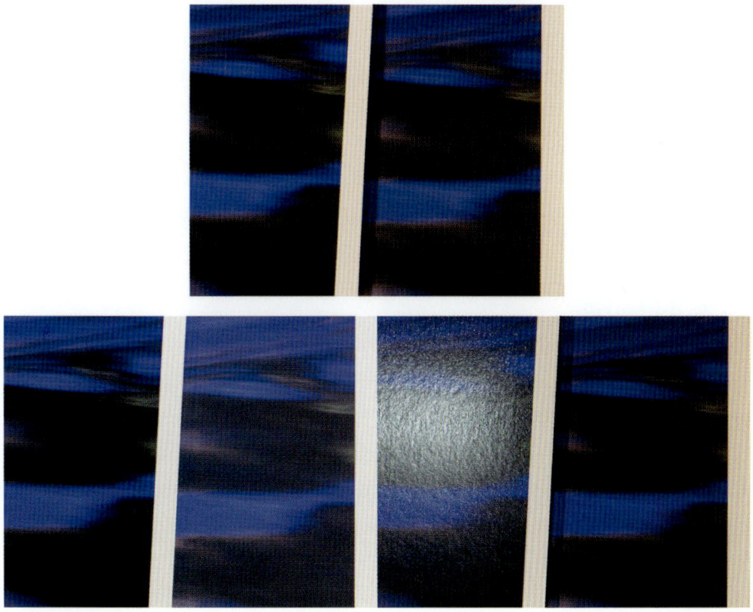

FIGURE 9-2: I compared the same image printed on two different papers. In each pairing, a fiber-based lustre (Epson Exhibition Fiber) is on the left and a matte paper (Moab Somerset Velvet) is on the right. The top pairing shows the prints in a diffused front light that is probably the closest to a normal viewing situation. The lustre (left) shows more contrast and deeper blacks, but not dramatically so. The pairing on the lower left was under a brighter light that was offset a little, and the difference between the lustre and matte is more apparent. The lower-right pairing shows the prints in more of a side light, and the lustre paper suffers from severe glare. The lesson: Test these papers yourself in different lighting conditions to see what the best fit is for your needs.

completed, it will stand alone and will not be next to the same image printed on a photo paper, so comparisons with photo papers become less important.

Print Mastery: Measured Black vs. Perception of Black

Photo papers unquestionably can produce deeper blacks than matte papers, and measurements will support that. The blacks on matte papers, however, can sometimes look blacker even though they aren't actually blacker (see Figure 9.2 also).

Those deep, solid blacks on a lustre or glossy surface will reflect so much light that you can lose some of that sense of blackness. Blacks on great matte paper seem to absorb the light rather than reflect it, and blacks can become almost velvety.

I've chosen matte black papers for some of my projects that are very dark. It isn't the best look for some photographs, but it can be for many. I encourage you to experiment with your own work.

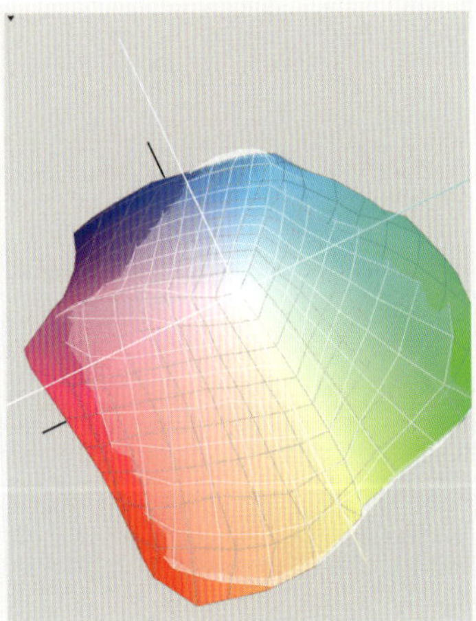

FIGURE 9-3: Using Apple's ColorSync, I've compared the color gamut of Hahnemühle Photo Rag (a matte paper, shown on the inner grayscale wireframe here) with Hahnemühle Photo Rag Baryta (a lustre paper, shown on the color wireframe here). In most regions the Photo Rag Baryta extends beyond the Photo Rag and thus can produce more colors, as one would expect from the lustre vs. matte paper types. But even in this situation there are certain regions where the Photo Rag goes a bit further out, meaning that for those specific colors the matte is more capable. Capability is complex and a paper being more capable in one way doesn't mean it is more capable in all ways.

Paper Capability

"Paper capability" is my phrase for the ability of a paper to show a range and intensity of colors as well as a range of tones via blacks, paper white, and dynamic range (based partially on the deepest possible black).

Generally speaking, photo papers have more paper capability than matte papers; photo papers have larger gamuts and deeper blacks as a class of papers, though of course some high-quality matte papers have capabilities rivaling or surpassing lower performing photo papers. To account for the reduced capability of matte papers, you may need to add increased contrast, increased saturation, and/or increased local contrast enhancement to create a satisfying print. The matte papers may never approach the range of the photo papers, but you can somewhat close the gap.

To best understand the capability of a paper, you need to work with it, but I find that the free Apple utility ColorSync (described below) provides a good way of approximating the differences between two papers (**Figure 9-3**).

Paper Substrates

Once you've decided on either a matte or photo paper, your next decision is about the substrate. There are a wide variety of paper substrates available for digital printing, giving you many choices to find a paper that matches your artistic intent for your print. I generally divide substrates used for inkjet paper into three general categories: art papers, resin-coated papers, and fiber-based papers.

Art Papers

Art papers include a wide variety of matte papers with natural substrates, and they vary with respect to surface texture from ultra smooth papers that are, well, smooth, to highly textured watercolor-type papers. At their best, art papers counter the disadvantages of matte papers with respect to capability with an elegant feel and a complete lack of gloss differential issues or reflections.

A common substrate for art papers is cotton rag. **Cotton rag** papers were traditionally manufactured from torn cotton rags but are now typically manufactured from a pulp of cotton linters, which are fibers that adhere to cottonseed after ginning. Cotton rag papers for digital printing are often traditional art papers (e.g., textured watercolor or other matte papers) on which an inkjet-capable coating has been applied to properly receive inks. Cotton rag substrates are overall the best substrates for art papers in terms of public perception and in the available papers, but 100% cotton rag is not a guarantee of quality, either—but it is a great starting point.

Alpha cellulose is another common substrate for art papers. Cellulose, the chief constituent of cell walls of plants, is the result of processing of plant tissue designed to yield cellulose. High alpha cellulose papers are a particularly pure form of wood pulp considered to have comparable longevity and archival characteristics as cotton or other plant fibers. A pulp is any cellulose plant fiber (wood, cotton, linen, and the like) that has been cleaned and beaten into a wet mixture. Alpha cellulose substrates vary in quality more than cotton rag. There are great papers with 100% alpha cellulose substrates, but papers that are higher in wood pulp content are usually less archival and less durable.

Other art paper substrates include bamboo (Hahnemühle Fine Art Bamboo), sugar cane (Hahnemühle Fine Art Sugar Cane), and mulberry plants (most rice papers).

Resin-Coated Papers

Resin-coated (RC) papers, by definition, utilize resined plastics in the paper substrate (sometimes along with a wood pulp sandwiched in between the plastic layers), and all that I have seen are RC photo papers rather than matte papers.

Much like in the traditional darkroom days, RC papers provide a combination of very good image quality with a reasonable price. Unlike the darkroom days, there are no particular concerns with longevity—good RC papers have comparable archival characteristics to the "fine art" papers. RC papers have a look and feel like some photo lab prints and thus seem like a "real" photograph to many. However, most (including myself) feel that the more plastic feel and look is undesirable when compared to art and fiber-based papers.

The advantage to RC papers, besides price, is that the plastic paper base allows for extremely smooth surfaces, making it very suitable for high gloss papers.

Print Mastery: Outgassing

An issue with RC papers that has not been entirely resolved is the issue of outgassing. The impervious polyethylene layer between the coating and the base of the substrate rejects glycol (a humectant) from inkjet inks, slowing the evaporation process. The glycols then evaporate off the print, so if you frame the print before the glycol has evaporated and the print is completely dry, it can create a fog on your glazing (glass or Plexiglass). So, what to do about this?

Letting the prints dry for a few days in a studio that is sufficiently warm can work in letting the prints completely dry, and many cure the paper to accelerate the process by laying a sheet of absorbent paper over the print for a day or two to avoid the possibility of fogging. Outgassing doesn't have a negative impact on your print, just potentially on the glazing, so there are no archival concerns with it in respect to the print. Outgassing is highly dependent on your paper and your drying environment so exact numbers are impossible to determine. Therefore, if you are having trouble, let your prints dry longer.

Outgassing can occur with any inkjet print but is much more of an issue on RC papers. That being said, I've never actually seen the fogging happen. My recommendation is to be cautious in letting all your prints dry for a bit before framing, and to be especially cautious with RC papers.

Fiber-Based (fibre-based) Papers

Fiber-based (FB) papers are relatively new category of papers that I characterize as photo papers (that use the PK ink) with an art paper substrate rather than an RC substrate. FB papers originated as an attempt to replicate fiber-based darkroom prints in the digital darkroom. FB papers typically have a glossy or lustre surface over a fiber-based cotton rag or alpha cellulose substrate, and they provide a "fine art" feel along with stellar image quality. They bridge the gap between RC and art papers by providing an art paper backing with a non-matte surface that can provide deeper blacks and a greater color range.

One type of FB paper that has become very popular recently is the **baryta** paper. Baryta papers have a multilayer coating that includes barium sulfate (which is a white clay-like substance) over a paper base such as alpha cellulose or cotton rag. The baryta gives the paper much of its smoothness, white point, and, interestingly, sometimes a smell just a bit reminiscent of the darkroom. Baryta (pronounced bah-RYE-tah) papers have their origin in the traditional darkroom as fiber-based silver gelatin prints typically used a white layer of barium-sulphate gelatin applied to the paper ground and beneath the light-sensitive layer to help provide pure whites and rich blacks. As such, the use of baryta in papers for photographic printing has a long history of archival permanence.

Baryta papers for the digital darkroom have all the archival characteristics you would like and importantly, have a very similar look and feel to great air-dried fiber-based silver-gelatin papers. Similar, mind you, is not the same as identical—while these papers do appear very similar to traditional darkroom papers, there are of course differences visible to the discerning eye, most notably in how the ink sits more on the surface rather than being embedded in the surface in a darkroom print. But they are, however, very close, and wonderful in their own right, and that is ultimately what is important to me as a printer and photographer—not how closely the end result matches traditional methods, but how it stands on its own.

Considerations in Choosing Paper

Surface Texture

Surface texture is an important consideration in choosing a paper. Papers range from very smooth to heavily textured, and the nature of the texture can vary in unique ways (**Figure 9-4**). Like many aspects of choosing a paper, the choice is a subjective one, though there are relevant technical considerations as well.

With respect to matte papers, nomenclature you often see is "cold press" papers and "hot press" papers. Cold press papers are textured (like watercolor papers) while hot press papers are smooth.

For my own photographic work, I tend to prefer smooth or lightly textured papers. I feel that a smooth matte paper lets your image "speak" more than any other type of paper because of the absence of texture or reflection.

More heavily textured matte papers can provide a lovely surface and are popular for art reproduction and fine art work. Surface texture can also help hide imperfections in your image, so consider a textured paper if you are

Figure 9-4: A close-up view of Epson Exhibition Fiber, a popular fiber-based lustre paper, on the left, and Moab Somerset Velvet, a textured fine art matte paper, on the right

enlarging beyond a comfortable range. Texture in more uniform areas such as a sky can help fill in the image, too.

With respect to photo papers, glossy papers provide very dramatic looks and high amounts of color and dynamic range ability. Lustre or semigloss surfaces break up the gloss somewhat, and I've found that individual preferences on lustre surfaces tend to be strong. With certain lustre surfaces I find the pebbled surface very attractive, but I find others distracting.

Paper Brightness, Color, and OBAs

Another significant factor to consider is the **color** of the paper. Papers often have a warm, neutral, or cool look, and your work may look its best on a particular one. With black-and-white printing, this choice is even more important as the overall look of the image will greatly depend on the paper's color characteristics.

The **brightness** of the paper—which is tied to the color of the paper—is another key consideration. White is not always white in the paper world, and papers tend to range from warmer to cool with more neutral choices in between. For many papers, brightness (i.e., how white the whites are) is achieved through the use of optical brightening agents (OBAs), an addition to the paper that helps make the paper brighter.

OBAs are clear or white dyes that activate under visible light (the ultraviolet spectrum in the light is what causes it) and make the white in a paper appear brighter and cooler (**Figure 9-5**). A paper with significant OBAs can look almost blue when compared to a paper without them.

Papers with OBAs often still have good archival characteristics, but testing has shown that OBAs will often fade before the rest of the print and the OBAs thus become the limiting archival factor. Additionally, testing indicates that OBAs don't simply fade away, but that a more complicated process occurs that can negatively impact your color over time in many cases, too.

What you plan to do with the prints is also important. Mounting papers with OBAs behind glass that filters ultraviolet radiation (which is good practice for preservation) reduces their effectiveness, as UV is necessary to activate the OBAs. With UV light no longer hitting the paper, they will appear less bright and perhaps have a slightly warm color shift.

I still recommend some papers that use OBAs for many purposes, but many artists prefer to avoid them entirely. For my fine art work, I strongly prefer papers that don't have OBAs (or at least minimal OBAs) unless I have a particular need for a paper with the extra brightness they provide. If you think your image looks better in print on a paper with OBAs, find one that has better archival ratings and go for it.

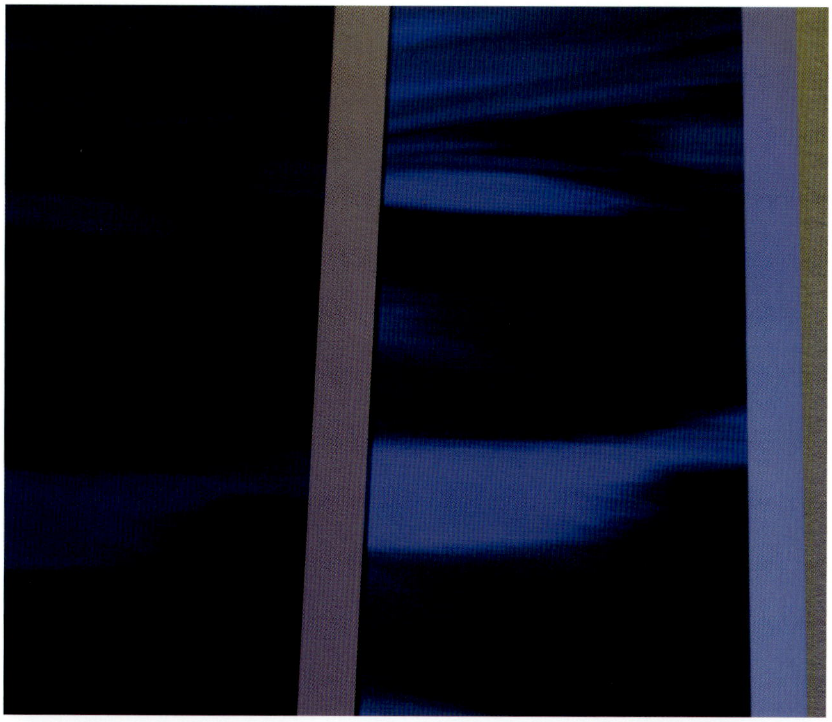

Figure 9-5: Moab Somerset Velvet on the left and Epson Exhibition Fiber on the right under a UV flashlight. The Epson Exhibition Fiber is clearly reacting strongly to the direct UV light as its OBAs are activated. UV flashlights are inexpensive (less than $10) and are often marketed as pet stain detectors.

Print Mastery: How Do You Know If OBAs Are Present?

Determining whether OBAs are in a paper is not a trivial task. RC papers almost always have them. Whenever a paper manufacturer has a Bright version and a Natural version of their paper, the Bright version will have OBAs and the Natural version will not. Many papers are marketed as OBA-free, but I haven't found one that brags about their presence.

Unless you want to do your own testing (with a UV light per Figure 9-5), I recommend looking online for reviews of the paper as they often mention the presence of OBAs or the lack thereof.

Paper Thickness and Weight

Thickness and weight are both indications of the relative heft of a paper. Most papers fall within a relatively small range of weights between about 150 grams per square meter (gsm) and about 310 gsm. Since gsm is a measurement of weight, papers with the same gsm rating can be different in thickness because the paper materials may have different densities.

Thicker papers (those with normal densities and weights from about 270 gsm and up) are often harder to handle in the printer (such as by having an increased chance of head strikes because of their thickness), but they often feel better in the hand. Paper thickness and weight are part of the **presence** of a paper—a more substantial paper can be very pleasing when compared to one that is thinner or more flimsy.

Archival Considerations and Print Permanence

Print permanence has been one of the most crucial issues, if not *the* most crucial issue, in acceptance of digital printing in the fine art world. Early versions of inkjet printers were plagued with horrible fading and color drift issues, and dedicated digital fine art printers are still fighting against that reputation to this day. Advances in technology now give us paper and ink combinations that are rated for many decades, or even centuries, before unacceptable fading occurs.

For those interested, I recommend the websites of Wilhelm Imaging Research (www.wilhelm-research.com) and Aardenburg Imaging (www.aardenburg-imaging.com) as excellent resources on the archival aspects of different types of prints. I find the Aardenburg Imaging site in particular to be very valuable as it provides more aggressive and more independent testing than does Wilhelm, but both provide valuable information. Many ink and printer combinations have been specifically tested already by these labs and can provide useful longevity information as you are deciding what papers to use.

Availability and Cost

Availability is another factor to consider. Is the paper available from your favorite retailer? Do they offer the sizes you need? Epson's popular Velvet Fine Art, for example, is only available in sizes up to 17" × 22". Do they make ICC profiles for your printer?

Cost can also be important as paper prices vary dramatically. Double-sided papers can also be more efficiently used for proofing, providing another opportunity to reduce cost.

Handling

Handling of papers is something that can usually only be determined from experience. How bad is the curl? How susceptible is the surface to scratching? How easy is it to put a kink into your big print when you are handling it? There are papers that I definitely use less of because the curl is so annoying.

Inkjet paper comes either in cut sheets or rolls, each form having its advantages and disadvantages. Cut sheet paper in the United States is usually available in 8.5" × 11", 13" × 19", and 17" × 22" sizes, with occasional variations such as 17" × 25" or a few larger options such as 24" × 30". For other sizes, you'll have to either trim an available cut sheet or print from a roll (if your printer supports it).

I prefer cut sheet papers because of ease of handling and because I find that they have less curl after the print is complete. Since I often change papers many times a day to serve clients, it is easier to use cut sheets as well since switching papers doesn't require switching out a roll. Rolls can be more efficient and are often the only choice for a larger print. Once the roll is loaded, printing is straightforward since you don't have to reload the paper for each print.

Choosing a Paper

When I was choosing a paper for my own landscape photography, I wanted a paper that had very good image quality characteristics as my work often relies on sharpness, detail in the shadows, and subtleties in color. I also wanted a relatively neutral (or slightly warm) color, a great feel in the hand, and a cotton rag base without OBAs. I ordered and tested a number of papers that met these criteria and laid them all side by side and chose my favorite. Some of the papers had more capability than the one I chose (Canson Platine Fiber Rag), but the surface texture of this paper was just perfect to my eye.

For my next bodies of work, I eventually decided that Canson Platine Fiber Rag was not the right choice because of its lustre surface. My Pyrotechnic project is printed on Hahnemühle Museum Etching, as its slight warmth and texture are harmonious with the warm-toned black-and-white images. Similarly, my Adventures in Celestial Mechanics series includes mostly minimalist photographs for the full moon inspired in part by Japanese woodblock prints, and a smooth matte paper like Canson Rag Photographique provided a closer match to that feel.

Principles of Printing #13:
Paper Choice Can Be Key for Achieving Artistic Intent

Paper choice is one of the most important decisions a photographer should make in realizing their artistic intent for a print. The right choice of paper, suitable for the image and supporting the artistic intent behind the print or portfolio, can raise a print to a new level of quality and impact.

If you view the print as the final and ultimate expression of a photograph as I do, the choice of paper plays an incredibly important role in the final print. Given how subjective your choice will be, I recommend considering these factors to narrow your selections down and then put ink to paper. Holding pictures printed on different papers side-by-side is the best way to make the choice. Most manufacturers also offer sample packs so that you may sample their papers without a major investment. Once you've chosen a paper or two, I recommend working with them for a while to really learn their abilities and idiosyncrasies.

Don't be wed to a paper, though. There is an obvious benefit to using the same paper for a long time to learn its intricacies, but you'll also learn by noticing differences with other papers. You may find some you like better, and paper technology is still advancing. You may want one type of paper for landscapes, another for black-and-white prints, another for portraits, and so on.

Recommended Papers

A list of papers that I use often and that I love is below. This is not meant to be an exhaustive list, and please don't be offended if your favorite is not on here:

- Canson Platine Fiber Rag for fiber-based lustre (also Hahnemühle Photo Rag Baryta, Canson Baryta Photographique, Ilford Gold Fiber Silk, and many others)
- Canson Rag Photographique for a smooth matte fine art paper (also Epson Hot Press Bright and Natural as well as Hahnemühle Photo Rag)
- Canson Aquarelle for a fine art matte with a watercolor texture
- Hahnemühle Museum Etching for a fine art matte paper with a little bit of texture (possibly my favorite paper)
- Harman by Hahnemühle Gloss Baryta for fine art fiber-based glossy

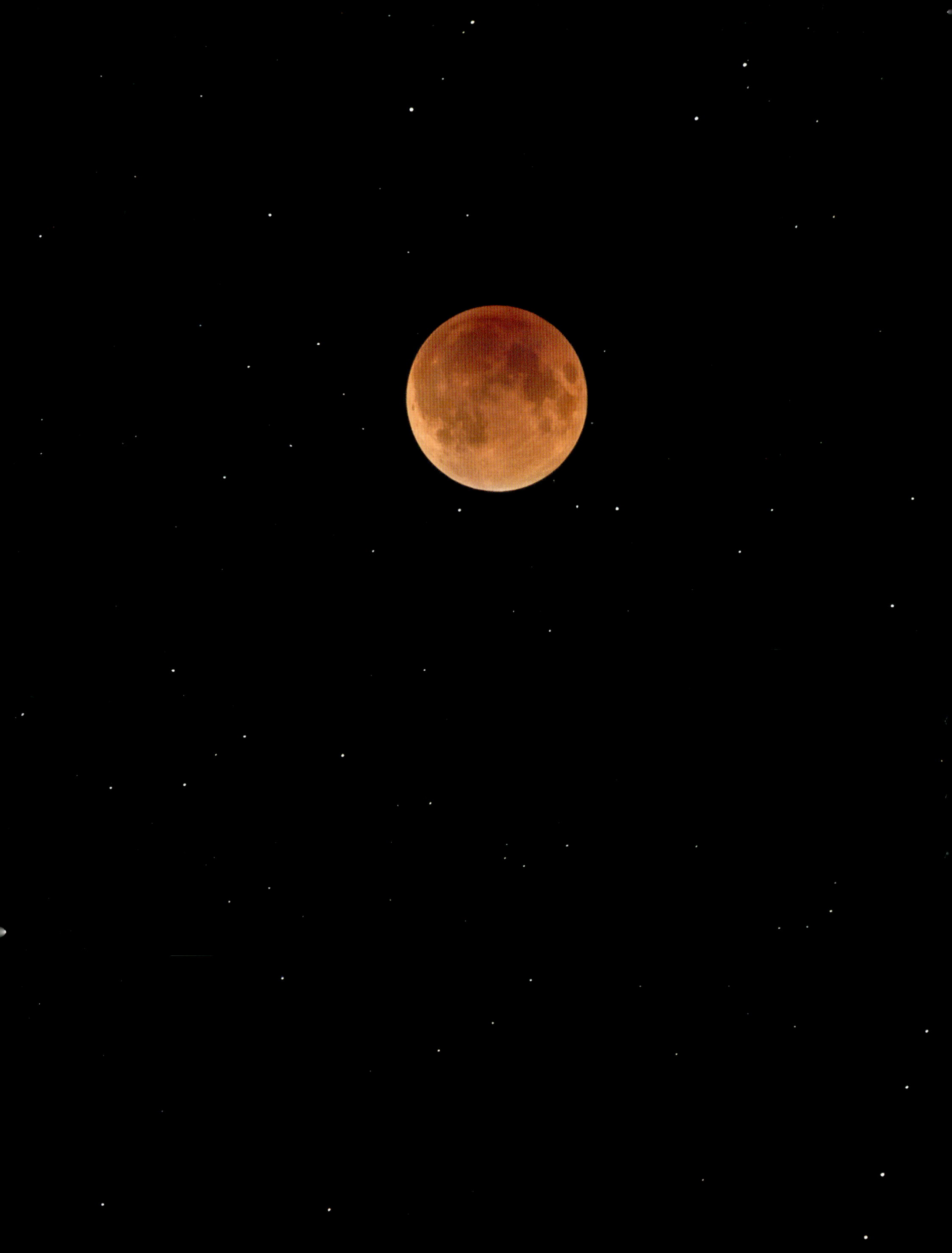

10

Editing for Print Interpretation

In this chapter we'll discuss specific examples of Print Interpretation where we edit images with the intention of making prints that are consistent with our artistic intent. As we discussed previously, Print Interpretation includes both Print Editing to match print to screen and Artistic Editing to further improve our prints and to align them with our artistic intent.

Artistic Intent and Print Interpretation

> *I photograph like a documentarian but print like a painter.*
> —Todd Hido

I believe that your **artistic intent** for your image should drive your decision making in the digital darkroom and during printing. Deciding how you want your print to look and developing the craft to make that look happen are both fundamental to the artistic process.

Print Interpretation is my term for making the necessary modifications and choices to realize your artistic intent in the final print, as discussed in chapter 5. My goal with Print Interpretation is simple: analyzing and evaluating my image and print to decide what can be done to make it more powerful and consistent with my artistic intent, and then implementing those changes. You are the director of your final print and you need to have your end goal in mind throughout the entire process.

Each image and each artist are different, providing for an unlimited number of choices in goals in editing an image for print. Print Interpretation is about judgment, and the more you think about it and implement it, the better you will likely become.

Principles of Printing #14:
Emphasize and Deemphasize to Direct the Attention of Your Viewer

Part of creating a fine art print is attempting to control how a viewer experiences the print. One successful method of doing this is to try to direct the attention of the viewer, whether it be by emphasizing things you want them to notice, deemphasizing things you don't want them to notice, directing their gaze around the image and keeping their gaze from slipping off the edge of the image, or magnifying or downplaying relationships between aspects of the image.

Print Interpretation Examples

Let's go through examples of Print Interpretation using some of the tools we've covered previously.

Mood and Feel

One common type of Print Interpretation is trying to achieve a particular mood or feel of the print. You may, for example, look at your image (or print) and decide that it needs to be brighter or darker to help change the mood or feel. Reducing the exposure and darkening the image may, for example, make a black-and-white landscape more foreboding and dramatic by making the blacks deeper (**Figure 10-1**). You may then wish to change the mood further by increasing the contrast to make the image even more dramatic.

A brighter version of an image can also have a much different mood and feel. A brighter image can feel lighter and airier than one that is a more typical exposure (**Figure 10-2**). These high-key images can evoke different emotions in a viewer.

You may also use *color* to effectively change the mood and feel of your images and prints. For the overall color, the most common tool is chang-

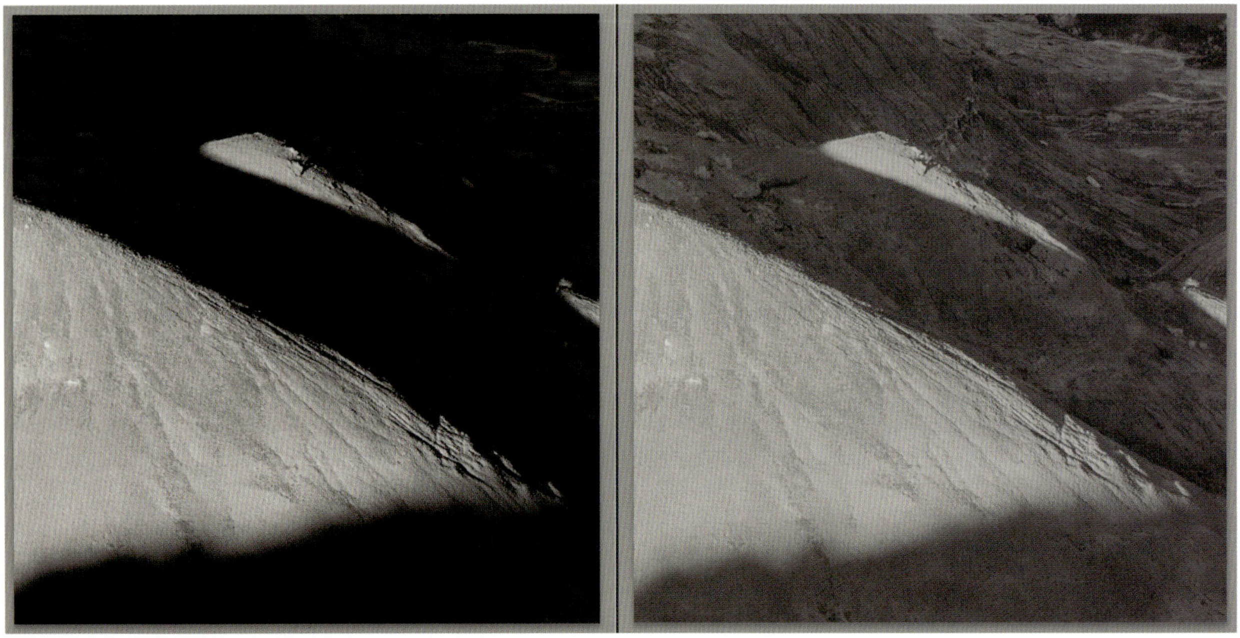

Figure 10-1: In these two versions of a rock formation in Petrified Forest National Park in Arizona, the version on the left is darker and more contrasty and the version on the right has been made brighter and less contrasty. The mood of each is different, with the darker one being more dramatic and mysterious and the lighter one revealing more in the shadows and being more balanced. The question of which is better is a subjective one.

ing the White Balance Temperature. Driving the White Balance Temperature toward blue makes the image cooler, and driving it toward yellow makes the image warmer (**Figure 10-3**).

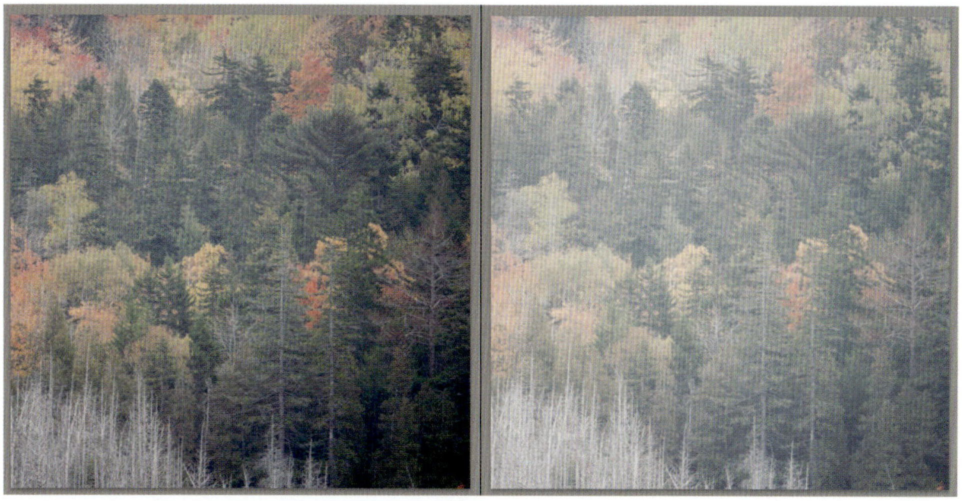

Figure 10-2: This quiet scene from a foggy day in Acadia National Park in Maine is represented in two versions. The one on the left has a relatively full histogram and tones ranging from shadows to highlights, while the one on the right is brighter and less contrasty (and incidentally much closer to the real life scene). The colors on the brighter version are more delicate, but it doesn't have as much drama as the other. The correct one to choose depends on your artistic intent.

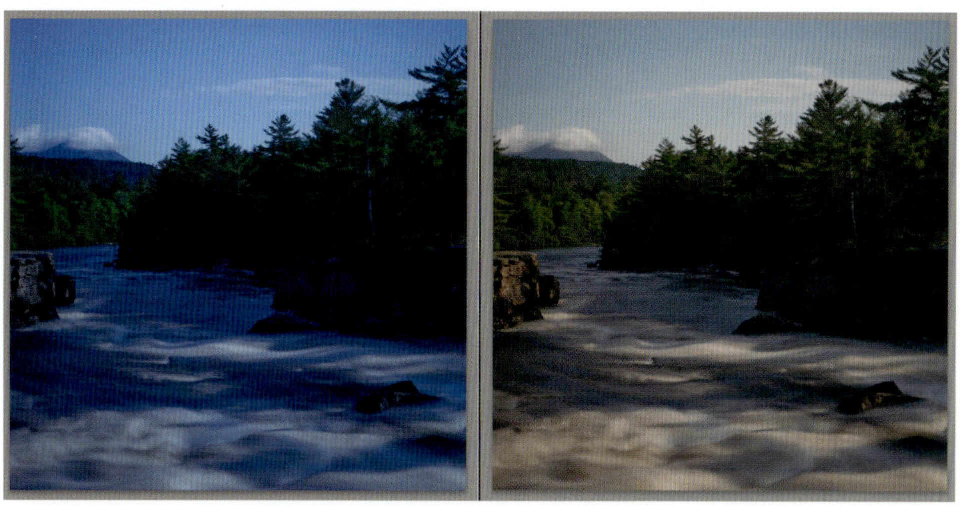

Figure 10-3: This night photograph from near Katahdin State Park in Maine illustrates the power of changing the white balance. The version on the right shows the white balance as captured by the camera, and since the scene was lit by the full moon, the color temperature resembled daylight. By driving the white balance toward blue on the version on the left, the look of the image changes dramatically, and to my eye feels more like night.

Color can be one of the most important elements of the look and feel of an image for black-and-white images, too. Many people print their black-and-white work as neutral in color, a classic look, but color toning can be a powerful tool for changing the visual impact of this type of image, too (**Figure 10-4**). A warm-toned black-and-white image feels entirely different than a cool-toned one, providing an excellent tool for black-and-white print interpretation.

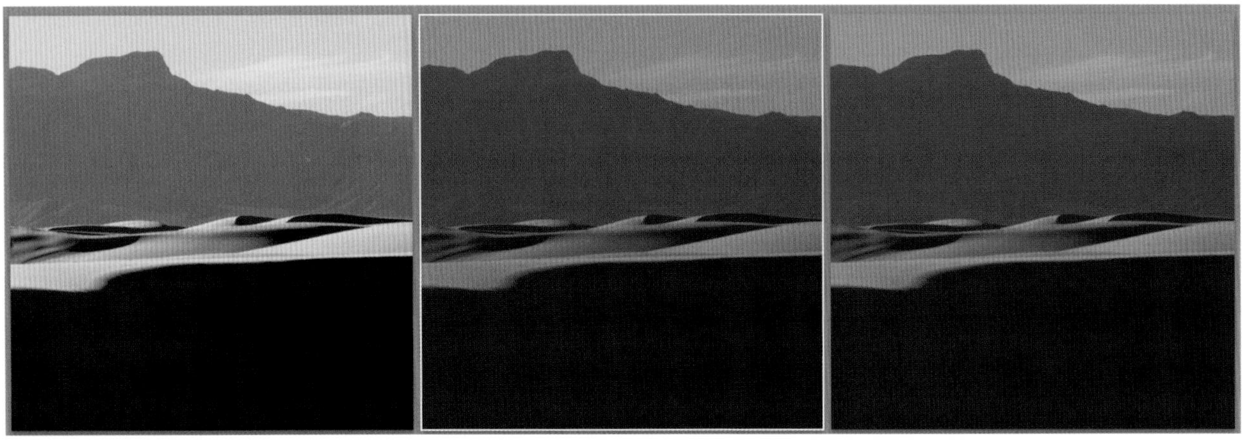

FIGURE 10-4: These three versions of a photograph from New Mexico's White Sands National Monument vary only in their tint. The version on the left is neutral, the middle one is from Lightroom's Sepia Tone preset, and the right version is based on Lightroom's Selenium Tone preset. All are valid interpretations of the scene, and personal preference, artistic intent, and the overall print statement can all drive you to choosing which one is best for you.

Visual Flow

When viewing a print, our eyes are drawn toward certain things beyond just the basic composition of the image. As a few examples, our eyes are drawn to the following features:

- Diagonal lines more than vertical or horizontal lines, as well as along lines of any sort
- Higher-contrast areas rather than lower-contrast areas
- Very bright objects rather than midtone areas
- Very dark objects rather than midtone areas
- Lighter areas rather than darker areas
- Sharper areas rather than softer areas
- Objects with more presence/clarity than those with less
- More intense saturation versus lower saturation
- Warmer colors rather than cooler colors
- Colors that clash or conflict with other colors in the print
- Objects that are out of place in their surroundings, such as a man-made object in a landscape
- Eyes in a portrait, particularly if the eyes are facing the viewer

If there is an object (e.g., a rock, the sky, or a car) in your print that you feel is too prominent in terms of visual flow, you can use the following tools to help emphasize that object or, instead, deemphasize the other things in the image. If the sky is too bright, you can darken it down or lighten everything else, or a combination of the two.

If, instead, you'd like to deemphasize an object, use these tools to do so, or use those same tools to emphasize everything else.

Below you'll find a few specific examples that modify the visual flow and I hope they will be an inspiration for editing your own images for print.

Vignetting and Edges

Another tool in Print Interpretation involves improving the **visual flow** of an image by helping to direct the viewer's eyes in particular directions. Let's say you want to have the viewer eye's naturally stay on the image and not to follow a visual path off the edge of the print. One way you could do this would be to add **vignetting** to the image to darken the edges (particularly the corners), which would help keep the viewer's eyes from trailing off the edge (**Figure 10-5**).

FIGURE 10-5: The original version of the image on the left appears fine, but a subtle darkening of the corners as seen in the version on the right helps keep the viewer's eye within the image area and to not follow the diagonal lines off the edge. To accomplish this in Lightroom/ACR, I went to the Post-Crop Vignetting Tool in the Develop module in the Effects panel and simply put in an Amount of –6 of a Highlight Priority post-crop vignette.

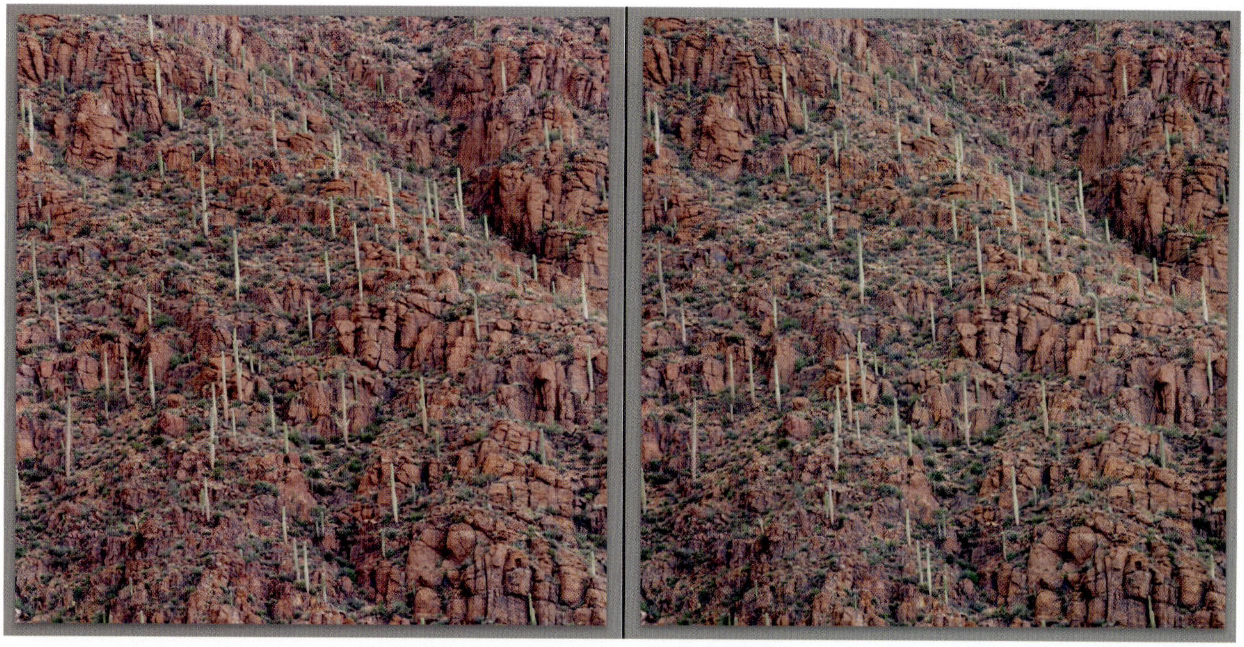

The eye tends to be attracted to brighter areas rather than darker areas, so darkening the edges of a print to help keep the viewer's eye from drifting off has been a classic technique for decades.

Instead of vignetting, you can also use the Gradient Tool or Graduated Filter to burn edges more consistently and flexibly than a vignetting tool. You can choose to burn all four edges of a print, for example, to place less emphasis on the corners, or you could only apply burning to some of the edges (e.g., burning the edge with sky but not the edge with foreground detail).

Bright and Dark Objects

The eye is also attracted to very bright or very dark objects, so reducing the impact of any of those could potentially improve the flow of the viewer's eye throughout the image. Similarly, if you'd like to attract the viewer's attention to part of the image, making it very bright or very dark can accomplish that.

Consider this winter landscape photograph from Marshall Point in Maine (**Figure 10-6**). I liked the original photograph on the left but felt that my eye was first attracted to the bright sky and then continued to leave the image. To help control the viewer's eye, I made two changes: First, I added a gradient to the sky that lowered exposure and highlights a little bit to tone down the sky so that it would not draw attention as much. Next, I added just a bit of

FIGURE 10-6: The original version of the image is on the left, and a version with enhanced bright areas in the foreground a darker sky is on the right

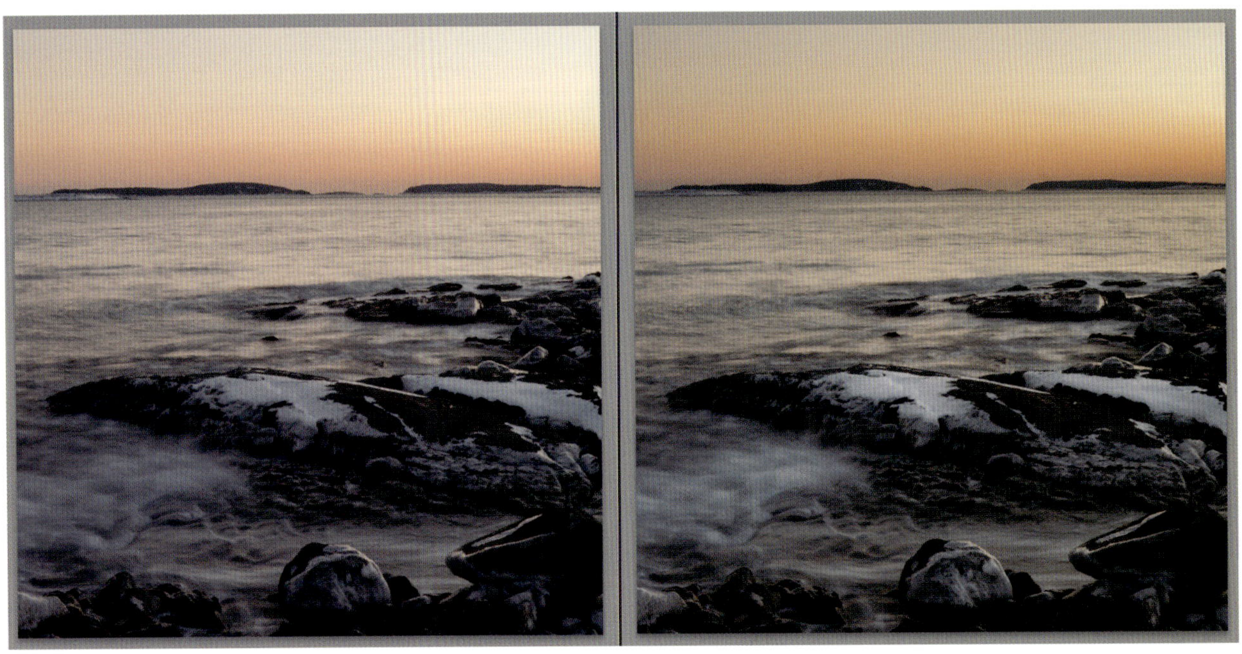

exposure to some of the rocks and waves using the Adjustment Brush tool (**Figure 10-7**).

I wanted to provide a roughly oval path of brighter areas of interest, so that the eye would go across the snow, down the wave, over the ice on the rock at the bottom, and then back up to the snow. The original image seems a bit flat in comparison to the edited version, and because of that flatness the viewer's eye was more static except for being drawn upward towards the sky. Even a subtle change can make a difference.

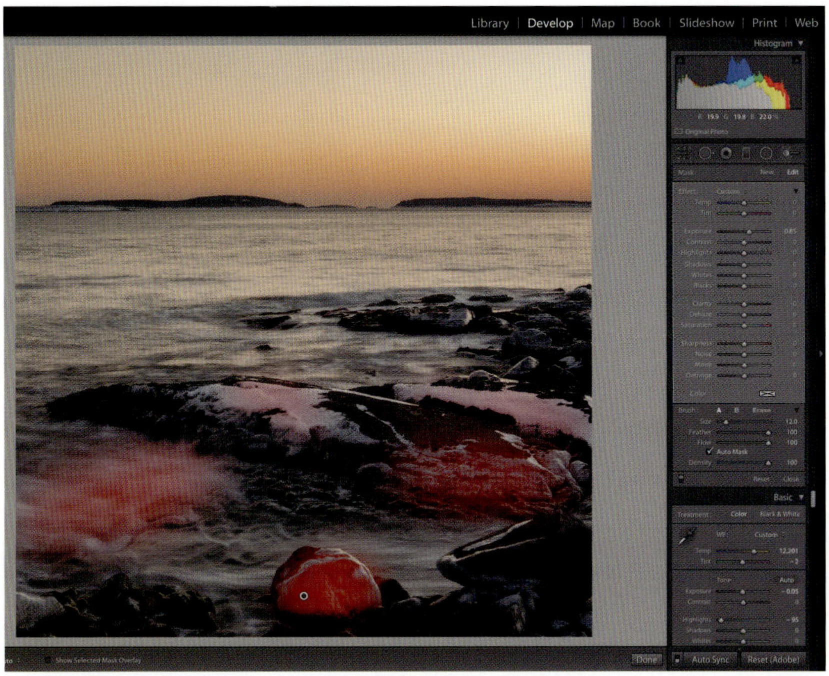

Figure 10-7: The red mask indicates where the Adjustment Brush tool is being applied. This mask is very rough and not at all precise, though the Auto Mask function of the tool helps keep even rough applications of the brush contained. The mask could be fine-tuned, but I want to illustrate how a quick mask can still be effective.

Emphasizing Existing Visual Flow through Composition

Another solution to downplay or enhance the visual flow of an image might be to change the crop or orientation. In one example, diagonal lines are a strong compositional element and heavily influence how a viewer's eyes move through an image. If a strong diagonal is present that goes to the edge, it can be such a strong element that it can easily lead the viewer's eyes right out of an image (**Figure 10-8**). Through judicious cropping, you can often change the dynamics of that type of image so that the diagonal is not so dominant, whereas in other images, you can crop to help create stronger diagonals when strong ones are missing and you want to intentionally use them for creative effect.

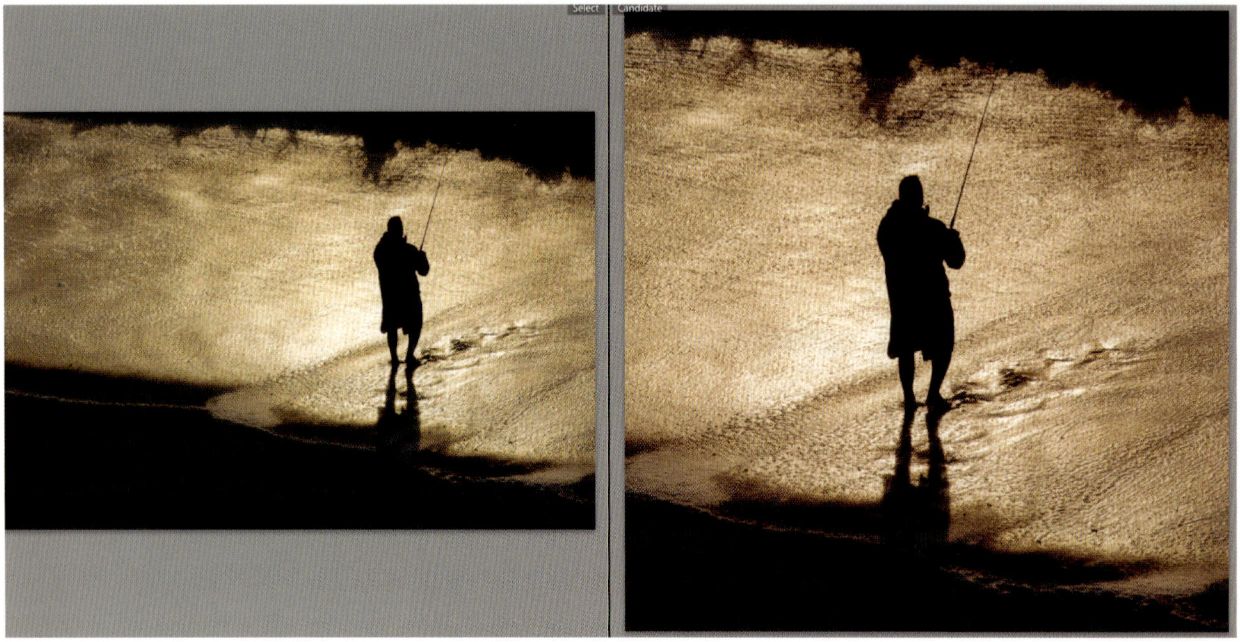

Figure 10-8: My original photograph on the left taken from the Pacific Coast Highway in California has lovely light but I find that the strong diagonal on the bottom draws the eye up and out of the left side of the image. By cropping to the square version on the right, the lower diagonal line is balanced with the upper one, and they work together to emphasize the fisherman without drawing the eye out of the image.

Changing Tonal Relationships

> *Dodging and burning are steps to take care of mistakes God made in establishing tonal relationships.*
>
> —Ansel Adams

A powerful method of Print Interpretation is editing the image to either emphasize or deemphasize **tonal relationships** within an image. For example, a seascape might have a very bright rock in the surf that attracts the eye, and burning the rock down to reduce its brightness might improve the image by making the rock less prominent. Rather than directing the viewer's path, this can be thought of as changing the focal points of the viewer's attention.

In another example, brightening the eyes of a portrait subject to draw the viewer's attention to the eyes is a well-known technique used long before digital processes. A similar idea of brightening an area of interest can be applied to landscape photography as well as any other genre (**Figure 10-9**).

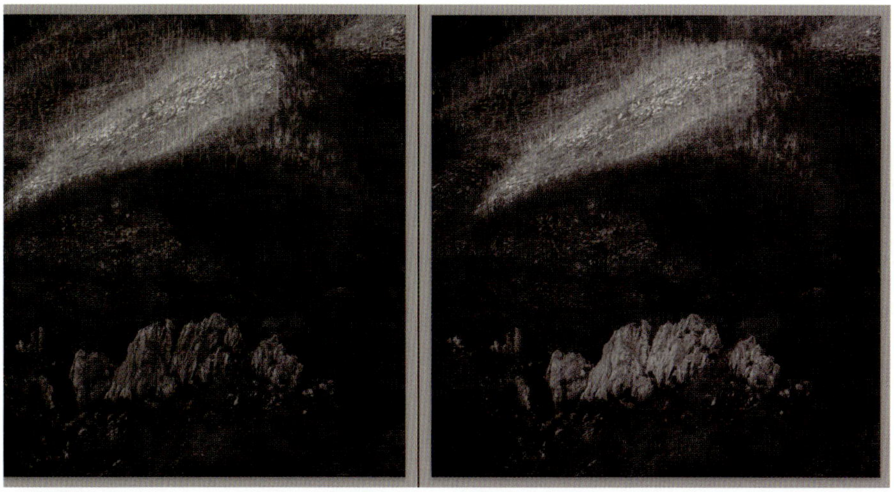

Figure 10-9: In the original version of the image on the left of this photograph from Chiricahua National Monument in Arizona, the interesting rock formation on the bottom half of the image blends into the surrounding landscape. By using an Adjustment Brush in Lightroom and adding a bit of exposure, those rocks can be emphasized, creating a better balance to the image.

Changing Color Relationships

We can also modify color relationships by adjusting color tint or saturation, such as by increasing the visual "pop" of yellow foliage, by making the blue of the sky more intense and saturated, or by reducing the emphasis on the sky by toning down blue saturation. If you have both warm and cool colors in your image, such as an image dominated by both yellow and blue, increasing the intensity of each color will highlight their complementary nature (**Figure 10-10**).

Just changing the white balance can change the color relationships, too. Making the white balance temperature bluer, for example, makes things in the image that are close to neutral somewhat blue, and items that are warm become a little less warm. The result of this can create a color contrast that did not previously exist (**Figure 10-11**).

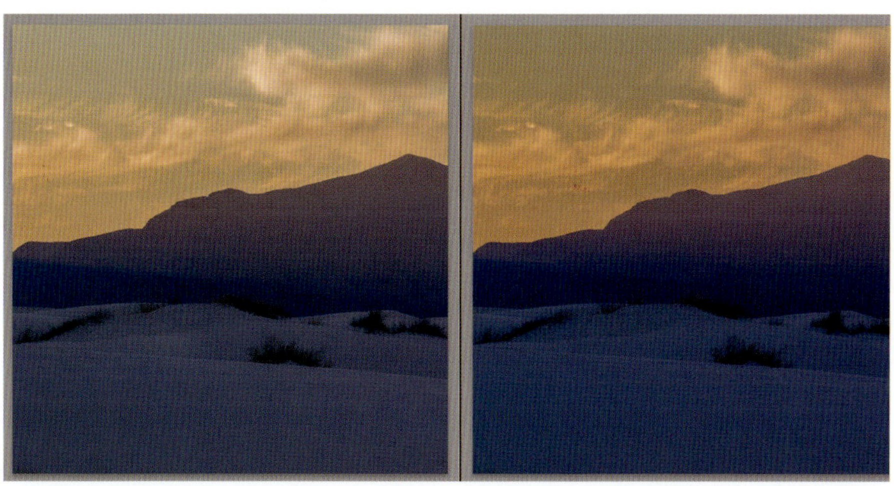

Figure 10-10: In this scene from White Sands National Monument in New Mexico, the modified version on the right emphasizes the striking combination of yellow and blue by intensifying it. In Lightroom, using the HSL > Color > B&W Panel, I increased the saturation of the Yellow and lowered the luminance to make the color deeper and richer. For the Blue color I only increased the saturation and did not change the luminance.

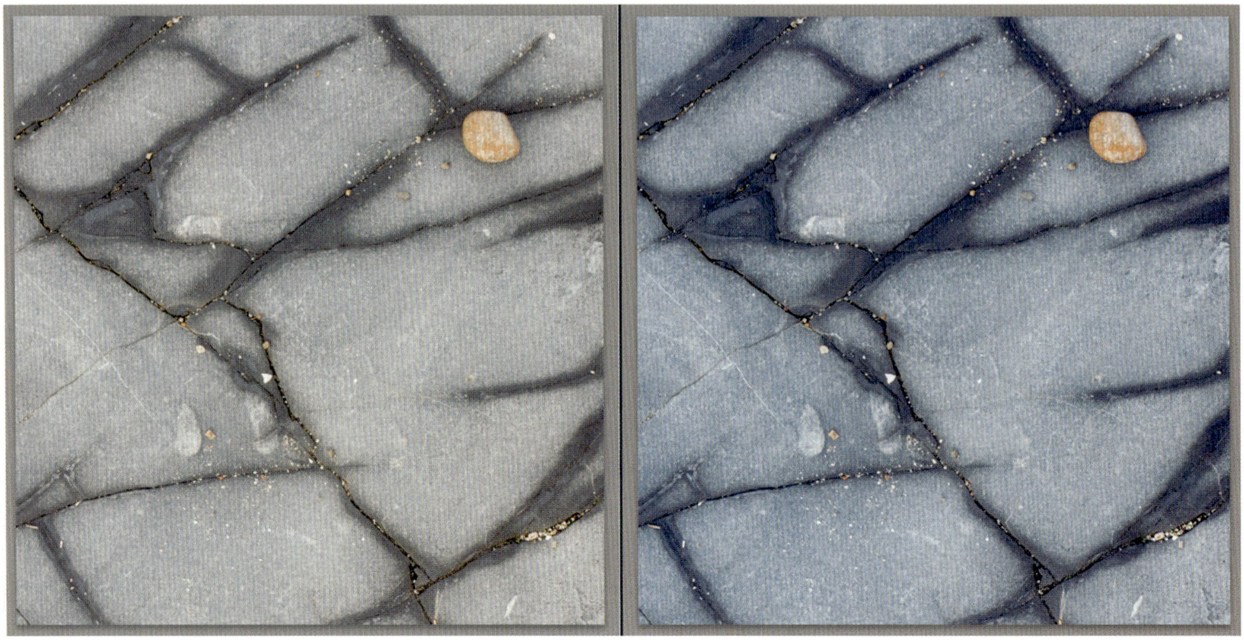

Figure 10-11: In this scene from Point Lobos in California, in the original version on the left, I felt that the orange rock did not stand out enough against the gray rocks. An increase in orange and yellow saturation did improve things, but only marginally. It was not until I shifted the white balance of the entire image toward blue that the contrast between the orange rock and the base rock became pronounced, as shown in the version on the right.

Creative Sharpening and Blurring

Another way of emphasizing objects in an image is to sharpen that object using selective adjustment tools. This is the **creative sharpening** mentioned previously as the optional second sharpening step. The eye is drawn to sharper things and this can help focus the viewer's attention.

Adjustments to midtone contrast and clarity can achieve a similar effect. Taking the improved photograph from Figure 10-11, I decided that the black lines in the rock were not prominent enough. I applied both clarity and sharpening using the Adjustment Brush tool all along those lines to create a new version with more pronounced lines (**Figure 10-12**).

When analyzed at the pixel level, you can see the increased sharpness and clarity of the modified image more obviously. In print, this will help those cracks be a more significant part of the image (**Figure 10-13**).

Editing Print Interpretation Summary

Print Interpretation, and particularly its artistic aspect, is infinite in its possibilities as to what you can and should do in editing each image, as it will vary for each and every print. Building off the examples above, here is a

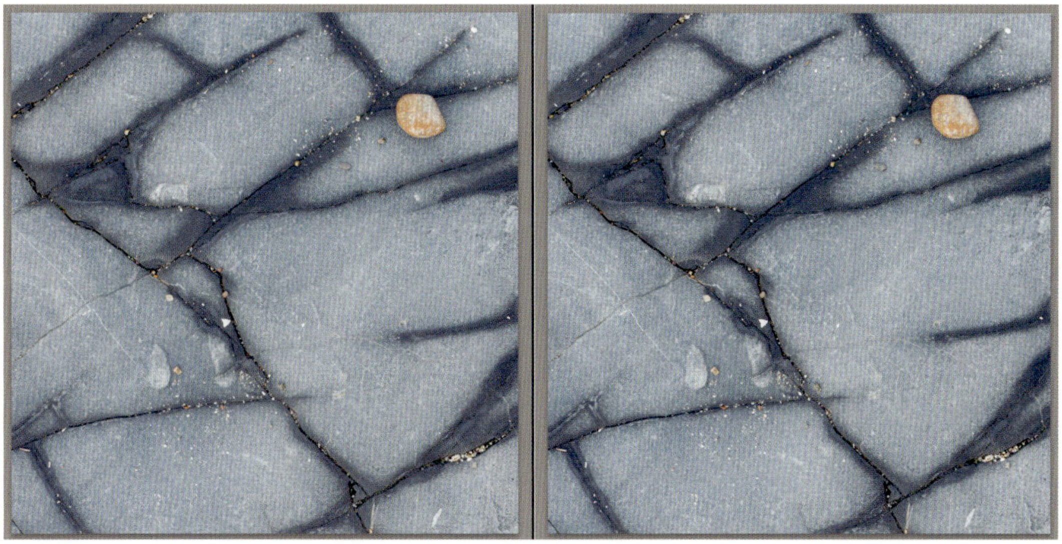

Figure 10-12: Building off the changes in Figure 10-10, I've added clarity and sharpness using the Adjustment Brush to the cracks in the rock. The version on the right with the additional clarity and sharpness emphasizes the cracks in the rock as compared to the original version on the left.

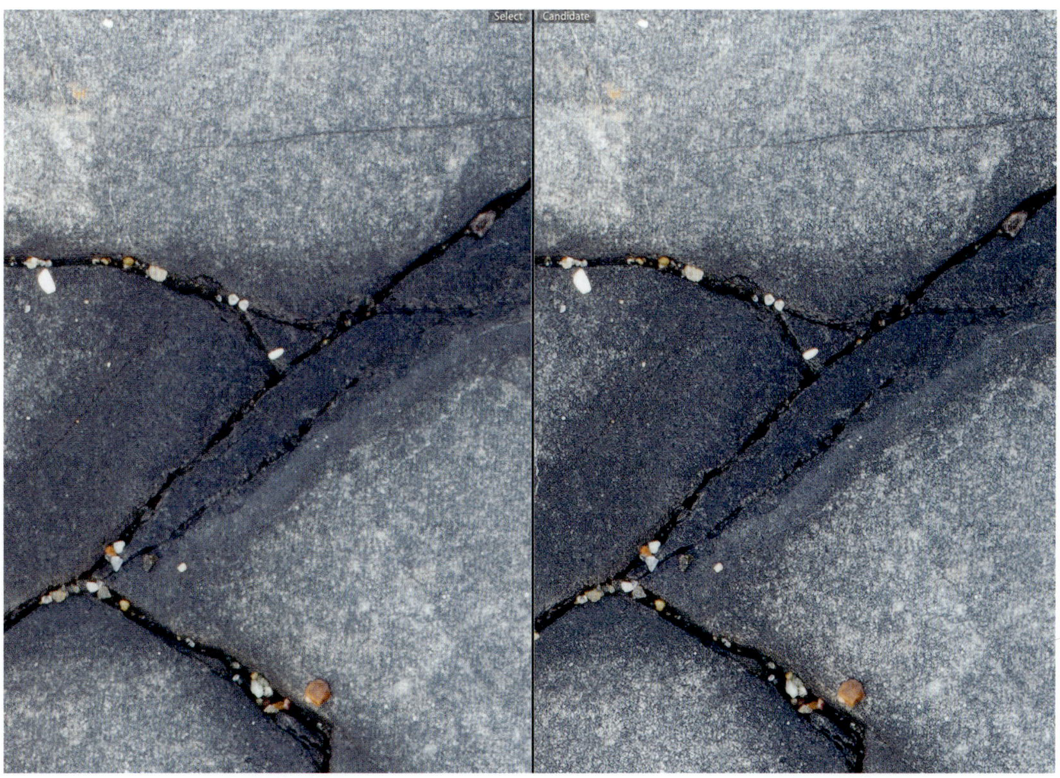

Figure 10-13: In this close-up of Figure 10-12, the increased sharpness and clarity can be seen in the new version on the right

summary of the types of things I consider in Print Interpretation to try to improve my prints:

- **Vignetting** – Add vignetting or gradients to help burn the edges to keep the viewer's eyes from drifting off the print
- **Brightness** – Adjust overall brightness to be consistent with artistic intent or print statement of portfolio
- **Compositional Changes** – Make changes to help direct the viewer's gaze either toward or away from objects
- **Tonal Relationships** – Change tonal relationships to emphasize or de-emphasize selected portions of the print, including removing overly bright tones that distract or adding brightness and contrast to areas that are more important
- **Color Emphasis** – Modify individual color channels to emphasize or deemphasize particular colors and change the color relationships in the print
- **Color Shift** – Adjust overall color (such as by modifying white balance) to change mood or feel or to change palette to be more consistent with artistic intent
- **Toning Black-and-White** – Adding a warm or cool tone to a black-and-white image for creative effect
- **Sharpness** – Modifying sharpness or clarity selectively to emphasize or deemphasize portions of the print
- **Cropping** – Crop to improve the visual flow of the print

These are just some of the many types of edits you can make as you interpret your own images for print.

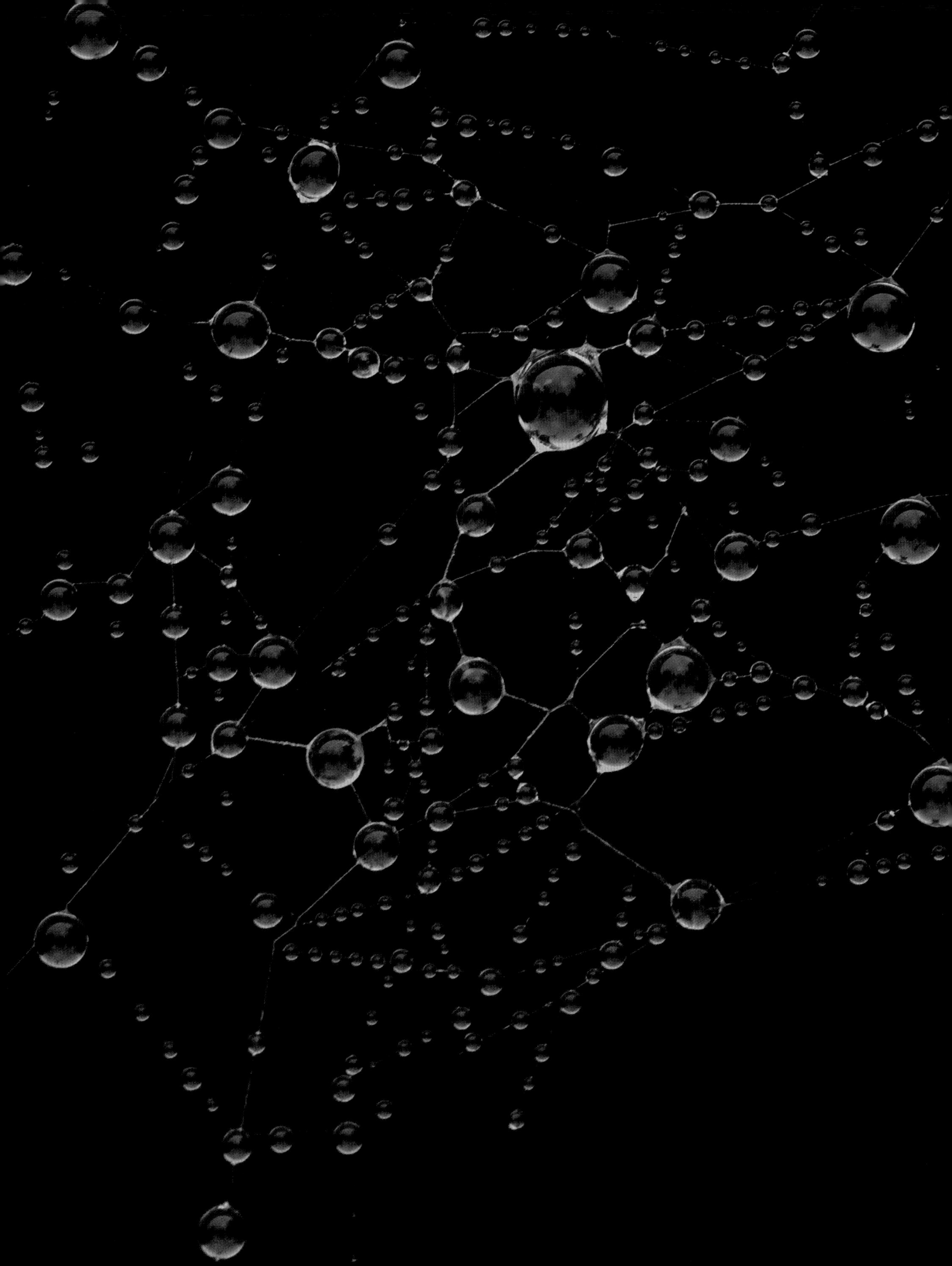

Printing Black-and-White Images

11

Photographers were quick to embrace color printing using digital technologies, largely because most photographers were not doing their own color processing and printing using traditional methods due to the hassle and complications involved. Black-and-white (monochrome) printing has been slower to gain acceptance for a variety of reasons, but in my opinion the technical limitations of digital black-and-white have disappeared and it is now considered to be an archival medium with a beauty all its own.

I don't think digital printing will ever completely replace traditional silver halide photography—nor should it—but it provides many photographers the opportunity to do high-quality, fine-art-quality black-and-white work without having to own or have access to a traditional darkroom.

> *Black and white are the colors of photography.*
> —Robert Frank

Challenges of Printing Black-and-White

Printing black-and-white images presents challenges different than those of color printing, and most of these issues stem from the fact that when we are making black-and-white prints using our normal inkjet printers we are using a combination of black and colored inks.

The use of color inks in black-and-white prints increases the possibility of metamerism, which results in black-and-white prints looking different in color under different lights (e.g., it appears neutral in one light, a little green in another light). The use of color inks also makes achieving a truly neutral print much more difficult, as even the slightest error in the printing path can result in a print that is visibly off. Looking under a microscope or strong loupe, you'd see little color dots mixed in with the more numerous black dots (**Figure 11-1**) to create the black-and-white image.

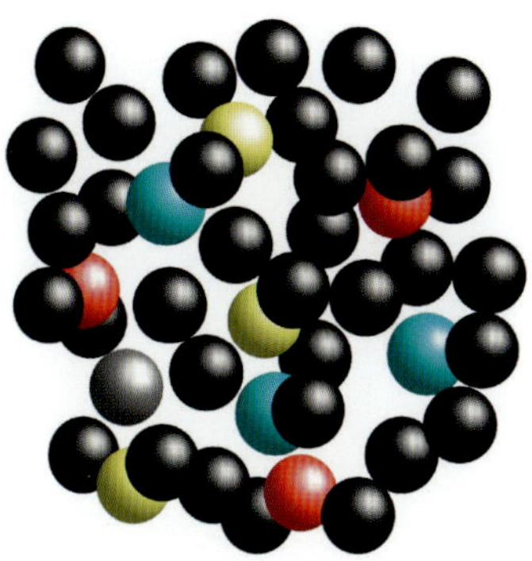

Figure 11-1: Highly stylized representation of dots of pigmented ink in an inkjet print made using a combination of color and black inks. The printer lays down mostly black dots but color is intermixed throughout. Color is necessary to offset the natural warmth of the black inks but can cause other issues.

Since most modern inkjet printers have three or four black inks, why can't we just use those inks and nothing else? There are two reasons for this. First, most software doesn't allow us to isolate the inks this way; second, these black inks are not actually neutral themselves, which means that some color ink is needed to neutralize them. Luckily, modern hardware and software have greatly improved this aspect of black-and-white printing.

Another issue with black-and-white printing is that the tone of the print is much more susceptible to the color of the paper than is a color print, particularly in lighter areas where there is less ink on the paper. An ink formula that is neutral on one paper won't be neutral on another paper that has a different color base. This effect can also be used to creative advantage—I often print a neutral image on a warm paper to get a subtly warm print that is a bit warmer in the highlights (where the paper shows through more).

Principles of Printing #15:
Paper Color Matters, Especially for Black-and-White Prints

Each type of paper has its own color, and even though we use printer-paper profiles and other techniques to minimize its impact, the paper color does affect the final print. This happens in two ways: first, the paper border is bare around the print, and warmer or cooler colors surrounding your print can impact the appearance of the image; and second, some of the paper's color shows through the ink, especially in highlight areas where there is less ink covering the paper.

The effect of paper color is even more pronounced with black-and-white prints as variations in color are more noticeable where there is less ink laid down in the image. I see this as a feature rather than a bug, though, and I use paper color for creative purposes.

The preceding discussion of issues is not meant to be discouraging—with modern printers we can make absolutely lovely black-and-white prints, and we can use a range of papers that would have been unthinkable in the traditional darkroom. Throughout this chapter we'll discuss ways of overcoming these challenges as you make your own black-and-white prints.

Black-and-White Printing Methods

Before you make a black-and-white print, you of course need a black-and-white image. There are hundreds of ways of making a black-and-white image from a color one and we won't address all of these choices here. As a custom printer, what I usually see are images that have either been converted in Lightroom or Photoshop to a neutral or toned black-and-white image, or those that have been converted using a plug-in such as Nik Silver Efex Pro.

What I would recommend is to use a method where you can exert some control over the conversion process—there are significant controls available to customize your black-and-white conversion that are not available if you just strip out the black-and-white information in Photoshop by simply making your image grayscale or pushing the B & W button in Lightroom

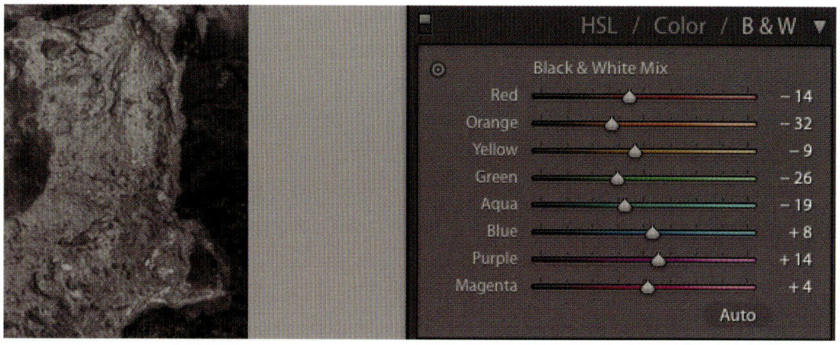

Figure 11-2: Lightroom's Black-and-White Mix (and Photoshop's similar adjustment layer) are surprisingly powerful in being able to precisely control the conversion to a black-and-white image from a color one

(**Figure 11-2**). You'll have more control if you take advantage of the Black & White Mix (in Lightroom) or converting via an adjustment layer in Photoshop.

Printing Using Color Profiles

Once you have a black-and-white image, there are four primary methods for making black-and-white inkjet prints, and I will describe them here roughly in the order of increasing complexity as well as increasing success. I've seen great prints made using each of these methods, and if you are serious about black-and-white printing I encourage you to experiment with some or all of them.

Toned Black-and-White

Many photographers producing black-and-white images utilize some sort of tone (rather than a pure neutral) for creative effect. Warm tones are very popular, as are cool tones and selenium tones (**Figure 11-3**). If you are producing black-and-white images using an app on an iPhone, or sending your DSLR photographs through a program such as Nik Silver Efex Pro, you might have a tone as well. Lightroom's split-toning functionality results in an image that has a color tone as well. In all of these cases, your resulting image is not a neutral, grayscale image but instead an RGB file with color information.

If your black-and-white image is a toned, non-neutral RGB file, then your best printing method is simple: print your toned black-and-white image **just as you would a color image** using your standard printer-paper profile and so on, and you can achieve a great print. Your image may

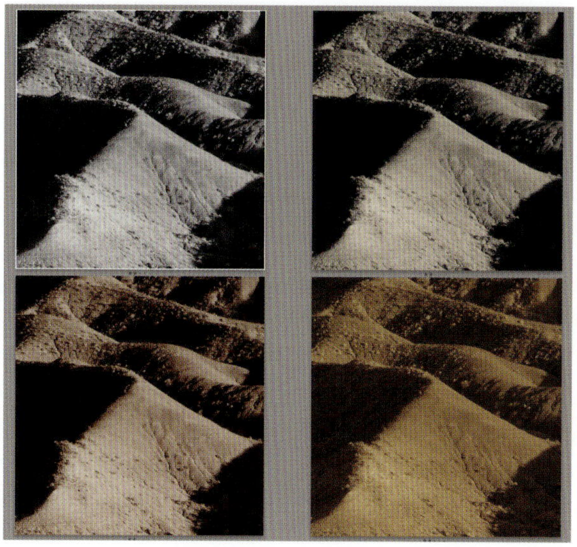

Figure 11-3: Photographers have embraced the creative possibilities of toning their black-and-white images, creating a wide range of possible tones and styles. I toned this photograph from Arizona's Petrified Forest National Park with (going clockwise) neutral tone, Creamtone, Sepia Tone, and Antique Light. These types of presets (and others in Silver Efex Pro, etc.) are great starting points to find a color tone for your black-and-white prints.

be a toned black-and-white one to your eye, but from the point of view of the printer it is a color image and should be treated accordingly.

Neutral Black-and-White

Just as with toned black-and-white images, you can also print neutral black-and-white images using your standard color profiles. Just a few years ago this was a pretty unsatisfactory solution, but printing technology has improved enough that you can now get decent results using this method. Any flaws in your printing path, such as a printer-paper profile that is not dead-on, will result in your print being off of neutral, and if it is off in a direction that results in the print being even slightly green or magenta, you'll likely be dissatisfied.

If you are seeking a truly neutral black-and-white print, I strongly recommend choosing any of the subsequent methods over your printer-paper profiles. Your prints using printer-paper color profiles might look neutral to you until you compare them with one using the later methods that is actually much closer to neutral.

Printing Using Epson Advanced Black-and-White Mode

Newer printers have more sophisticated software that essentially optimizes black-and-white printing by minimizing the use of colored inks. Epson's implementation of this in their print driver is called the **Advanced Black & White (ABW) mode**, and it does a better job of achieving a neutral print than does the color print driver. Canon's Monochrome Photo is similar in concept and execution.

Because printer driver methods such as ABW mode use less of the color inks, the resulting print should have better archival properties than one made using a traditional color profile (and independent testing has confirmed this) when using quality print media.

A disadvantage to using a print driver method such as ABW mode is that you are dependent on hardware to make additional prints—if you made small prints on your Epson printer using ABW mode and then want to make big prints of the same image on a friend's Canon printer, there might be differences between how the respective print drivers handled contrast, tone, or other factors, therefore a match would be more difficult to achieve. Moreover, if Epson changes how ABW works in their printer driver or if you move to a new Epson printer, there is a possibility that new prints might come out differently.

Printing using ABW mode does not use any type of printer-paper profile—the inks that are laid down are independent of, say, the color of the paper white. A neutral ABW print on warm paper will therefore be at least a little warm, as the print itself takes on color from the underlying paper, particularly in the highlight areas where there is less ink laid down. Eliminating the need for a printer-paper profile is a nice bonus when no such profile exists for a paper you'd like use for a print, such as a new paper or a paper without profiles for your printer.

To print using the ABW mode, you should have a neutral image as your starting point, whether it be a grayscale file or an RGB file (such as one that just came out of Silver Efex Pro). In ABW mode, if your image has any color information, that information will be stripped out and the image will be treated as a neutral image.

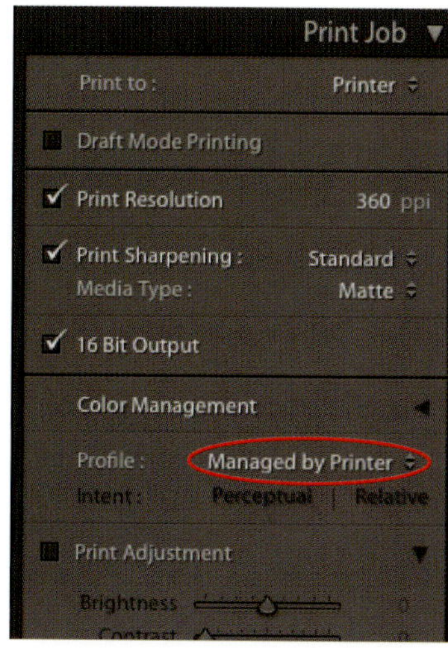

FIGURE 11-4: Lightroom's Print Job panel. Select Managed by Printer for Profile in Color Management to enable ABW mode.

Accessing ABW Mode

Accessing the ABW mode requires bypassing color management in Lightroom and Photoshop and instead relying on color management in the printer driver and printer. In Lightroom, when in the Print module, select Managed by Printer for your Profile in the Print Job panel (**Figure 11-4**). This will let the printer driver manage the printing, and you cannot use the ABW mode without making the choice here.

In Photoshop, when you call up the Print dialog, select Printer Manages Colors in the Color Handling selection of the Color Management box (**Figure 11-5**) and for your Rendering Intent choose Relative Colorimetric.

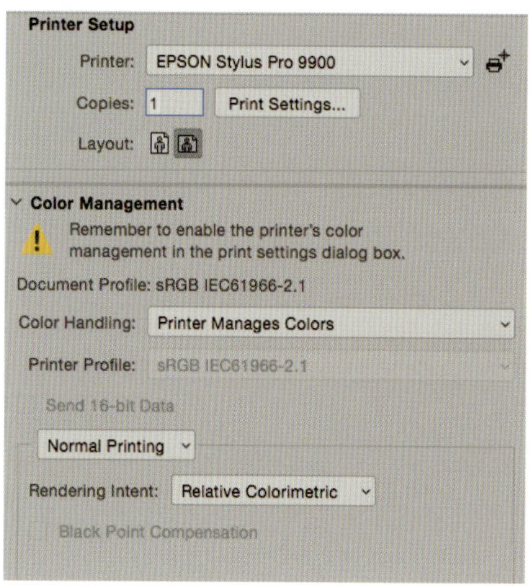

FIGURE 11-5: Photoshop's Print dialog, where you need to set Color Handling to Printer Manages Color to enable ABW mode

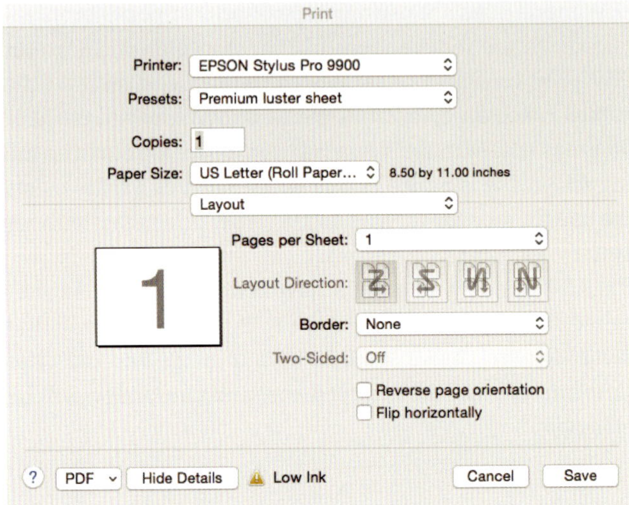

FIGURE 11-6: The main panel for Epson's print driver. Once here, you can confirm that you have the correct Printer selected, too.

After turning on printer color management in Lightroom or Photoshop, we need to enter the Epson printer driver (**Figure 11-6**). To do this in Lightroom, select the Print Settings button in the lower left and that will open up the Epson printer driver interface. Similarly, in Photoshop click the Print Settings button in the Printer Setup panel to enter the printer driver.

Once you are in the Epson print driver, the first step is to choose Color Matching in the pull-down menu near the center (that defaults to Layout). (If you don't see this choice, make sure you've selected to Show Details). While in Color Matching, click the radio button for EPSON Color Controls (**Figure 11-7**). If you can't make a change here, cancel out of this and go back to make sure that you have selected Printer Manages Colors/Managed by Printer. If

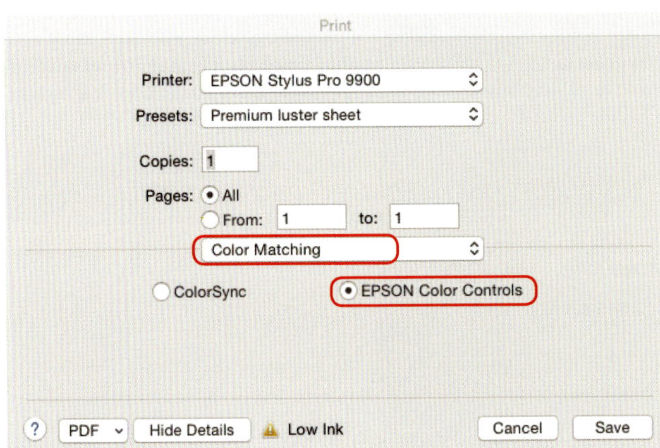

FIGURE 11-7: The Color Matching panel in Epson's print driver, where you ironically need to select EPSON Color Controls to enable black-and-white printing using the ABW mode

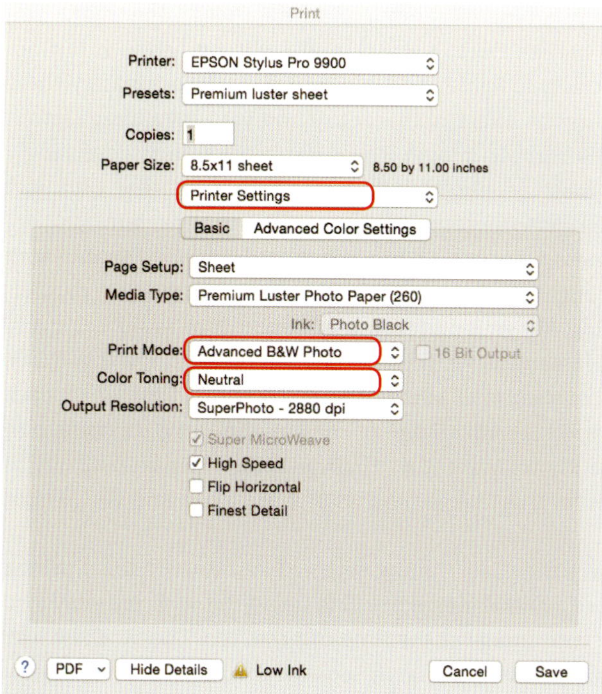

FIGURE 11-8: The Basic panel for Epson's ABW mode. You can choose from the preset tones here, including Neutral.

that choice is not made correctly, you won't be able to choose EPSON Color Controls here.

After selecting EPSON Color Controls, click the pull-down menu currently on Color Matching and choose Printer Settings instead. To enter ABW mode on the Printer Settings screen, change the Print Mode to Advanced B&W Photo (**Figure 11-8**). We've now entered the ABW mode.

Controlling ABW Mode

I like to handle the ABW from its more advanced screen, which you can get to by clicking the Advanced Color Settings button (**Figure 11-9**).

The Advanced Color Settings panel is where you can fully control the implementation of Epson's ABW mode, including tonality and color (though everything is somewhat confusingly named). The primary control for tonality is the Tone drop-down menu, which defaults to

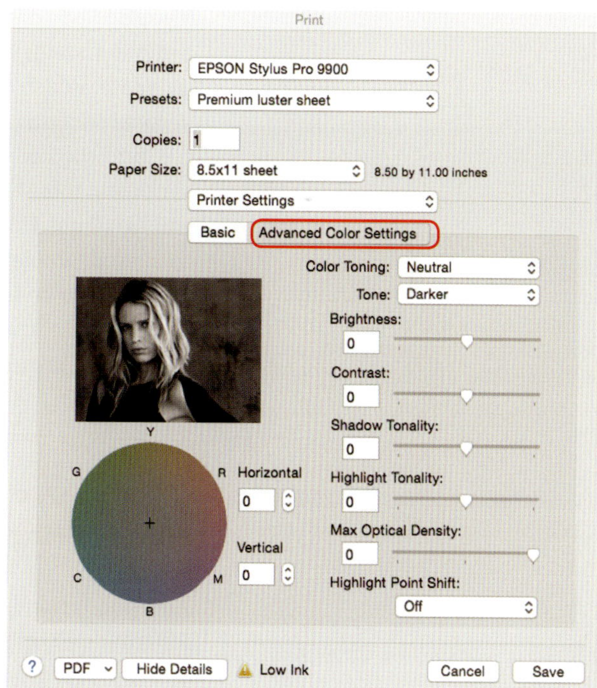

FIGURE 11-9: The Advanced Color Settings panel of the ABW mode gives you finer control over color tone and tonality

Darker. This is basically a type of gamma and brightness adjustment. You can choose Darkest, Darker, Dark, Normal, and Light, and they vary from darker and more contrasty to lighter and less contrasty. Unfortunately, there is no way of previewing the effect of this setting on your own image (but it does preview it on the sample image). The default position is confusingly Darker, not Normal; most people, including myself, believe that Dark is a setting more consistent with a properly calibrated printing system.

ABW offers Brightness, Contrast, Shadow Tonality, Highlight Tonality, Max Optical Density, and Highlight Point Shift tools to control tonality in addition to the Tone setting. My general recommendation is to avoid using any of these controls and instead leave them at their default settings. If you, say, feel you need more contrast after seeing the print, I would rather go back to your original file and take advantage of the superior tonality correction tools in Lightroom or Photoshop rather than utilizing their equivalents in the Epson print driver, as they are somewhat of a black box and you cannot preview their effects.

The default position the Color Toning setting in ABW is Neutral, which will print the closest to neutral image possible using the tool. You may also apply a color tone to your image at the time of print, too. The quickest way of doing this is changing Neutral to one of Sepia, Warm, or Cool. The preview on the left will show an approximation of the effect on the standard image. If you'd like to choose a different tone (and I do as I find the default ones very heavy-handed), you can click on the color wheel and move the + sign around to create a custom tone or manually input numbers in the Horizontal and Vertical sections.

I find the color toning to be a bit frustrating with ABW. It is a relatively simplistic tool that requires some trial and error, but once you find a setting you like (I use Horizontal 2, Vertical 10, for a more subtle warm tone), it is an easily repeatable setting.

Once you've finished with your settings, simply hit Save and move on to making your print. For neutral prints, I find ABW mode to be consistently superior to printing with printer-paper color profiles. If you can find a tone you like with the ABW mode, the tool works well and provides a high-quality print.

Printing Using RIPs

Another option is to use special software (called a raster image processor, or RIP) that will optimize the inks in your standard color ink set for black-and-white printing without using the printer driver. This is essentially the same principle as using Epson's ABW mode but instead bypasses the Epson print drivers themselves. Why do this? Because these specialized tools can do a better job of making black-and-white prints than can the manufacturer's tool.

My recommendation for an RIP for black-and-white printing is **QuadTone RIP (QTR)** by Roy Harrington (www.quadtonerip.com), which is available for both Mac and PC and is compatible with professional and prosumer Epson printers. As a reasonably priced $50 piece of shareware that offers a free trial, it is definitely worth investigating if you take black-and-white printing seriously and have an Epson printer.

ImagePrint RIP

ImagePrint by ColorByte Software is another RIP often used for making black-and-white prints. It is relatively expensive (you buy it separately for each printer, and the price depends on the size of the printer) and by all accounts it does a great job using its own profiles for black-and-white printing. Many swear by this software for both black-and-white and color printing and I encourage you to investigate it if you are comfortable with the pricing. As someone who regularly uses four printers in my studio, their pricing model is not a good fit for me so I've pursued other solutions.

What QTR does is act as a separate printer and print driver made specifically for black-and-white printing. On the Mac, it actually installs as a separate printer. On my system, I have my Epson 9900 and then another printer installed (which is the same physical printer) called Quad9900 (**Figure 11-10**). QTR uses the standard Epson inks and, to my eye, does a better job of managing them than does Epson's ABW mode in the print driver. The recommended

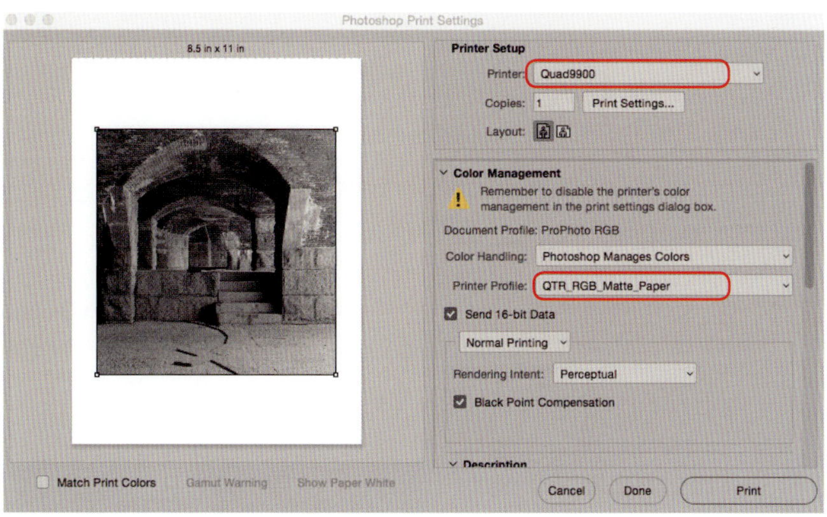

FIGURE 11-10: QTR acts as a separate printer on Apple computer, so you would select it just like any other printer in the Printer Setup menu of the print driver

settings for Color Management are Photoshop Manages Colors, the QTR printer profile for either photo or matte paper, Perceptual Rendering Intent, and Black Point Compensation turned on.

Once you've selected your QTR printer, when you click on Print Settings you'll see a modified version of the Epson print driver available. Change Layout to QuadToneRIP and you'll see the interface with QTR (**Figure 11-11**). QTR works by using one or more of three toning curves (specific to a type of paper) and applying them to your black-and-white image. You can use a warm, cool, or sepia curve; you can blend a warm and cool curve together with 50% of each for neutral; or you can do something more complex like split toning. There are many creative possibilities available with QTR and I've found that it produces fabulous results both for neutral prints and toned black-and-white prints, even when compared to Epson's ABW mode.

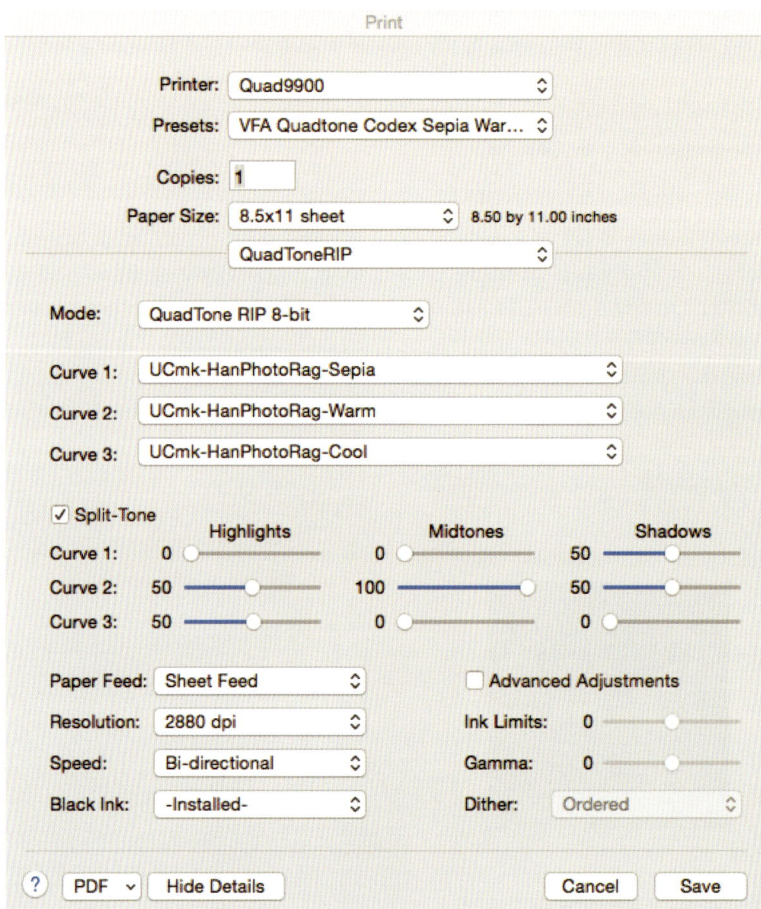

FIGURE 11-11: The QuadToneRIP panel gives you precise control over toning of your image at the time of print, including blending up to three tones into the highlights, midtones, and shadows

Dedicated Black-and-White Ink Sets

The final and most complicated option for black-and-white printing is to replace the color inks in your printer with a dedicated black-and-white ink set. The two most popular inks are Jon Cone's **Piezography** system (www.piezography.com) and the ink sets from **MIS** (www.inksupply.com). Both have their adherents, but I personally have used only the Piezography system, and it can produce absolutely stunning results. Both systems require you to replace the inks in your printer, making a dedicated printer necessary (and thus making these options best for those very serious about digital black-and-white). Dedicating an old printer to one of these inkjets is a popular option.

The Piezography system uses six or seven black inks rather than the three inks of the standard Epson printers, providing smoother tonalities and transitions and a very long tonal range. One downside of the Piezography printing system is that you are limited in terms of tones to whatever tones you can achieve from the particular inks you bought and your choice of papers. The lack of color inks in the system makes it less flexible, but it has the benefits of eliminating all of the issues inherent in printing black-and-white images with color inks.

Post-Printing

12

Once you've completed your fine art print, it's time to properly handle it. After spending so much time getting it perfect, you don't want to damage your print or treat it in a way that doesn't do it justice. In this chapter we'll explore how to finish your print and how to properly handle, store, and ship it.

> *Writing is a craft and, like all craft, proceeds by stages: conception, material selection, rough shaping, detailed shaping, sanding and finishing.*
> —Richard Rhodes

Handling the Print

Many perfectly fine completed prints have been damaged during handling by myself and others, so I'd like to share some of my hard-earned tips on handling your finished print.

Suggestions for Handling

Once your print is completed, you will need to move it to a place where it can safely dry and be evaluated. You can never have too many flat surfaces for this type of purpose in your print studio. The most difficult aspect, however, is actually moving the print from one place to another without damaging it.

One way of damaging your print is by touching its surface with your fingers. Inkjet prints are surprisingly delicate and susceptible to scuffs and scratching from your fingers, fingernails, or anything else. Additionally, oils on your fingers can be transferred to the print and cause immediate impact (visible fingerprints) and long-term impact (archival concerns from the oil). Wearing **gloves** will help prevent fingerprints and other damage from happening to your prints (**Figure 12-1**).

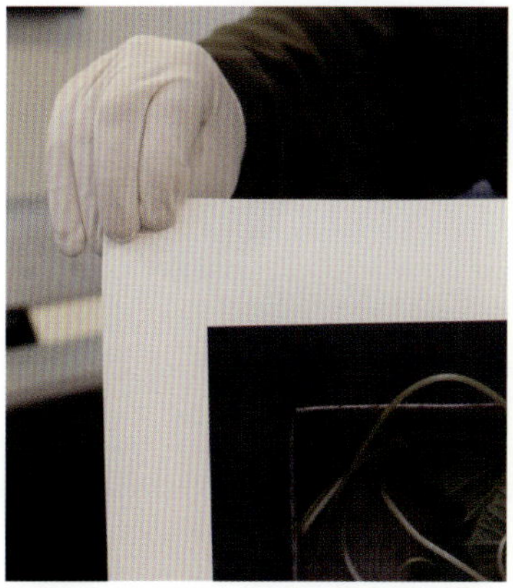

Figure 12-1: Handle prints with gloves to protect the print from oils from your skin

Even for smaller cut sheets, I usually will handle them just at the edges, with gloves on, to help prevent inadvertent damage. For larger prints that come off a roll, I handle them one of two ways. The first way is, when the

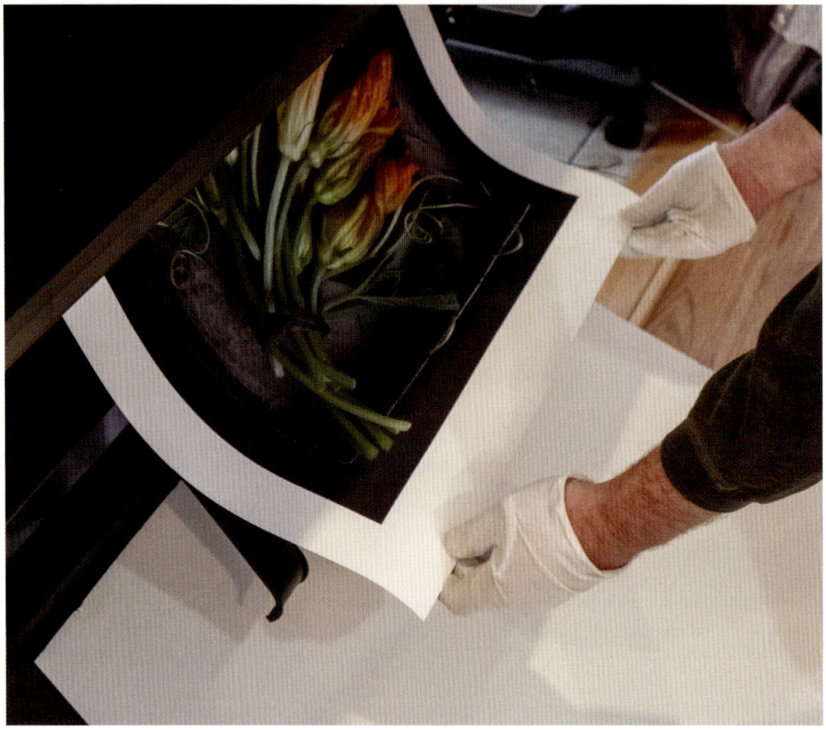

Figure 12-2: A demonstration of "catching" the print from roll paper as it is about to come off of the Epson 9900 printer. For thicker paper, I prefer to hold the paper by the leading edge corners for moving it from the printer to the cutting station. Photograph courtesy of Lynn Karlin.

print is coming off of the printer and about to be cut, I'll grab the leading edge's corners and catch the print as it comes off of the printer (**Figure 12-2**). At this point, I'll be standing and holding the print vertically by the upper corners. I'll then traverse my studio and gently place the print on a flat surface for further treatment.

I tend to use thick papers and this method works for me. For those using thinner paper that is more prone to getting dimples, consider trying to hold the print by opposite corners when moving it around.

For large prints, I like to use either a big piece of **foam core** or even thin **plywood** to catch the print coming off the printer and then to safely and easily move it around my studio (**Figure 12-3**). I have a few of these pieces in my studio so that I can have multiple prints drying and being handled at the same time. I lost many prints before finding this solution, and I highly recommend it for large prints.

Another way that using a catching surface can protect your print is in preventing the print from going into the printer's print catcher. My big 44" Epson is designed to drop the print face down into a basket of sorts, but I found that surface markings were inevitable from the straps when I used this catcher. Directing the print onto a piece of plywood keeps the print face up at all times and prevents damage in this fashion. It also facilitates moving the print once it is done.

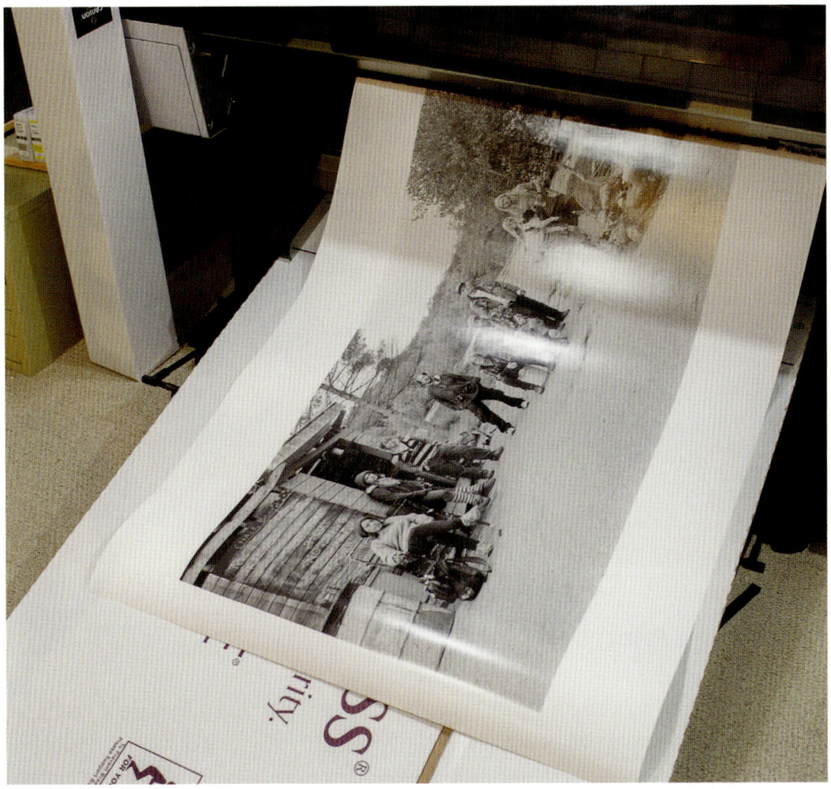

Figure 12-3: For this 9-foot-long panoramic print (photograph courtesy David Brooks Stess), I had to make an extra-long print catcher beyond my normal 4' x 4' plywood and 3' × 3' foam core. This box from my framer is not as stiff as I would have liked, but it did the job of holding the print and allowed me to avoid using the printer's print catcher.

Trimming

Very often you will need to trim a print with some sort of cutter to make the paper the right size. One common example is when you print on 17" × 22" paper but need to fit the prints into a 16" × 20" portfolio. Other common reasons for trimming paper are when you print multiple images on the same piece of paper and would like to separate them or when using roll paper and you need to trim off extra space.

A good cutter is worth its weight in gold, particularly if you are using roll paper that needs trimming. From personal experience, I can recommend Rotatrim rotary paper cutters, and Dahle rotary cutters also come highly recommended. Make sure you buy one larger than the carriage width of your printer (e.g., if you have a 44" printer, get the 54" cutter).

Low-quality cutters can be very frustrating so I recommend purchasing a nice one if at all possible. They do last a long time so it is a worthwhile investment—I've used my Rotatrim just about daily for eight years and have had no issues, and the self-sharpening original rotary blade still cuts as well as when it was new. You can also trim with an X-Acto knife, a good ruler, and a self-healing mat.

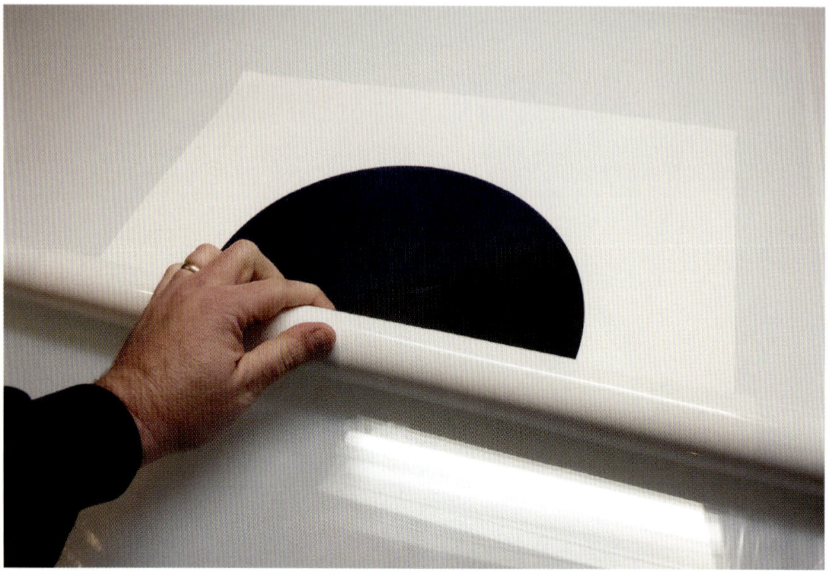

Figure 12-4: The De-Roller in action, imparting a reverse curl to the print. (I usually use two hands for this process but only used one here for visibility purposes.)

Flattening a Print

Often, you need to flatten a print that is curling from humidity, paper design, or from its time on a paper roll. This is usually an issue with roll paper rather than sheet paper, but I've definitely had instances where sheet paper had an undesirable curl at the corners that I wanted to flatten out. There are two basic options for flattening a print. The first option is to, after putting your print in a sleeve or otherwise protecting the surface, place weight on it and let time slowly flatten the print. I have found that for many papers even days of flattening with weights do not result in a truly flat print.

For these more stubborn curls, I recommend a device such as the Bienfang De-Roller. A D-Roller (or De-Roller) is a long metal rod with a plastic sheet wrapped around it many times (**Figure 12-4**). You roll out the plastic sheet, and with the curl facing down (usually this would be with the image facing up), place the print within the plastic sheet, roll the entire assembly up tightly, and then unroll it. Your paper, given enough time (usually 10 seconds or so), will have the curl permanently removed. The De-Roller imparts a reverse curl to counteract the original curl, resulting in a flat print.

As with anything touching the surface of a print, you need to be careful while reversing the curl so that you do not damage the print. Check the surface of the De-Roller for any objects on it (in my studio, dog hair and dust) before subjecting the surface of your print to being pressed up against it. I also recommend letting your prints dry as much as you are able before using this device so that the surface is as strong as possible.

Signing the Print

For many artists, signing their print is an essential step in the artistic process, marking approval of the print as a completed work of art. Typically in the fine art world, the artist signs the print outside the image area on either the front or back of the print rather than on the image itself.

The classic method of signing any kind of print is with a pencil, and that is the choice I make when I am able to do so. It is worth going to an art supply store to try different kinds of pencils as you'll find that coated inkjet paper varies dramatically in how it receives pencil.

For glossy and lustre prints, pencil doesn't really work on the front, as the surface coating rejects every pencil I've tried. Most pens do work but, unfortunately, most (including Sharpies) are not very archival and you don't want to bring questionable elements into an archival fine art print. The solution? Archival pens.

My favorite choice among archival pens are the Sakura Pigma Micron pens (**Figure 12-5**). These pens use pigments inks similar to the inks used in the Epson, Canon, and HP high-end printers. I use the black inks and the 02 thickness—much smaller of a point and I find that it doesn't write smoothly, and much larger of a point I find to be distractingly visible. Try some out yourself and see which one works best for you. I wish we could just use pencil with these lovely new lustre and glossy papers, but the Sakura pens provide a great archival alternative.

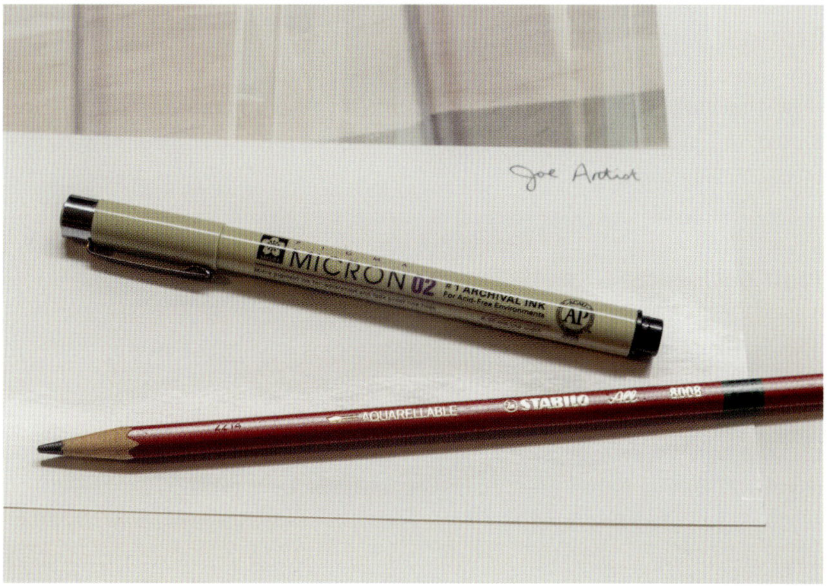

FIGURE 12-5: A signature on the lower-right corner of a print using one of the Sakura Pigma Micron pens as well as an excellent Stabilo pencil for signing matte papers

Protective Sprays

Many fine art printers apply a coating to their prints after they are completed. These coatings are usually applied via a spray can (Hahnemühle, PremierArt, and Moab, among others, make the coatings). In theory, applying a coating to a finished print can help provide protection from pollutants (and thus improve longevity) and also offers at least some protection from abrasion. The coating can potentially help reduce gloss differential and bronzing as well as improve the deepness of the blacks and colors on the image.

So why not do this for every final print? For me I do have a little fear—fear of adding an unknown substance to my prints, and fear of an uneven application ruining the print (especially for large prints). I don't apply the spray on every print but tend to limit my application to prints that I know are going to be handled frequently, such as portfolio prints.

I haven't yet been convinced that the benefits are worth the risks. Many fine art printers disagree, though, and they swear by these sprays, so you should certainly consider experimenting on your own. The recent archival testing results I've seen are pretty positive, so I'll probably start experimenting more with these protective sprays myself.

On lustre papers and matte papers, the application of the coating is pretty much invisible (not so for glossy or metallic papers). With all types of coatings, I recommend multiple passes of a light coat. I've had the best results with three coats or so of the spray, about five minutes apart.

Storage

Now that you have a beautiful, final print, you want to store it in a protected and proper manner, so I will offer some things to consider and some recommendations.

Print Enclosures

The first step in protecting your fine art prints is having something that will protect the relatively delicate surface of the print. What I typically use for finished prints are the clear plastic (and archival) Crystal Clear bags from ClearBags (www.clearbags.com), which are available in a wide range of sizes (**Figure 12-6**). I've found them to be very successful in protecting the surface

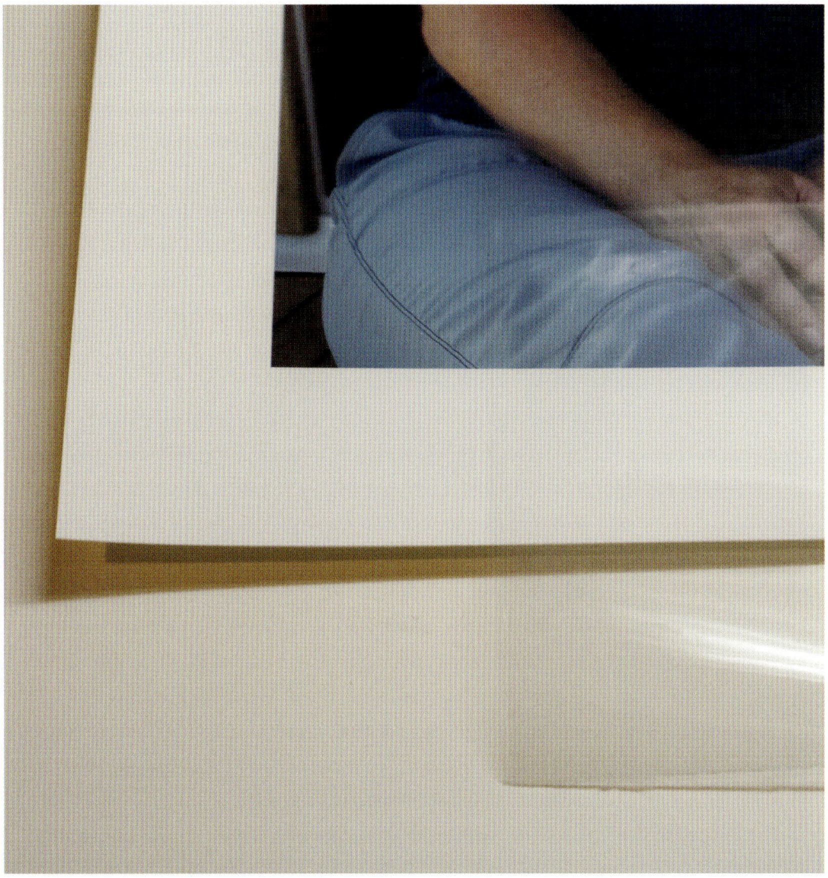

Figure 12-6: A print partially enclosed in a plastic sleeve from ClearBags.com

of the print during storage, handling, and shipping, though of course they won't prevent all types of damage.

I like to wait for a few hours, if possible, to make sure everything is absolutely dry before putting prints in sleeves, but I have never seen a problem in cases where I did not do that.

Many also use interleaving sheets or tissue over the surface of the print in addition to or instead of plastic bags. I recommend acid-free, buffered (see the following sidebar) interleaving material, but it is more important to use high-quality materials that are acid-free from a reputable manufacturer. The tissue is somewhat translucent so you can partially see your image through them, and both tissues and sheets again provide some protection for the surface of the print when the print is not being viewed.

Print Mastery: Buffered vs. Non-Buffered Materials

Should you use buffered or non-buffered (unbuffered) materials (matboard, interleaving sheets, etc.) for your digital pigment prints? The answer to this question is not absolutely clear cut, but I recommend **buffered** materials for use with digital prints.

Buffered materials are materials in which calcium carbonate (a chalk) or a similar material has been added to paper pulp during the paper-making process to act as a buffering agent. The calcium carbonate raises the pH level of the resulting material to the alkaline side of things, making it non-acidic, and acts to counter acidic substances or pollution in the environment (such as smog) from impacting the buffered material. Many inkjet papers themselves are buffered for this reason.

Historically, conservators preferred buffered materials for conservation purposes to help combat acids coming from materials in the environment, unless a particular material required non-buffered materials around it. The most common exclusion from being used with buffered materials is any item with components made from animals (i.e., protein-based materials), such as silk or leather. Photographic prints in this category include albumen prints, cyanotypes, and dye transfer prints because of their component materials.

In the 1980s, many conservators started recommending non-buffered materials for use with albumen, cyanotype, dye transfer, and chromogenic (color) prints by extrapolating from damage done to various albumen prints in storage. Additional research in the 1990s by the Image Permanence Institute (IPI) (www.imagepermanenceinstitute.org)—the same researchers who made the initial determination that buffered materials were the culprit—led to the IPI to withdraw their recommendation to use unbuffered materials.

The IPI now contends that either buffered or non-buffered materials are acceptable for all photographic prints except for dye transfer and cyanotypes. They now instead recommend the use of high-quality materials—museum quality board, acid- and lignin-free, and ability to pass their Photographic Activity Test. They also recommend buffered materials for photographic enclosures (which would include matboards and interleaving paper) as a means to help prevent acid from within an enclosure from damaging a print and possibly to help absorb environmental acids.

A consensus also seems to have formed around the fact that the buffering issue is actually not that important for digital prints—many other factors are much more important in determining print longevity, including exposure to light or sunlight, humidity, temperature, the particular paper and ink combination, and the like.

My recommendation is to use buffered materials with your pigment-based digital prints, though non-buffered materials should also be fine if you'd rather use those.

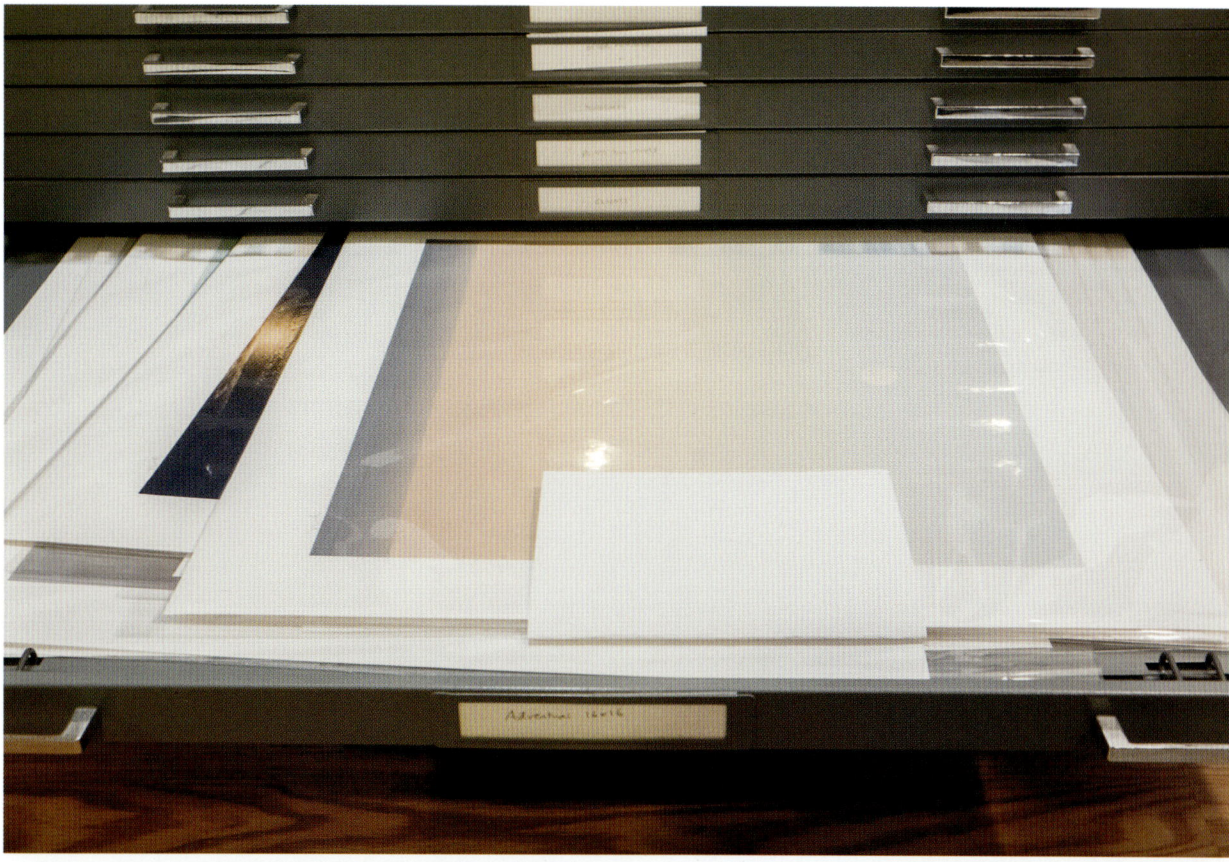

FIGURE 12-7: Completed prints stored in a flat file

Long-Term Storage

I recommend storing your prints **flat** rather than rolled if at all possible (which admittedly becomes difficult for very large prints). I prefer storing my prints either in flat file drawers or in archival storage boxes (**Figure 12-7**), both of which allow for flat storage and provide significant protection for the prints within. I keep the prints in their plastic sleeves during this storage as well. Long-term storage in a roll applies some stress and fatigue to the print and will over time make it more difficult to remove the curl from the print.

Very large prints of course take up more space and you may not have enough space in your studio to store them flat—in that case, I would accept the risks and store them rolled. Rolling in a strong tube does provide significant protection for a print, as large flat prints are more susceptible to being kinked or otherwise damaged.

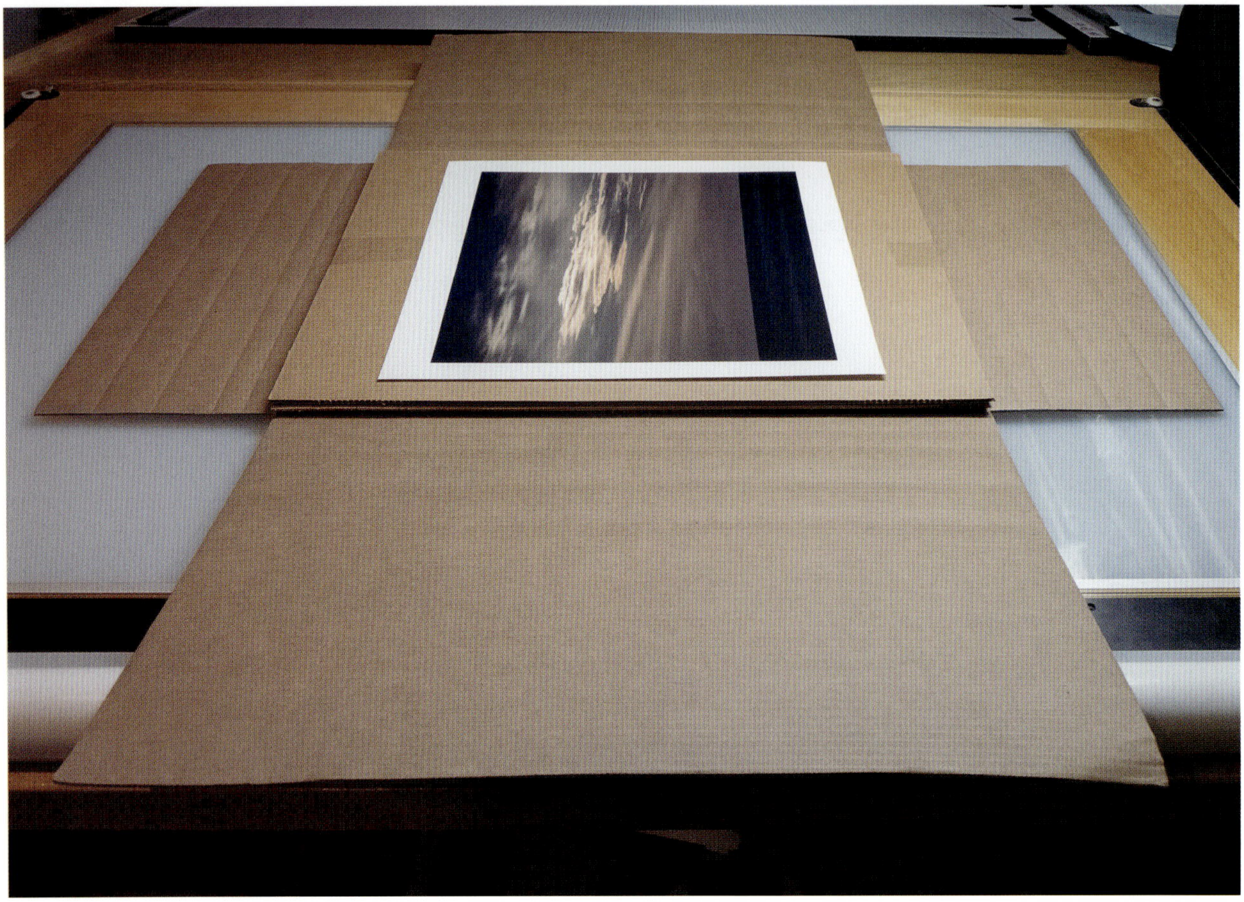

FIGURE 12-8: For flat shipping of prints, I love using Uline's Jumbo Easy Fold Mailers, along with pieces of cardboard within for stiffening. You secure the print in a plastic sleeve in the middle of a sandwich of four or more pieces of cardboard, and then wrap the mailer around the sandwiched cardboard and secure. I prefer to have at least a 1-inch border of cardboard around the print as a buffer if at all possible in case of bumps and dings.

Shipping

I ship my prints either rolled or flat, depending on size and cost limitations, and within their plastic sleeves (**Figure 12-8**). As prints become larger, the price to ship flat becomes much higher than shipping rolled. Shipping a print rolled in a strong tube is also less likely to be damaged in shipment than a flat print. So, even though I prefer to keep the print flat as much as possible, I'll usually switch to a tube once I reach more than 20" × 30" or so in size.

Whichever shipping method you use, you should use materials than can withstand shipping. I use the very strong shipping tubes from Yazoo Mills (www.yazoomills.com) in addition to the flat shipping boxes from Uline (www.uline.com).

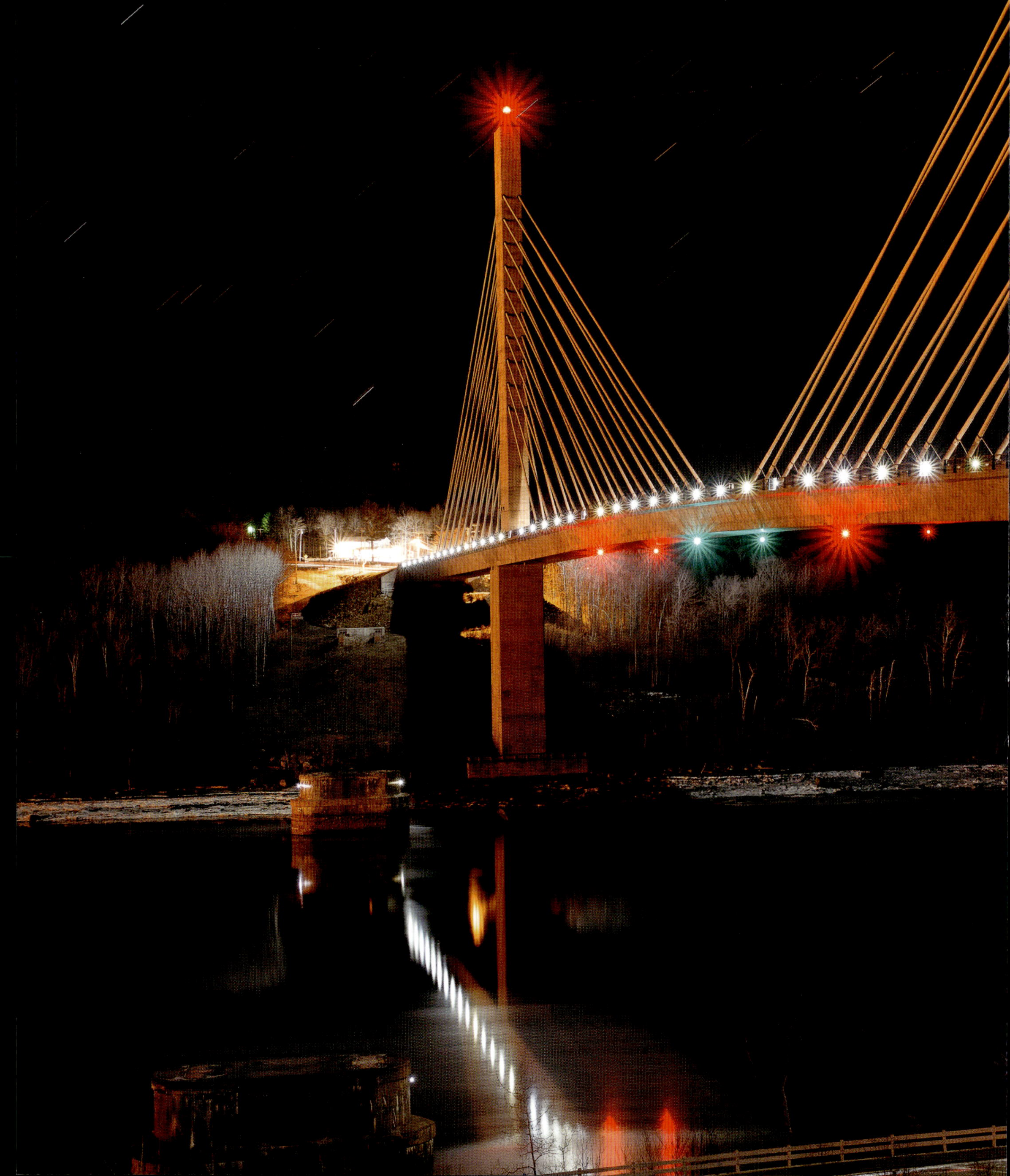

13 The Next Level

One of my favorite aspects of printing is the ability to create beautiful and meaningful objects that rise above the constant stream of imagery that we all experience daily in the modern world. In this chapter we'll discuss methods to help accomplish this task and help take your printing to the next level, whether it be by improving your technique and judgment, printing large, emphasizing the physical aspects of the print, or integrating your print into a larger body of work that raises the level of everything within.

> *What I think is so extraordinary about the photograph is that we have a piece of paper with this image adhered to it, etched on it, which interposes itself into the plane of time that we are actually in at that moment. Even if it comes from as far back as 150 years ago, or as recently as yesterday, or a minute before as a Polaroid color photograph, suddenly you bring it into your experience. You look at it, and all around the real world is humming, buzzing and moving, and yet in this little frame there is stillness that looks like the world. That connection, that collision, that interfacing, is one of the most astonishing things we can experience.*
>
> —Joel Meyerowitz

Getting Better at Printing

> *The function of the overwhelming majority of your artwork is simply to teach you how to make the small fraction of your artwork that soars.*
>
> —David Bayles and Ted Orland, *Art & Fear*

The best way I know to get better at printing is to make a lot of prints. Whenever you prepare an image for print and actually make the print, you learn more about how to edit an image and how those edits will manifest themselves on paper. You'll learn a little bit more about what works and what doesn't work, about how ink lays on paper and how the paper reacts to ink, how shadows and highlights translate from the backlit screen to paper and ink, and how changes in color or saturation on the screen cause changes in the print itself.

Principles of Printing #16: Keep On Printing

Putting in the hours, running through the paper or ink...however you want to phrase it, the best way to become a good printer is to keep on printing. The more you print, the more you'll learn what works and doesn't work, and the more you'll face challenges that require you to learn a new skill or technique.

Malcolm Gladwell posited in his book *Outliers* that, generally speaking, people needed 10,000 hours of doing anything before becoming great at it. While that theory is somewhat controversial and is not exactly an ironclad rule, its general application to printing—that most people have to make a lot of prints in order to become great—is a principle with which I completely agree.

To make great prints, it helps to know what great prints look like, too. I strongly encourage you to seek out great prints at museum exhibitions, from your peers, or anywhere you can find them. And I don't mean just inkjet prints—I've found inspiration in other types of photographic prints like platinum prints or cyanotypes, as well as other art forms such as charcoal, oil paintings, woodblock prints, and many other genres.

When you look at a great print, try to determine what makes it great. Would any of those aspects be applicable to your prints? When you look at a print that is less than great, try to determine what makes it fail. Do any of your prints suffer from the same flaws?

Principles of Printing #17: Look at Great Prints

Looking at prints as much as possible is a valuable exercise. There are many places to see great prints, such as galleries, museums, or in the studios of your photographic friends. You will also see many not-so-great prints, which is a useful exercise in itself. The more you look at prints, the more you'll be able to tell the difference between a great print and a not-so-great print.

Printing Large

The visual impact of a large print can be immense. A large graphic image can be very striking when viewed from a distance and the large size allows it to be seen and appreciated from a distance. When viewed more closely, a large print can be an immersive experience for viewers as it can encompass their field of view, and the increase in size also allows for smaller details of the image be better seen and appreciated.

We've previously discussed many of the technical challenges in enlarging an image for print, as any flaws in your image will become more evident

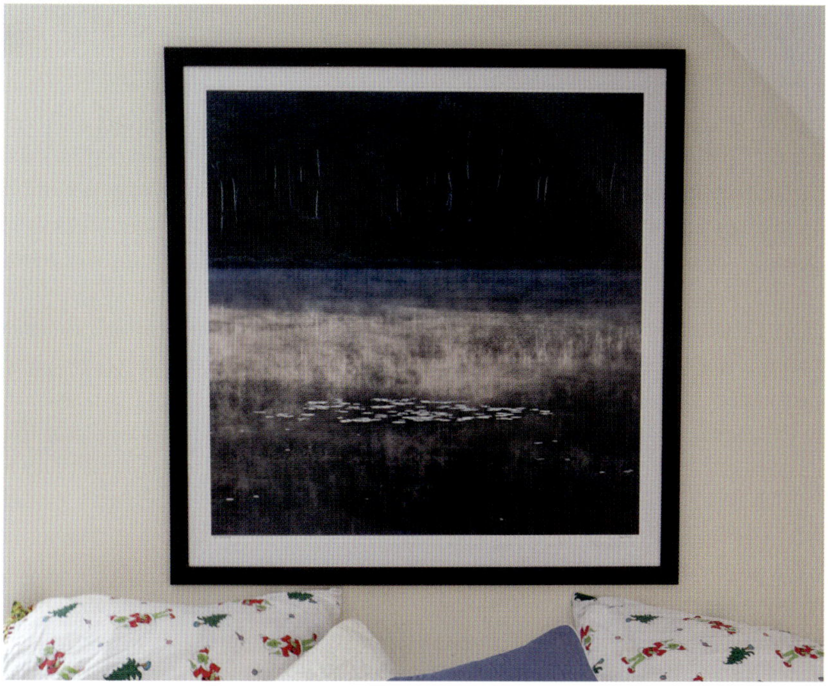

FIGURE 13-1: Large framed 36" × 36" photograph by the author hanging on a wall

the larger you go. Moreover, difficulties in handling the print and expense in shipping and framing also go up with size and can be quite daunting at very large scale. Once these challenges have been overcome, printing and presenting your prints at a large scale is one of the most powerful presentation methods.

Emphasizing the Print as a Physical Object

Making a print in a world where the vast majority of images are shared electronically is a statement that the *physical print matters*. Any things we can do to help emphasize the physical nature of the print will help viewers better appreciate the difference between viewing an electronic image and a beautifully made fine art print. In this section we'll discuss a variety of ways of accomplishing this emphasis.

Principles of Printing #18: Embrace the Physicalness of the Print

In this increasingly digital world, emphasizing the physical aspect of your print can heighten its impact to viewers. Reminding the viewer that prints are tangible and precious objects helps combat the ephemeral nature of most imagery.

Borders

I strongly recommend leaving a border (i.e., paper around the edge that has no ink on it) around your image for a variety of reasons. First, I think a border looks good aesthetically and helps to set off the print from its surroundings. This can *emphasize the physicalness* of the print, as prints online are not often viewed in this way, and even if they are presented with white borders, it is usually an extremely bright, featureless pure white rather than the more natural white of the paper.

A generous border also helps with handling of the print and makes it far less likely for someone to touch the image area of your print, providing protection for your print. A touch by a human hand to the print area can leave damaging oils and even a gloved hand can scuff or otherwise mar the surface.

Borders can make your print more archival as well. Conservators prefer a border around the image to keep any sort of contaminants that attack the edge of the paper as far from the image as possible.

Another advantage of borders arises if you are framing your print with an overmat, as a border area gives a larger surface upon which the mat can press down on the print, helping to prevent curling or rippling in cases where you are not dry-mounting.

I recommend a 1" border around the entire image as a minimum, with 2" preferred if possible, particularly for large prints (**Figure 13-2**). To make a basic border in Lightroom or Photoshop, you can simply print an image centered on the page where the paper size is larger than your print size. You may also bottom-weight the border for a more pleasing unframed appearance. If you are printing multiple images at once in Photoshop or want to more carefully control your border, I add white canvas for the border area and then a thin, 2-pixel black canvas so I know where to trim after printing (**Figure 13-3**).

FIGURE 13-2: Portfolio prints of the author presented at 12" across on 17" × 22" paper, giving a generous minimum 2½" border

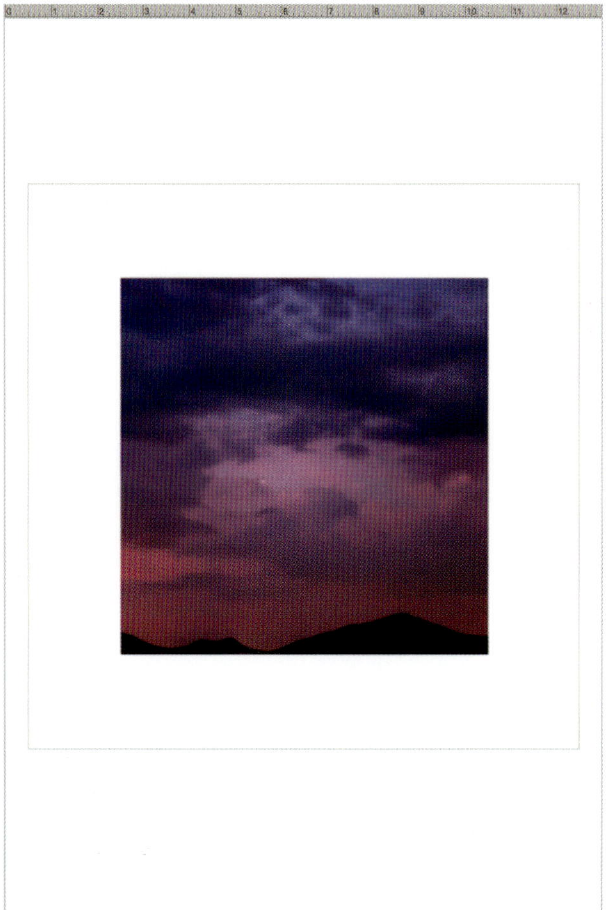

Figure 13-3: A photograph prepped with trim lines in Photoshop to provide exact directions for trimming. I use the Add Canvas, White to create the border, and then add a Canvas extension in black of just 2 pixels to create the trim line. For this print, I've set it up as an 8" × 8" image area with a 2" border all around and printed on a 13" × 19" piece of paper.

Using Unique Inkjet Papers

Taking advantage of the many unique and lovely inkjet papers available now is an excellent way of emphasizing the physicalness of your print. LCD screens are so perfectly smooth that any character of your papers will become evident, even if only subconsciously. This character is evident in the image area itself with how the paper receives inks and will usually be even more so in border areas where the paper is the only thing visible.

There is no one way for a paper to exert its character, with styles ranging from delicate watercolor textures to the sparkle of many luster papers. I love experimenting with other more exotic choices like metallic papers and (even better) delicate and semitranslucent rice papers (**Figure 13-4**). Careful choice of paper can help you achieve your artistic intent with your print and also help viewers better appreciate that your print is a physical object worthy of respect.

Figure 13-4: A close-up of a print on Epson Japanese Kozo paper, backlit on a transparency table. Because rice papers such as this are semitranslucent, the backlighting reveals the many fibers of the paper. A normal presentation of a print on this paper hides some (but not all) of its differences with more traditional paper, so seeking more unusual framing methods that reveal the character of the paper is worth trying. I've seen this type of paper hung like a scroll, backlit on a light box, and wrapped over a wooden frame.

Using Uncoated Art Papers

Many printing books and resources (including this one) advise against using papers that are not coated to receive inks as the inks may bleed a bit, reducing sharpness, and inks on uncoated papers may not produce as intense and saturated a mix of colors, nor as deep of blacks, as would coated papers. They are right about these downsides, but I think that the upsides of using these types of papers can often overcome these downsides.

For printing on an uncoated paper, I recommend going to an art supply stores and seeing what papers they have available to get a feel for the choices. There are so many choices available in terms of size, texture, weight, and feel that it is tough to know where to start. What I did was simple—I tried a smooth paper and a watercolor textured paper that felt good in the hand, printed a variety of images on both, and then evaluated them to decide which pieces of my work were best on the different types of paper.

To me, the biggest advantages of using uncoated art papers is that they can have amazing character and can add a feeling of uniqueness when compared to coated papers. These papers can have a presence and weight to them, and the textures of the papers can be absolutely beautiful. Many come with one or more natural deckled edges as well.

These uncoated papers are also likely to be very archival—some recipes have been around for centuries so there is lots of real-world data—but few have been tested with modern inks. Many of these papers are very substantial and much thicker than inkjet papers, which can be powerful in a final print.

Besides the possibility of loss of color saturation and sharpness, the other downside to uncoated papers is the necessity for more trial and error in settings and in color management, as the manufacturers do not provide information for inkjet printing, as that is not their intended purpose for these papers.

What I recommend is to just pick an inkjet paper that is roughly similar in color, weight, and surface, and use the profiles and settings for that paper as a starting point and then refine the settings as necessary. The types of settings you should consider adjusting are ink loading (trying to balance out dot gain—how much the ink spreads—and the maximum density of colors and blacks achieved) and of course paper thickness and/or platen gap, if you are using a thick paper.

I've used Moulin du Roy and Arches uncoated papers successfully (**Figure 13-5**), and I've seen recommendations to try Arches Watercolor Hot Press, Arches Cold Press Somerset Velvet, Arches Aquarelle, Lanaquarelle papers, and Japanese Washi papers. You are likely to get the best results from papers that are sized, preferably with both surface sizing and internal sizing.

I think it is important to add that the purported disadvantages of uncoated papers can actually be advantages for certain types of prints and images. Let's say the images you wanted to print were soft and dreamy in nature—a print method that softened the image in color and sharpness might actually be closer to your artistic intent than, say, an inkjet paper that was more perfect.

Like so many things in printing, you'll have to experiment to see if you like the sort of effect achievable with uncoated papers with your own images.

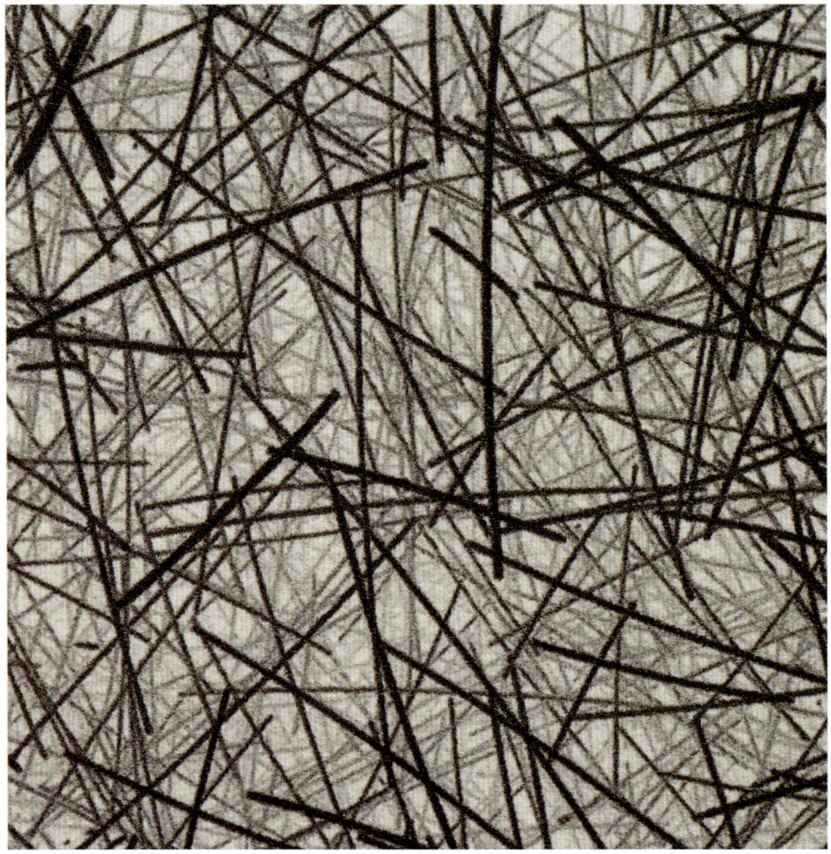

FIGURE 13-5: A close-up of a print on the Arches Watercolor paper. From this close you can see the softness of the lines that should be distinct, yet from a normal viewing distance the print appears sharp.

Print Mastery: Sized Papers

Art papers are often described as "sized," which means they have been specially treated with (typically) a starch or gelatin to help reduce the spread of inks of whatever sort that are applied to the paper. Sized papers are better able to resist the spread of inks—not as much as a coated paper would, but they can significantly reduce the gap. The added sizing material changes the absorption characteristics of the paper to help prevent absorption of the inks so that the inks dry on the surface rather than sinking into the paper to dry.

Using Alternative Substrates

One area where many artists are experimenting now is using alternative substrates rather than paper for making their fine art prints. The way this works is that you take some sort of flat material (that you feed through your printer—a straight feed path helps!), apply your own coating, and then print. I haven't done this myself, but there is a small and thriving community of people pushing into this new area.

The types of materials that are being used are fascinating, ranging from metal sheets to birch bark to stone to acrylic sheets. You would usually apply the coating with a brush (one popular coating is from a company called InkAid) and let the coating dry before printing.

Many people also use this technique on uncoated papers, too. For me, when I'm using uncoated papers, I'm trying to take advantage of their qualities and how they handle ink in their uncoated state, so this path has not been of interest to me.

While I haven't attempted this method of applying coatings myself, I've seen beautiful results from others. One reference on this process is titled *Digital Art Studio: Techniques for Combining Inkjet Printing With Traditional Art Materials* by Lhotka, Schminke, and Krause, published by Watson-Guptill, 2004.

Deckled Edges

Deckled edges are irregular edges of papers that are usually formed by tearing and are homages to classic papermaking methods. A deckled print is a print that has one or more edges that are torn instead of being a straight edge. Traditional mould-made papers often had a soft, feathered edge where the deckle (or belt) was used along with a mold to gather up wood pulp from a vat for pressing and drying into sheets. When the paper was torn into separate pieces, a tear deckle was created in addition to the natural deckle formed during manufacture of the paper.

When compared to the straight and perfect edges of a normal paper, deckled edges provide a uniqueness to the paper (as each tear is different) and also provide a strong emphasis on the *physicalness* of the print. Because of its historical origins, deckling is often associated with fine art papers, and deckling of paper edges can add an organic feel to a digital print.

Deckled edges can either be offset from the image itself (i.e., separated by a border) or can even be torn into the image area itself (**Figure 13-6**). The choice is purely an artistic one.

Any paper can be deckled using a deckling device to assist or a metal ruler (perhaps facilitated by wetting the crease or pre-scoring where you will tear) (**Figure 13-7**). Another method is to use a straight edge to guide an X-Acto knife to partially break through the paper so as to weaken it for tearing purposes.

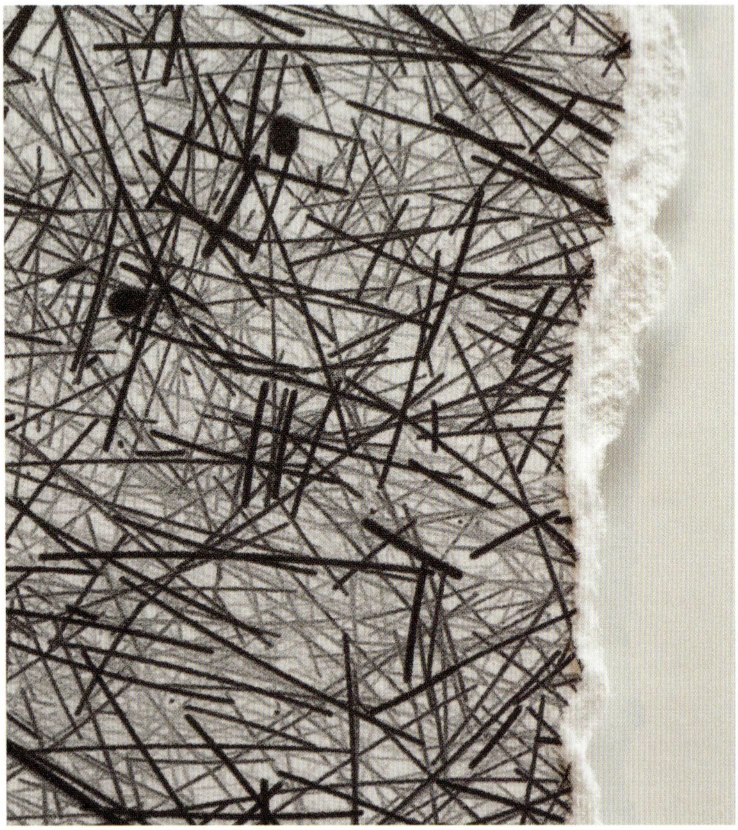

Figure 13-6: A deckled print on Arches Watercolor paper, with deckling torn into the image area using the deckler from DualEdgeRipper.com

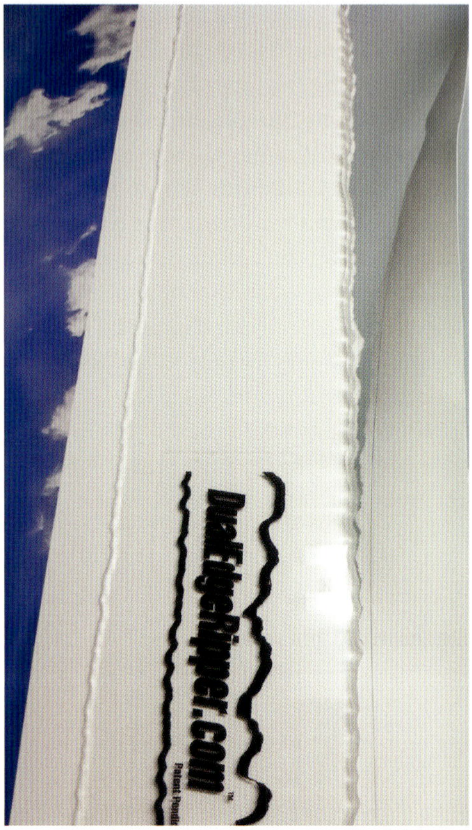

Figure 13-7: Deckling a print on Canson Print Making Rag (f/k/a BFK Rives) using the deckler from DualEdgeRipper.com. The printed trim line is visible to the right of the deckler.

I personally find deckling to be much more aesthetically pleasing with a heavyweight matte paper, particularly one with at least some texture, but there is no one right choice. Hahnemühle also has a pre-deckled selection of papers, so if they have a size and paper that you like, it is a very good, albeit expensive, option.

I usually need to make a deckled edge of a custom-sized paper. What I've found to be the best method for doing this is to create a thin black line on my print roughly where I would like the tear to be located. So, if I wanted two inches of space around the image, I'd make a black line about 2 1/4" from the edge of the paper when I printed, and then use that black line as a guide in tearing, as shown in **Figure 13-7**. The black line is the same line that I make for marking a trimming border as described earlier in this chapter.

This technique works if you are deckling the paper by tearing toward the front of the paper, a method that is easier to do and results in a more visible deckled edge that shows more of the inside of the paper. For a different look, deckle from the back of the print by laying the print face down and tearing toward yourself and away from the printed side.

Practice in deckling will help quite a bit in being successful in deckling your paper without damaging your print. For framing, consider a float mount that allows the edge of the paper to be seen—a traditional frame with an overmat hides the deckled edge.

Going Small

Prints can have a big impact on viewers when they are smaller than normal, not just when they are large. A small print (**Figure 13-8**) invites the viewer to step in close to study the print more carefully. It almost seems counterintuitive, but I had the experience myself and I've seen it happen with others—small prints can be captivating in their own unique way and can establish an intimacy with the viewer.

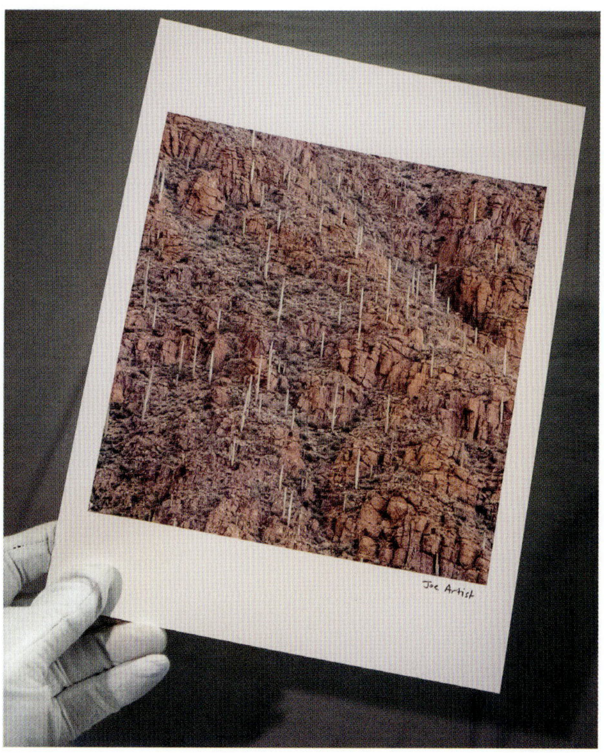

FIGURE 13-8: A print on 8.5" × 11" paper is easily handheld

When the image is framed, the viewer feels invited to come right up to the image and study it closely, looking for small details and subtle aspects. When in the hand, the small print has a preciousness to it as well—it feels like one is holding a valuable and treasured object.

Alternative Framing Options

There is no limit to the types of presentation styles for artwork, but photographs in fine art galleries have historically trended toward a relatively standard presentation of a wooden or metal molding with the print sandwiched between a backing of some sort and an overmat with a cutout revealing the image, with glazing (glass or Plexiglass) covering the print. Moving away from this standard can help emphasize your print as an object.

One popular technique used today is to frame with molding and glazing but with no overmat (**Figure 13-9**). Instead of an overmat, you print a

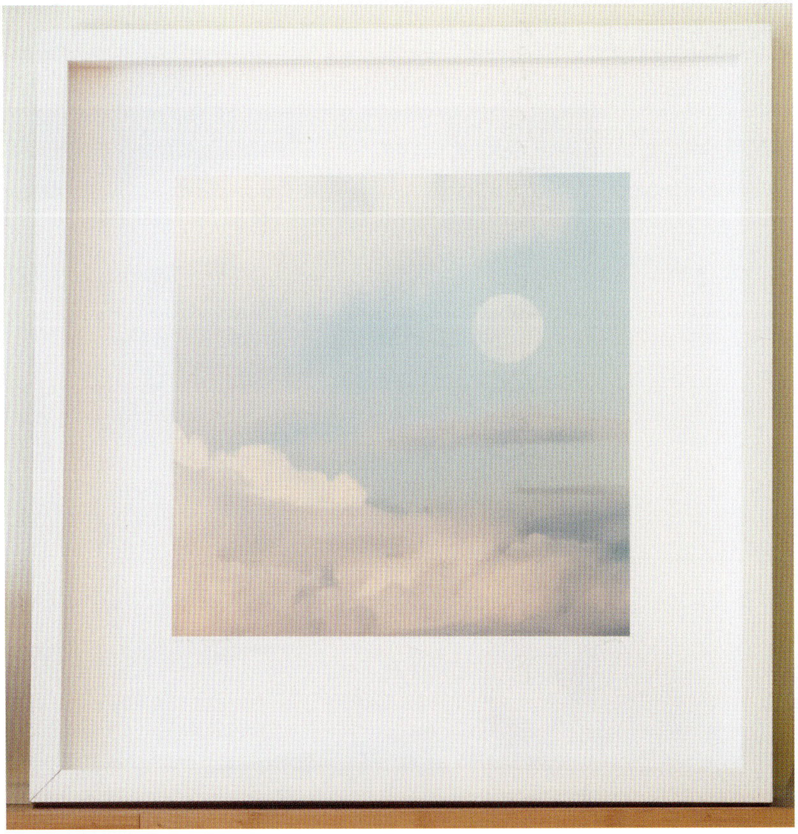

FIGURE 13-9: Photograph by the author framed in a shadowbox-style molding with no overmat

larger border of paper that acts as your mat in terms of visual impact, and include a spacer along the edges of the piece to keep the glazing from touching the print. This is relatively subtle in effect, but it allows your paper to shine instead of the mat and bring more emphasis to the fact that the print is made on paper. If you've chosen a paper perfectly suited to your print, why cover it with a mat?

Another framing technique to emphasize the print is a float mount where the print appears suspended within the frame (**Figure 13-10**). A spacer is required here, too, to keep the glazing off the print itself. This is a particularly useful effect with a deckle edged paper as the edges of the paper are completely revealed.

For exhibition purposes, many are using a mounting panel where the print is mounted flush to a piece of wood and hung directly on the wall with no glazing (**Figure 13-11**). The advantage of this method is that the print and its surface are immediately accessible to the viewer—you can't help but notice the print and the paper. This method is not good for archival purposes

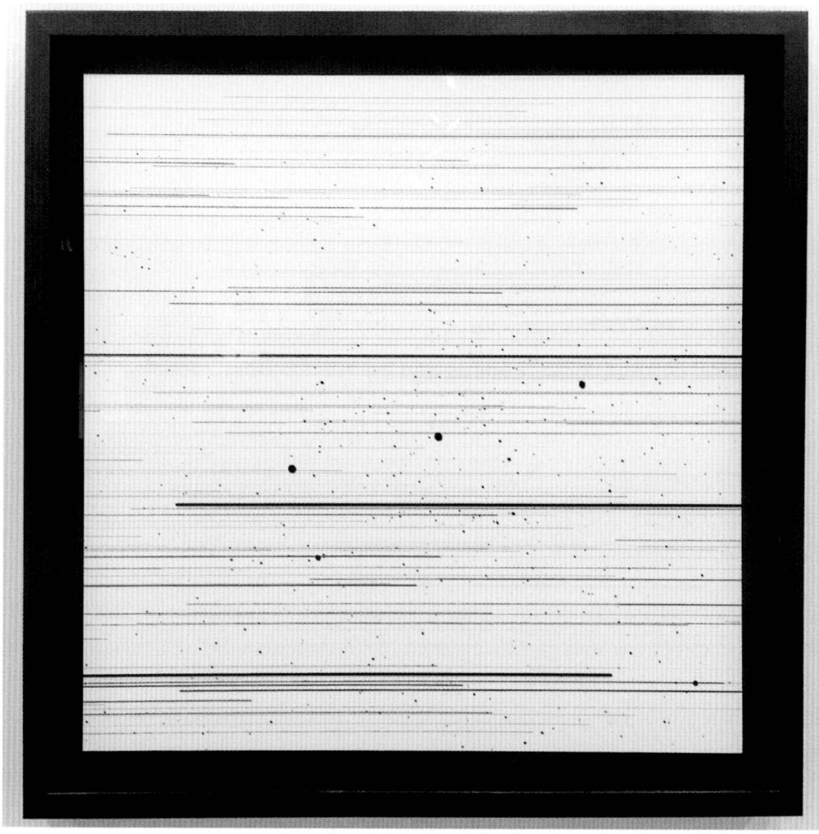

FIGURE 13-10: Photograph by the author framed in a shadowbox-style molding and float mounted on a piece of foam core with no overmat

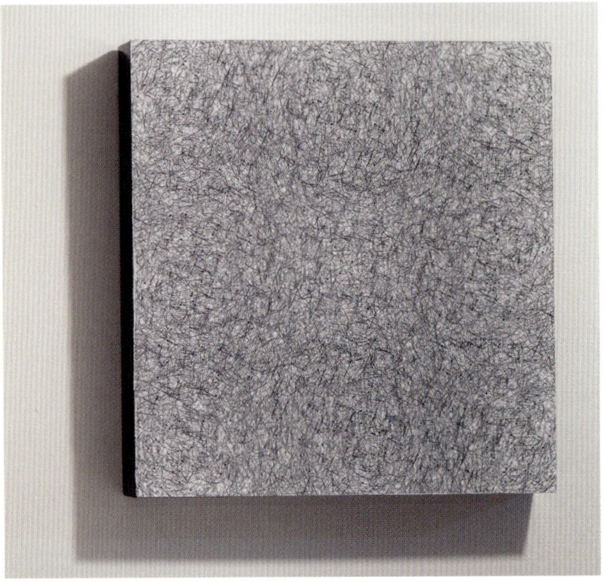

FIGURE 13-11: A mock-up of a mounting panel with a print trimmed to have no border and glued to the wooden base. This is a great contemporary way of presenting work, but it would not be good for archival purposes and it also does not allow for a signature verso (i.e., on the printed side).

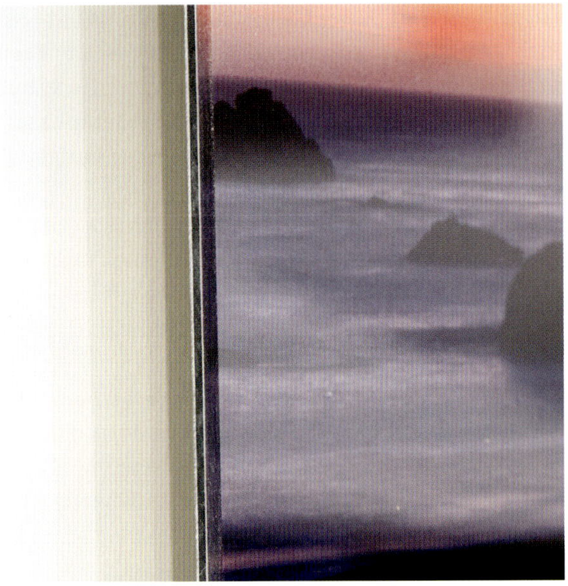

FIGURE 13-12: A close-up of a face-mounted piece. On the edge you can see the metal backing and Plexiglass sandwiching the paper print.

without further treatment (such as using the encaustic technique to cover the print with a beeswax and resin mixture), as there is no UV protection and anyone could touch and damage the print. Mounted prints can be very striking and contemporary looking and are worth considering for temporary exhibitions.

An alternative to the mounting panel is a well-established face-mounting method where a print is sandwiched between an aluminum backing and a glazing of Plexiglass (**Figure 13-12**). This dramatic and contemporary look is relatively expensive and nonreversible but can be quite powerful in visual impact.

Another exhibition-style framing solution that is increasing in popularity is to avoid the framing entirely and to instead attach the print directly to the wall. Like a mounted panel, this is not good for archival purposes, but it dramatically highlights the print itself (and it is obviously less expensive than framing). I usually see pins holding the corners to the wall, but I prefer very strong rare-earth magnets holding the corners via either a metal wall or a nail in the wall hidden under the paper (**Figure 13-13**).

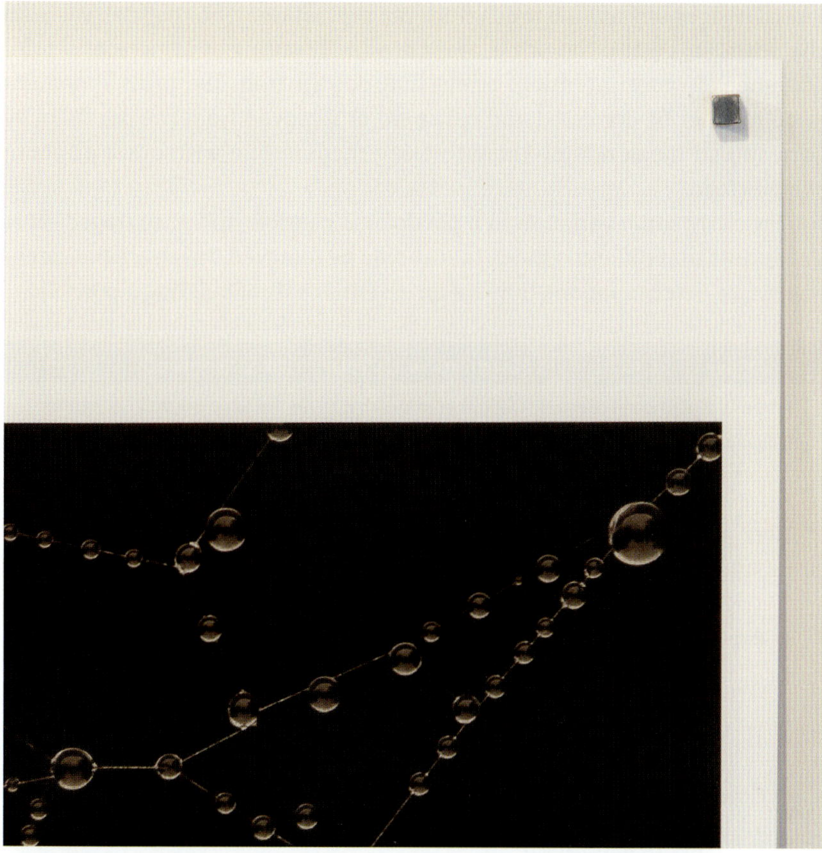

FIGURE 13-13: A rare-earth magnet holding up a print with a metallic item underneath, such as a steel nail or wall

The Print Statement

The **print statement** is artistic intent manifested in a portfolio of fine art prints. Much like the artist statement does with words, the print statement conveys to the viewer a *consistent printing style and look* applied to an entire portfolio. When done well, a print statement consistent with your artistic intent can raise the level of both the individual prints and the entire portfolio.

Everything we've done in our printing process ultimately goes into our print statement when dealing with a portfolio of prints: our processing, the materials such as ink set and paper, our toning of black-and-white prints or our color palette for color prints, our print and border size, and our presentation method.

When these aspects are harmoniously applied and when they support the artistic intent, the print statement for the portfolio is a success; when individual images deviate too much from the print statement, they detract from the portfolio, even if the prints are individually strong. If a successful print statement is your intention, prints that detract from the print statement should either be corrected and reprinted or removed from the portfolio. By correction, I mean editing them to bring them in line with other prints in the portfolio.

Obviously some variation in a portfolio is possible and encouraged—it is only prints that differ too much that should be removed. These are the sort of subjective determinations that are an essential part of building a portfolio.

Principles of Printing #19: Harmony with Your Print Statement

Your print should be in harmony with other prints that are in the same portfolio as part of your print statement. Doing so will help each print rise as part of a greater whole.

Here are typical factors to consider when matching prints as part of a print statement:

- Paper type, size, and border
- Overall tonality, including brightness and contrast
- Toning of black-and-white prints
- Color palette
- Intensity of saturation
- Sharpness or lack thereof
- Presence of bright highlights or solid blacks
- Aesthetics, such as traditional vs. contemporary, edgy vs. conservative, minimalist vs. complex
- Level of abstraction vs. level of descriptiveness

Let's talk about a few specific examples to illustrate this using my own work.

In deciding on a new photograph for my *East of the Sun, West of the Moon* project, I considered my overall print statement of dark and mysterious prints with deeply saturated and relatively monochromatic colors (**Figure 13-14**). The prints on the left and right are already in the project, and I was trying to decide on whether to include the photograph in the middle (shown in three different versions). My first attempt is in the center, and when compared to the prints to the left and right and the overall print statement, I felt

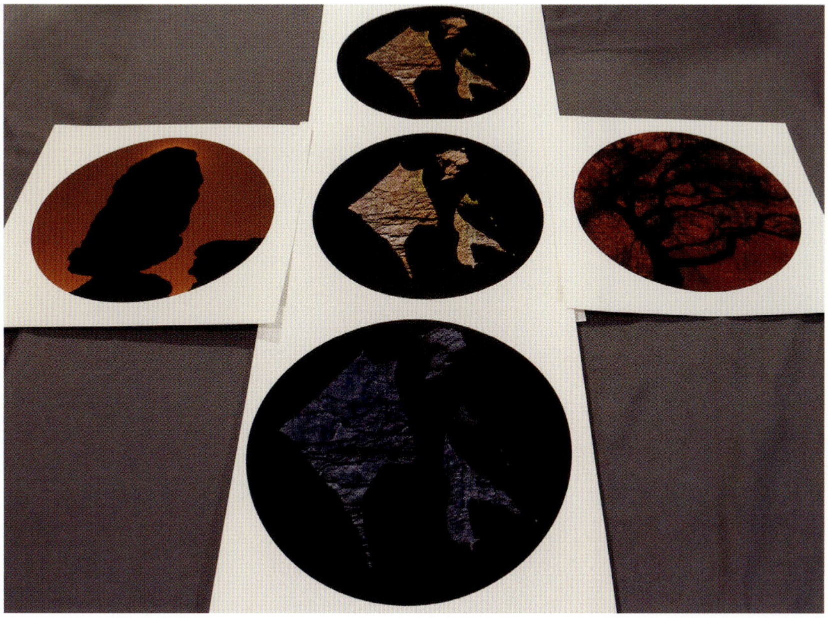

FIGURE 13-14: Potential new prints in my *East of the Sun, West of the Moon* project positioned vertically in the center, bracketed on the left and right by existing prints in the series

it was too bright and too descriptive. Instead, I wanted a darker image to create mystery and ambiguity.

I next tried darkening the print, resulting in the print on top. I thought this print was more in-line with its neighbors but still was too descriptive and a bit jarring. Last, I tried to abstract that one more by stripping out the color and adding a blue tone. A variation of this is what ultimately made the portfolio, as I believe its additional abstraction and complementary color worked well in series with the others. There is no right answer, of course, and it is a subjective decision and ultimately up to you as the artist.

Consider these two prints from my *Codex Natura* series (**Figure 13-15**). The print on the left is typical of photographs in the project as being very dark, with even the highlights being somewhere around the middle of the histogram and with nothing brighter. When looking to add the print on the right to the portfolio, I realized that its brighter highlights were not consistent with the print statement. So, over a series of prints, I kept on printing with darker and darker highlights until I found a print that would fit within the project—it is still a bit brighter than others, but some variation can be beneficial if it doesn't rise to a level where the print does not seem to fit.

As you make these sort of evaluations for your own prints and projects, consider seeking out input from others, though the ultimate decision is a subjective one and is up to you. I also recommend not deciding too quickly and to live with the prints for a while. Similarities and differences between prints have a way of emerging over time.

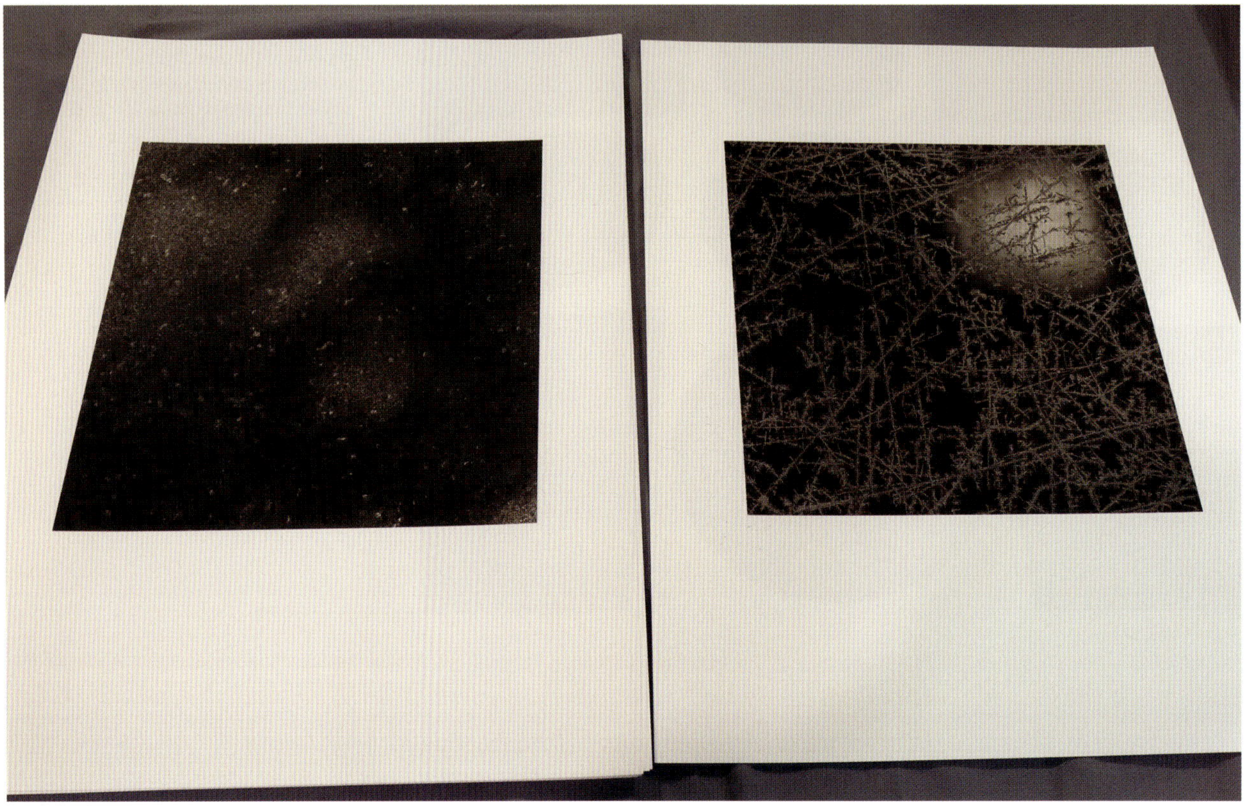

Figure 13-15: Prints from my *Codex Natura* project in portfolio size. The print on the right took multiple iterations to bring it in line with my overall print statement.

A new tool in Lightroom added in December 2016 facilitates editing your prints to be consistent with an overall print statement. The new **Reference View** in the Develop module allows you to compare two different images while editing one to facilitate editing your image to match something else (**Figure 13-16**). To use it, select the Reference View dropdown (the "R" and "A" separated by a line) in the lower left of the Develop module while you have your image active. You can then select a reference image to compare with it by dragging and dropping the image from the Filmstrip at the bottom of the screen. By choosing a "standard" image from your portfolio as the Reference Image, you can edit new ones while simultaneously viewing another image in the portfolio, making it easier to match color, contrast, brightness, and the like. The print itself will still dictate the right fit, but software tools such as this can help in eliminating some of the proofing steps.

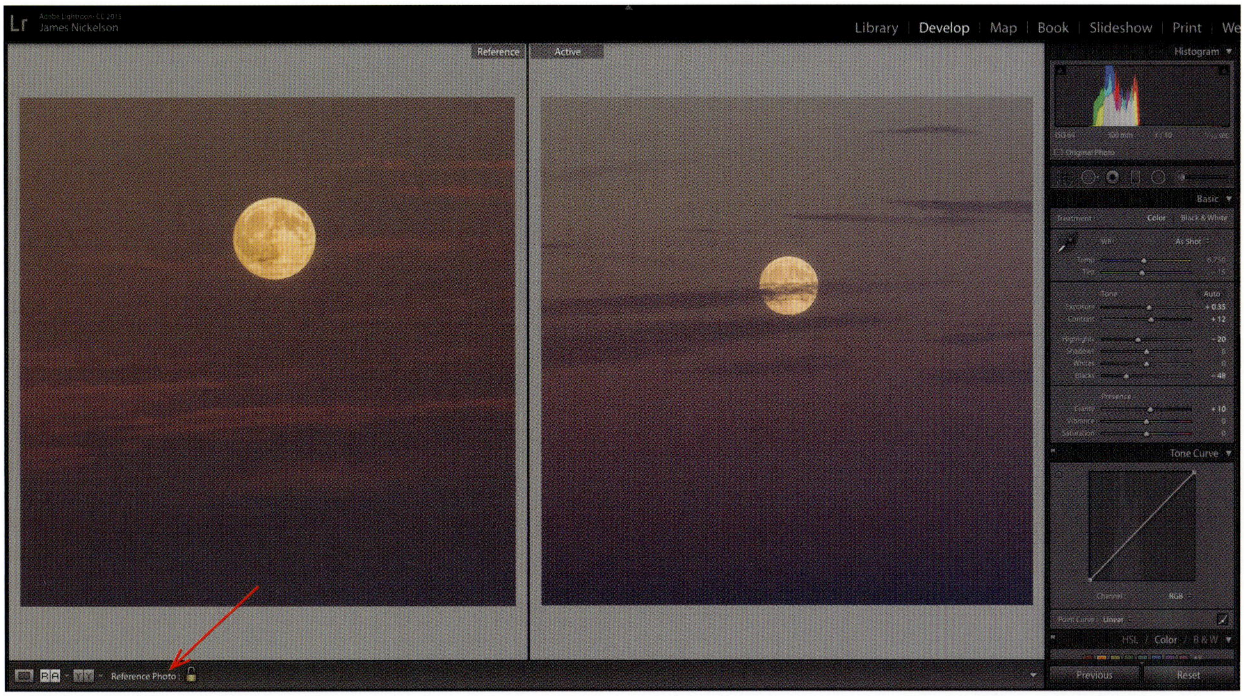

FIGURE 13-16: Lightroom's new Reference View, which allows you to edit the image on the right to match another reference image on the left. This looks to be a powerful tool in helping to establish a consistent print statement.

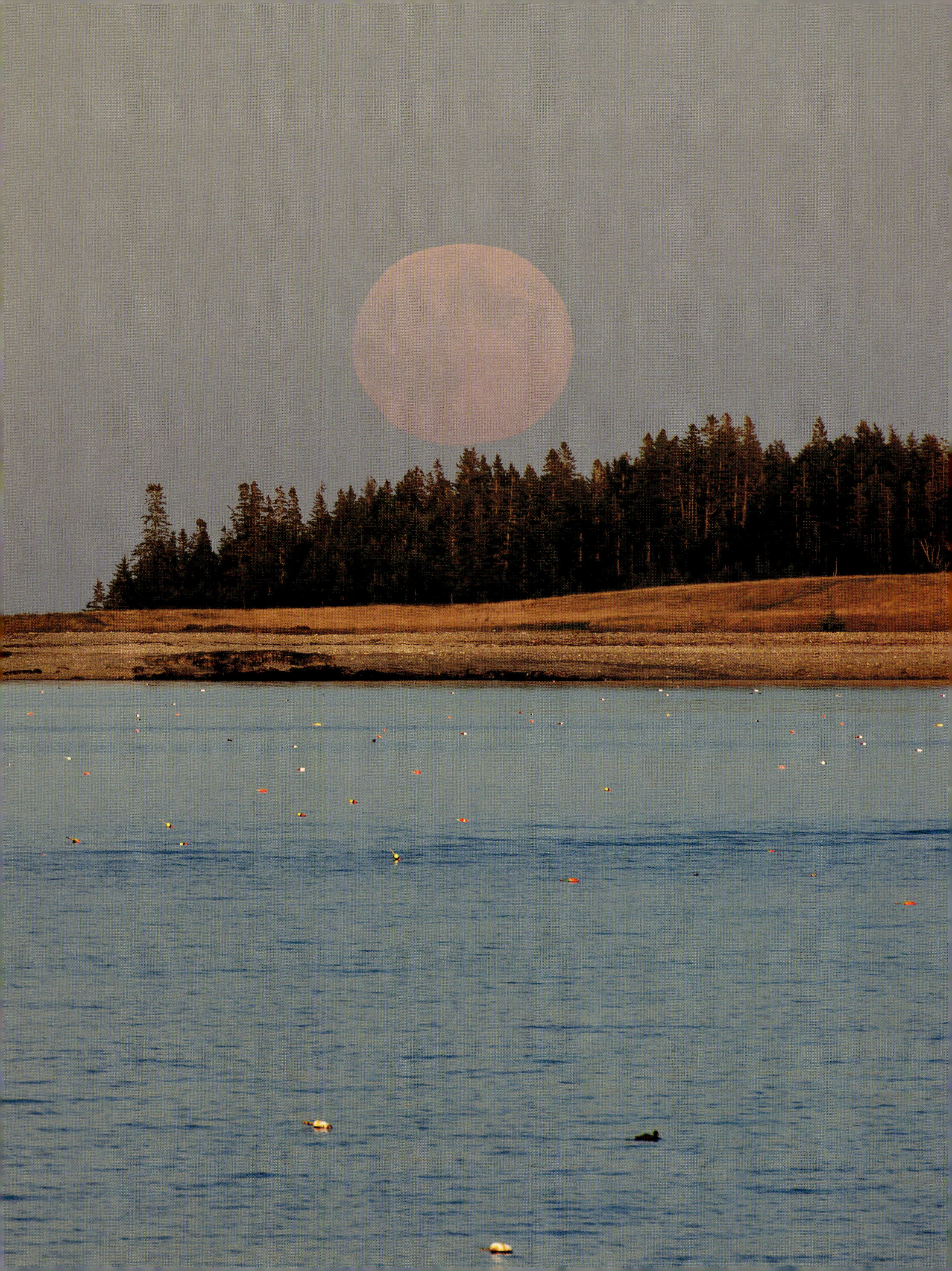

14 Considerations for the Fine Art Market

In this chapter we'll discuss presenting the prints you've worked so hard on perfecting to the fine art market. Over the past decade I've been working to place my own photography in that fine art market, and I've learned a lot throughout as part of my research as well as my successes and failures. I work with scores of clients, too, as part of my custom printing business and have learned immensely from my clients and their stories.

Many of these skills we've learned so far will help in producing the best possible portfolio, and here we'll discuss how to create marketing materials for the fine art market that will allow you to present your prints in a way that is worthy of them.

> *Photography to the amateur is recreation, to the professional it is work, and hard work, too, no matter how pleasurable it might be.*
> —Edward Weston

Signatures, Edition, and Other Information on the Print

In this chapter we will cover a variety of topics relevant to the fine art market, including editioning of prints and signing your prints.

Signatures and Titles

One of the most common issues for fine art photographers is deciding how to sign and edition their prints. It is well established in the art world that an artist sign a completed print in some fashion. This **signature** indicates to galleries, curators, and collectors that the piece is a completed work and provides an authentication that it was approved (if not also created) by the artist. While there are some exceptions, I've found that the fine art gallery and museum world expects a finished print, particularly a photograph, to be signed by the artist.

I would also interpret "signed by the artist" to mean signed *by hand* by the artist, not adding a scanned signature to your print. There are markets where an electronic signature makes sense, but I do not consider the fine art world to be one of those markets. We talked about pens and pencils you can use to sign your print back in chapter 12, "Post-Processing."

Many artists also put the **title** of their piece on their final print. I would consider this an optional step that you should do if you'd like or if your gallery or collectors require it.

Another option would be a date, usually in the form of just the year, which is usually meant to indicate the date of printing, not the date of creation of the image.

Limited Editions

Editioning of fine art inkjet prints means putting some limit on the number of prints that you will make. This **limited edition** creates an exclusivity that can increase the value to collectors (and thus the price you can charge for your work) and all the galleries I've dealt with have strongly encouraged, if not required, their artists to edition their prints. An **open edition** is a print that is not limited in any way; that is, you can make and sell as many copies of it as you want.

The requirement of editioning is less consistently applied than that of the signature. With inkjet printing, the trend has been that many galleries are requiring artists to limit their edition to help justify higher prices and eliminate the perceived value gap between inkjet prints and traditional analog prints. Ultimately the question of whether to create a limited edition is up to you.

A further complication for editions is how to handle multiple sizes of prints. The multiple sizes can be part of the same edition (all counting toward the same limit) or each size can be a separate edition.

Whatever you end up choosing to do with respect to creating a limited edition, it is important that you honor the limit. The entire premise of the limited edition for inkjet prints requires your collectors to know that you will maintain the integrity of the edition and you will not produce additional prints beyond the limit. It is also important that you disclose your edition so that buyers know the limits of your edition. Check also to see if there are any local laws that may put additional requirements on selling limited edition prints, particularly if you live in California or New York. Please note also that nothing in this book should be considered legal advice—please consult an attorney for advice specific to your situation.

I recommend producing your fine art prints in a limited edition rather than an open edition. There is always the risk that you will sell out a very popular print, but I put that in the category of a good problem to have. It will be the rare artist who consistently sells out her editions, no matter what the size.

Let's go over a few examples of how I've seen artists assign editions to their work as well as a few guiding principles:

- The trend at present is for smaller editions rather than larger. Many fine art galleries and collectors don't view editions of 30 or more to be particularly limited, and what you'll instead see are editions in the range of 5, 8, 10, 12, and 20.
- A common edition would be a simple number that covers all prints of that image. This would apply for cases when you always print that image the same size, or in rarer cases, when you print different sizes and have them all count toward the same edition. A limited edition of 12 in this case would mean the edition would only have 12 prints, regardless of size.
- Another common edition would have separate editions based on size. You could have an edition of 10 of a smaller size and 5 of a larger size, for example. If you wanted an open edition as well, I've seen people have an open edition for their smaller size and then a limited edition for their larger sizes.
- There is a trend now in bigger markets for escalating prices within an edition; in other words, the price increases as you get closer to the end of the edition. You could increase the price with each print, once you pass the halfway point, or whenever else it might make sense to you. It is more complicated to manage and document escalating prices but it does make intuitive sense that the last print in a limited edition could have an increased value.
- One way of making an open edition that helps protect early purchasers is to apply the escalating prices to the open edition. If the price goes up for each print, the edition will be essentially self-limiting as the price increases, but the option will be there for a very motivated collector.
- Limited editions are ultimately dependent on trust of the artist by purchasers, so I always tend toward being conservative when gray areas arise. When I have a question about how to handle a particular question about editioning of my own work, before I move forward I ask myself how a collector who paid for one of my prints would feel if they found out about a sale I had made.

Print Mastery: Artist's Proofs and Printer's Proofs

A limited edition will typically also allow the artist to make artist's proofs (usually labeled as A/P) and/or printer's proofs (P/P). The intention behind an artist's proof is for the artist to retain a copy of their print for their personal collection, museums, gifts, and the like. Usually the artist's proofs are not intended to be sold and, therefore, they don't impact the market for the print edition, but it does frequently happen. Printer's proofs are essentially a subset of artist's proofs and are meant to be a copy retained by whoever is doing the prints to match with any future prints.

Customs on these proofs are all over the place, from some people strictly limiting them to, say, 10% of the edition size (two proofs for an edition of 20, in this example), to artists in New York City galleries with a very small edition (3 or 5) and with more artist's proofs than sale prints. My opinion is that you can do whatever you'd like as long as you disclose to purchasers what you are doing. For my work I usually have 1 or 2 artist's proofs (per size, if applicable).

Where to Sign and Edition Your Prints

Now that you are going to sign, title, and/or edition your prints, you need to decide where and how to do so. Whichever way you decide to go, I recommend being subtle and tasteful as to how you sign and edition (with a pencil or fine point archival pen). I'd rather have the image itself speak louder than the signature and other information.

The three possible locations for these items are within the image area itself, on the front of the print outside the image area, and on the back of the print. Here's what I recommend for each:

On the front of the print, outside the image area: The front side of a print is often called the recto, as in the print is signed recto. This is probably the most common solution, and the most common location is outside the image area and below the print. I usually see the edition on the lower left, title if any on lower center, and signature in the lower right, but this of course varies. Depending on how close your information and signature are to the image area, and how it is framed, it may or may not be visible after framing (**Figure 14-1**).

On the back of the print: The back of a print is often called the *verso*. With a print that is signed verso my recommendation is to make sure that any information is located outside the back of the image area so there is no ink bleed-through or indentation to the image itself. Artists often prefer signing verso if they do not want the signature and such to interfere with the viewing of the image, or if the print is presented in a way that doesn't allow a

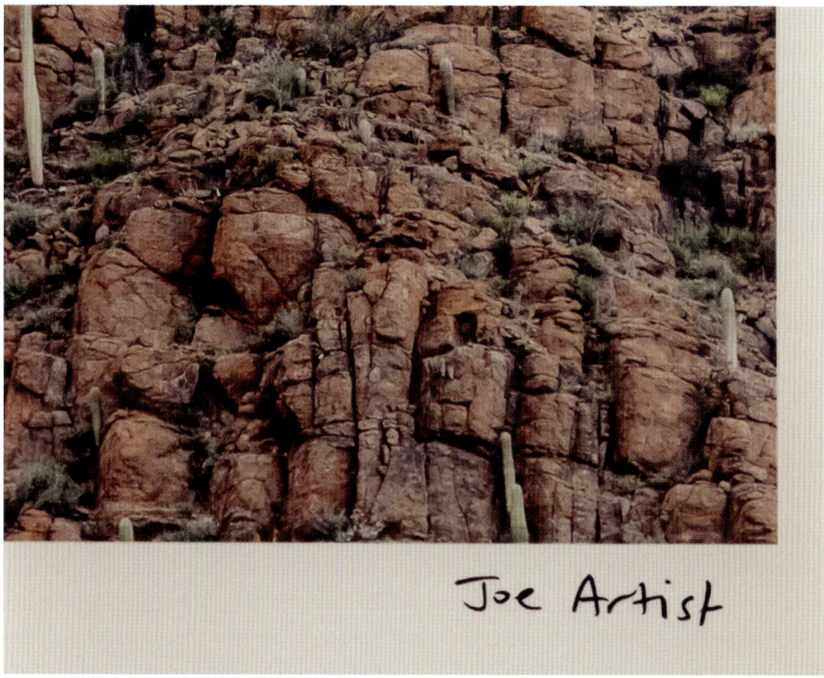

FIGURE 14-1: A verso signature on a print, to the lower-right side of the image

recto signature. A print that is borderless and mounted could be signed verso on the back of the matboard (if dry-mounted) or very lightly in pencil on back of the print itself to prevent any indentation (and because pencil marks do not bleed as do inks).

Within the image area: I strongly recommend against doing this. If your goal is to be in the fine art market, the vast majority of people in that field consider a signature of other information *within the image area* of a photograph to be amateurish. There are certainly some exceptions, and some types of framing might not give much else of a choice, but I would try very hard to avoid this solution.

Archival Considerations for the Fine Art Market

Archival considerations become paramount when you are participating in the fine art market. With print prices in the hundreds and thousands of dollars here in the United States, collectors expect to be purchasing an investment that will last. Careful attention to the archival qualities of print materials, storage materials, and framing materials are part of a professional approach to selling fine art prints.

Conservators (such as those maintaining collections at museums) also appreciate information about the production of a print (if we are lucky enough to have conservators care about our work). To help anyone in the future know more about your print, providing information such as the printer model, paper name, and date of printing all can help conservators in their efforts. None of us know if anyone will care about our work down the road, so providing information helpful to these professionals is advisable.

Printing for Portfolios

Very often an artist has a chance to meet in person with a gallery owner or curator and show them their work. This might be a scheduled meeting, part of a portfolio review event, or something less formal, but in these situations the artist usually only has a few minutes in which to pique the interest of the viewer. A printed portfolio is the vehicle of choice for showing your work to someone, and if you get this type of face-to-face time, I recommend you use it to your best advantage with a beautifully printed and presented portfolio.

Using actual prints, on the paper you normally use, is much more powerful than a printed portfolio book. Print-on-demand books have definitely gotten better in terms of image quality but they still pale in comparison to a custom inkjet print. When you present your work, the prints will be handled individually, and loose prints allow for pulling out particular prints or reordering them, too.

I recommend a print of at least 8" × 8" or 8" × 10" in size on paper of at least 11" × 14" so that it has a generous border. The white border around your print improves the presentation and sets the print off from its surroundings (**Figure 14-2**), and it also provides a place where people can handle the print without touching the image itself.

From my experience, a 17" × 22" sheet is close to the upper limit for normal portfolios, as larger sizes become hard to handle. There are nice portfolio boxes available in standard sizes such as 11" × 14", 13" × 19", 16" × 20", and 17" × 22".

Principles of Printing #20:
Don't Let Your Presentation Bring Your Prints Down

After you've spent all this time and effort making your prints perfect, don't let sloppy or inappropriate presentation choices diminish your prints.

Experiment with different types of portfolio boxes and other presentation materials to find one that works well for your prints and for your style of presentation.

FIGURE 14-2: A portfolio print from my Codex Natura space, printed at 12" × 12" bottom-weighted on 17" × 22" paper. Bottom weighting (larger margins on the bottom than the top) is a classic method for improving presentation of a print.

I prefer the prints to be loose in the box rather than enclosed in plastic sleeves during the presentation time. Plastic sleeves are great for protection, but they slightly dull, the print and taking them off and putting them back on eats up valuable time. Since you are reading this book and printing yourself, you can always make replacement prints if they become damaged during handling.

Printing Your Own Marketing Materials

You can use the skills you've developed to prepare your own marketing materials, too. Taking advantage of your own ability to produce prints that look just like you want them to, you can create handouts or other marketing items that are of a higher quality than you can get from the mass production online sources.

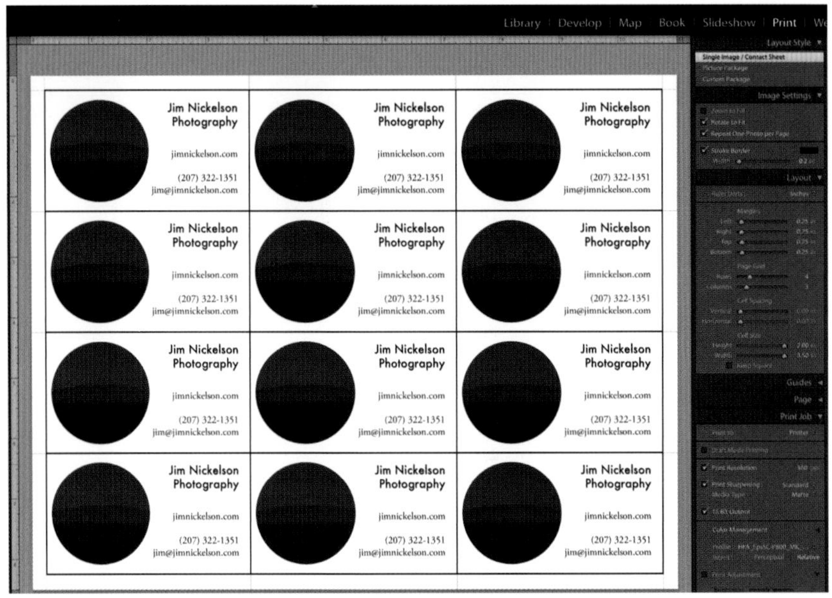

FIGURE 14-3: My business card in a print template. I create a single image in Photoshop where I can lay down text and an image together. I print 12 per page using Lightroom, and then I trim them to size.

Those online places can do a pretty good job on business cards and the like, and the prices are great, but you will end up with quality that is the same as everybody else. Taking the extra step to make your own where it makes sense can help your marketing rise above others.

I've include a few sample ideas for doing your own marketing pieces that will hopefully be a springboard and inspiration for making your own materials.

Business Cards

Business cards still find a use today, and it is great to have one printed on high-quality paper. For a standard 2" × 3.5" business card, you can fit 12 of them on one sheet of 8.5" × 11" paper (**Figure 14-3**).

Depending on your preferences, you can even print your business card on the exact same paper you use for your larger final prints. The tiny 2" (or so) gem-like prints of your image are a great marketing tool for your fine art prints. When compared to buying a box of 500 from an online retailer, it doesn't make financial sense—but most people do not pass out very many cards these days, and the visual impact of these make the extra time and cost worthwhile.

FIGURE 14-4: My template for the Museo Artist cards (the square card version). Using layers in Photoshop, you can precisely place text and images to design the exact card you'd like. Whenever I want to change the image, I just drop a new one in a layer and delete or turn off the old layer (and I change the text as appropriate).

Notecards

Notecards for holidays and marketing are less common now than they used to be, and that is an opportunity for those who do make them. I've found that I pay more attention to mailings that don't look like they were mass-produced and have actual human writing on them, and I suspect others do as well.

You can easily make your own notecards using high-quality paper on your inkjet printer (**Figure 14-4**). I've set up a template in Photoshop to use standard-sized cards—companies like Museo and Moab that sell notecards usually provide a blank template, too. Once you have a template, it is easy to add a new image to the card so you can make cards using fresh images. One limitation to note is that the bigger wide-format printers often do not accept paper smaller than 8.5" × 11". I use my 17" printer for this task.

Leave-Behinds

It is a common practice in the fine art photography world, after meeting with a gallery owner or curator for a portfolio review, to give them something that has your contact information on it and perhaps an image to trigger their memory. These "leave-behinds" can be a simple as a business card, but many photographers are coming up with creative designs to make an impression (and to make it more likely that your leave-behind isn't tossed in the trash).

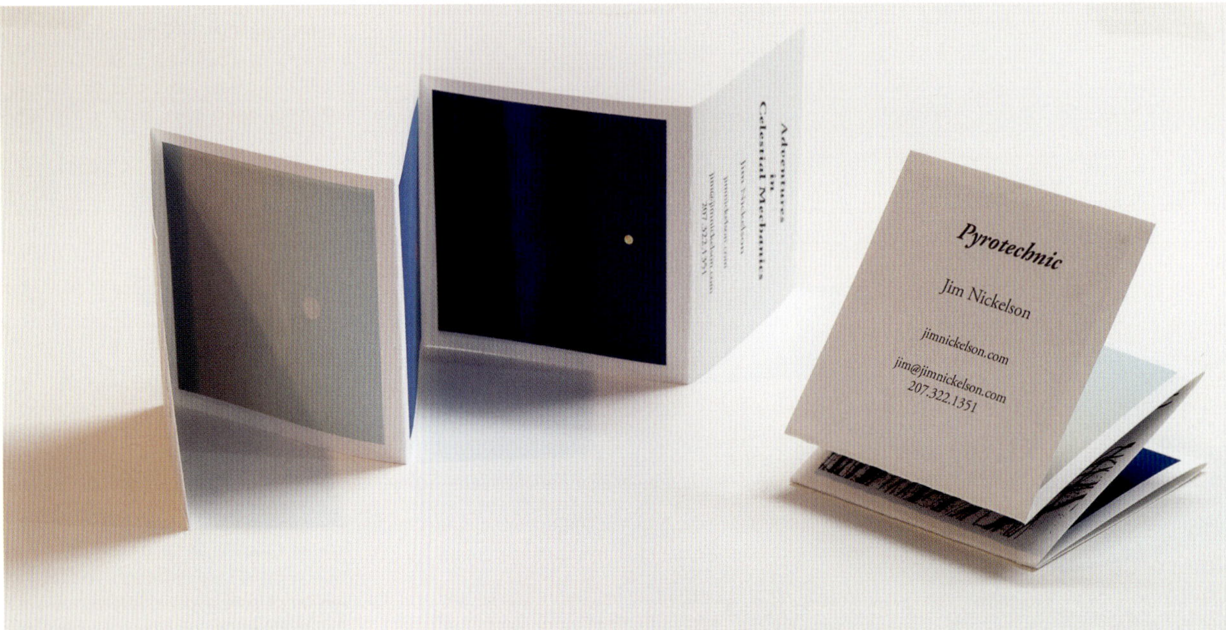

FIGURE 14-5: Sample accordion-style leave-behinds that I made using my inkjet printer. These are actually double-sided so there are different images front and back. To do this, you have to create a template for both sides, print one of them on double-sided paper, turn the paper over, and print on the other side. Getting the alignment correct for this takes a lot of trial and error, but it is a great effect.

This is another opportunity to showcase your printing skills, too, to help differentiate yourself from the crowd. As one example, I've made a very small accordion book of my images that I pass out to people who have reviewed my portfolio (**Figure 14-5**). I include contact information and four images, and its more unusual design makes it more likely to have an impact.

To make these accordion books, I design one in Photoshop using my desired dimensions, and I sized this one to fit four on a single 17" × 22" piece of paper (**Figure 14-6**). After printing, I cut each of the four pieces apart and then use a straight edge to add a crease where I'd like each fold to be. It does not have to be perfect since this is a simple handout.

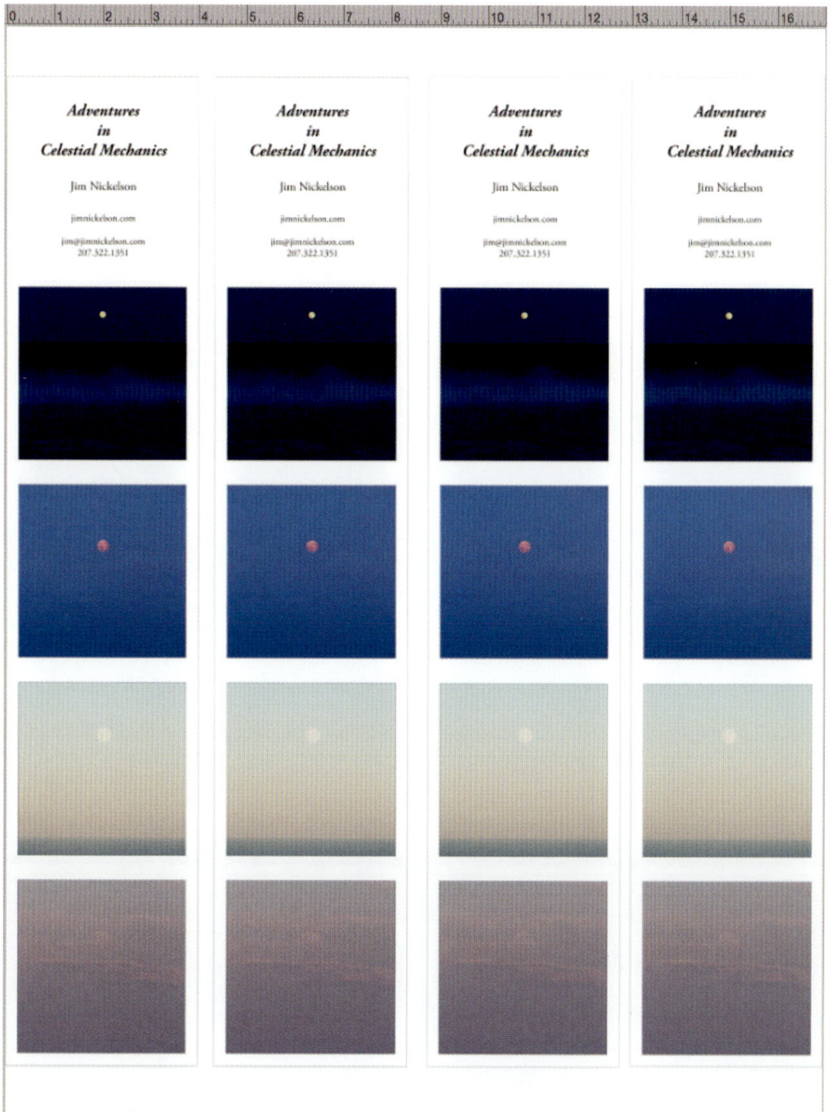

FIGURE 14-6: Four of my accordion-style leave-behinds batched on a 17" × 22" page. The trickiest part is to fold in the right spot, which I do by estimation and practice. I fold each up toward me so that I can see where I'm folding, and then I reverse the folds for the ones that need to go the other direction to create the accordion-style presentation.

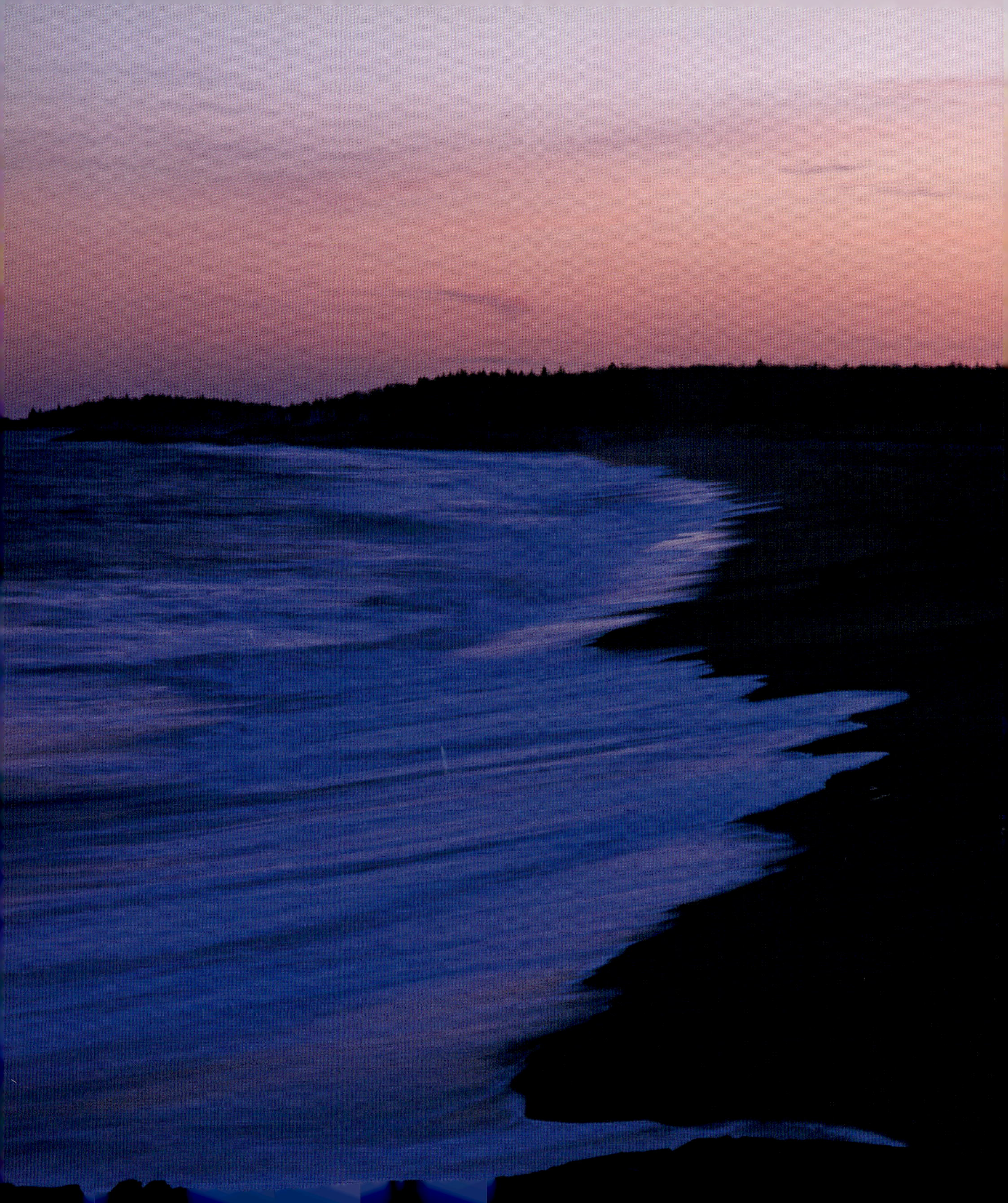

Appendix

Throughout this book you have come across callouts called "Principles of Printing." They are listed here for your convenience should you wish to reference them again.

Principles of Printing #1:

Artistic Intent Should Drive Your Decisions

Your artistic intent for your work should drive your decisions throughout the entire printing process. Everything from how you process an image, how large you print it, and what paper you use for the print should be guided by your own artistic intent.

Each photographer has a purpose for choosing to shoot a photograph and then for choosing to print that particular photograph. A fine print helps any photograph realize its fullest expression, and the nature of that expression depends on the artist. By taking control of the process, the artist can serve as the director of his or her final print.

Principles of Printing #2:

You Have to Know Where You Are to Know Where to Go

Consistent and accurate color management is essential to successful printing. If you are not looking at an accurate version of your file, your edits will give you results in the print that you don't expect.

Principles of Printing #3:

Optimize Your Starting Position

The better the quality of your original file, the better off you will be with your final print. Faults in your original capture can result in problems in your final print, or in significant time spent trying to overcome those faults during image editing and printing.

Principles of Printing #4:

Do No Harm

Don't do anything to your file that you can't reverse in some way.

Principles of Printing #5:

There Are Many Ways to Get There from Here

I'm a firm believer that with today's tools we have many good ways of performing our tasks in editing and printing, and you should choose what works best for you. For editing software, I think Photoshop and Lightroom are both great, but you may find that other programs give you better results for your particular camera or type of print, or they just make more sense to you in terms of workflow. Go for it.

Lightroom and Photoshop are immensely powerful and flexible tools, and there are always multiple ways you can accomplish any particular task. I often joke with my workshop students that you can do anything in Photoshop 20 different ways, and 18 of those ways are good. Some methods may be better than others in terms of the impact on image quality or ease of use, but I believe photographers should work with the methods with which they are most comfortable. I always recommend experimenting with other methods to see if they offer improvement over what you are doing, but also don't feel the obligation to use every recommended technique if what you are doing is working fine.

Principles of Printing #6:

Consistency, Usually

Work toward your goal in a consistent fashion, but don't be afraid to veer off the path, either. I typically perform the same basic edits to each image in a particular order. I do this to establish a routine and because it is an editing order that makes sense to me, but there is nothing magical about the order in which I personally edit. Using a consistent approach also reduces the probability that you will forget something.

Principles of Printing #7:

You Have to Go Too Far to Know That You've Gone Far Enough

As an editing philosophy, the photographer and publisher Brooks Jensen said it best:

> *You don't know if you've gone far enough unless you've gone too far, and then come slightly back.*
> —Brooks Jensen

Experimentation in the digital darkroom is essential in learning how the software works and in finding what settings will work best for a particular image. This can apply not only to noise reduction but to every step of the editing process.

Principles of Printing #8:

Problems Are Opportunities

Encountering a problem provides an opportunity to learn a new technique. Most things I've learned about image editing have been the result of researching and trying out different things when faced with problems on particular images. In a simple example, early on, I increased saturation in an image and was frustrated that all of the colors were increasing in saturation when I just wanted to increase the greens. Learning how to increase the saturation in only the Green channel taught me about channels, an idea I then could apply to other problems.

Learning how to make an HDR image to deal with a large dynamic range can, for example, open up the ability to use HDR techniques to solve other problems or can give you ideas on whole new bodies of work. Problems can be frustrating at times, but remember that all of those frustrations are making you better at performing processing and realizing your vision.

Principles of Printing #9:

Live with Your Prints

One of the best pieces of advice I received (and I wish I could remember the source) was to live with my prints for a while before making any final decisions. Print your work and then hang your print somewhere you can see it, and aspects of the print that can be improved will very likely become evident. Similarly, putting a bit of time between making a print and evaluating it can help you look at the print more objectively.

Principles of Printing #10:

The Print Is What Matters

You are the artist and it is up to you—you must be the final arbiter of your own print. Don't worry about what is on the monitor, and don't worry about what others say. All the decisions you make during the printing process lead to the actual physical object of the print.

Principles of Printing #11:

It's Only Paper

It's only paper. While there is nothing in photography I like better than a fine print, don't worry about when one is lost or when you end up making a small change and getting rid of an earlier version. Ink and paper aren't free, but a fine print will last and be appreciated for a lifetime and is thus worth the extra effort and possible wastage. Get your final image to where you like, but don't be afraid of making further modifications to improve it after you've had a chance to live with your print for a while.

Principles of Printing #12:

If You Think You've Seen Every Printing Problem Occur, You Are Wrong

I print almost every day and I see many of the same problems occur over and over with paper, printers, or files. And yet, I'm continually surprised when there is a new situation where a print has gone wrong and I can't figure it out. When these sorts of situations inevitably occur, it helps to logically work through the problem, eliminate variables, and hopefully find a solution.

Principles of Printing #13:

Paper Choice Can Be Key for Achieving Artistic Intent

Paper choice is one of the most important decisions a photographer should make in realizing their artistic intent for a print. The right choice of paper, suitable for the image and supporting the artistic intent behind the print or portfolio, can raise a print to a new level of quality and impact.

Principles of Printing #14:

Emphasize and Deemphasize to Direct the Attention of Your Viewer

Part of creating a fine art print is attempting to control how a viewer experiences the print. One successful method of doing this is to try to direct the attention of the viewer, whether it be by emphasizing things you want them to notice, deemphasizing things you don't want them to notice, directing their gaze around the image and keeping their gaze from slipping off the edge of the image, or magnifying or downplaying relationships between aspects of the image.

Principles of Printing #15:

Paper Color Matters, Especially for Black-and-White Prints

Each type of paper has its own color, and even though we use printer-paper profiles and other techniques to minimize its impact, the paper color does affect the final print. This happens in two ways: first, the paper border is bare around the print, and warmer or cooler colors surrounding your print can impact the appearance of the image; and second, some of the paper's color shows through the ink, especially in highlight areas where there is less ink covering the paper.

The effect of paper color is even more pronounced with black-and-white prints as variations in color are more noticeable where there is less ink laid down in the image. I see this as a feature rather than a bug, though, and I use paper color for creative purposes.

Principles of Printing #16:

Keep On Printing

Putting in the hours, running through the paper and ink... however you want to phrase it, the best way to become a good printer is to keep on printing. The more you print, the more you'll learn what works and doesn't work, and the more you'll face challenges that require you to learn a new skill or technique.

Principles of Printing #17:

Look at Great Prints

Looking at prints as much as possible is a valuable exercise. There are many places to see great prints, such as galleries, museums, or in the studios of your photographic friends. You will also see many not-so-great prints, which is a useful exercise in itself. The more you look at prints, the more you'll be able to tell the difference between a great print and a not-so-great print.

Principles of Printing #18:

Embrace the Physicalness of the Print

In this increasingly digital world, emphasizing the physical aspect of your print can heighten its impact to viewers. Reminding the viewer that prints are tangible and precious objects helps combat the ephemeral nature of most imagery.

Principles of Printing #19:

Harmony with Your Print Statement

Your print should be in harmony with other prints that are in the same portfolio as part of your print statement. Doing so will help each print rise as part of a greater whole.

Principles of Printing #20:

Don't Let Your Presentation Bring Your Prints Down

After you've spent all this time and effort making your prints perfect, don't let sloppy or inappropriate presentation choices diminish your prints.

Experiment with different types of portfolio boxes and other presentation materials to find one that works well for your prints and for your style of presentation.

Index

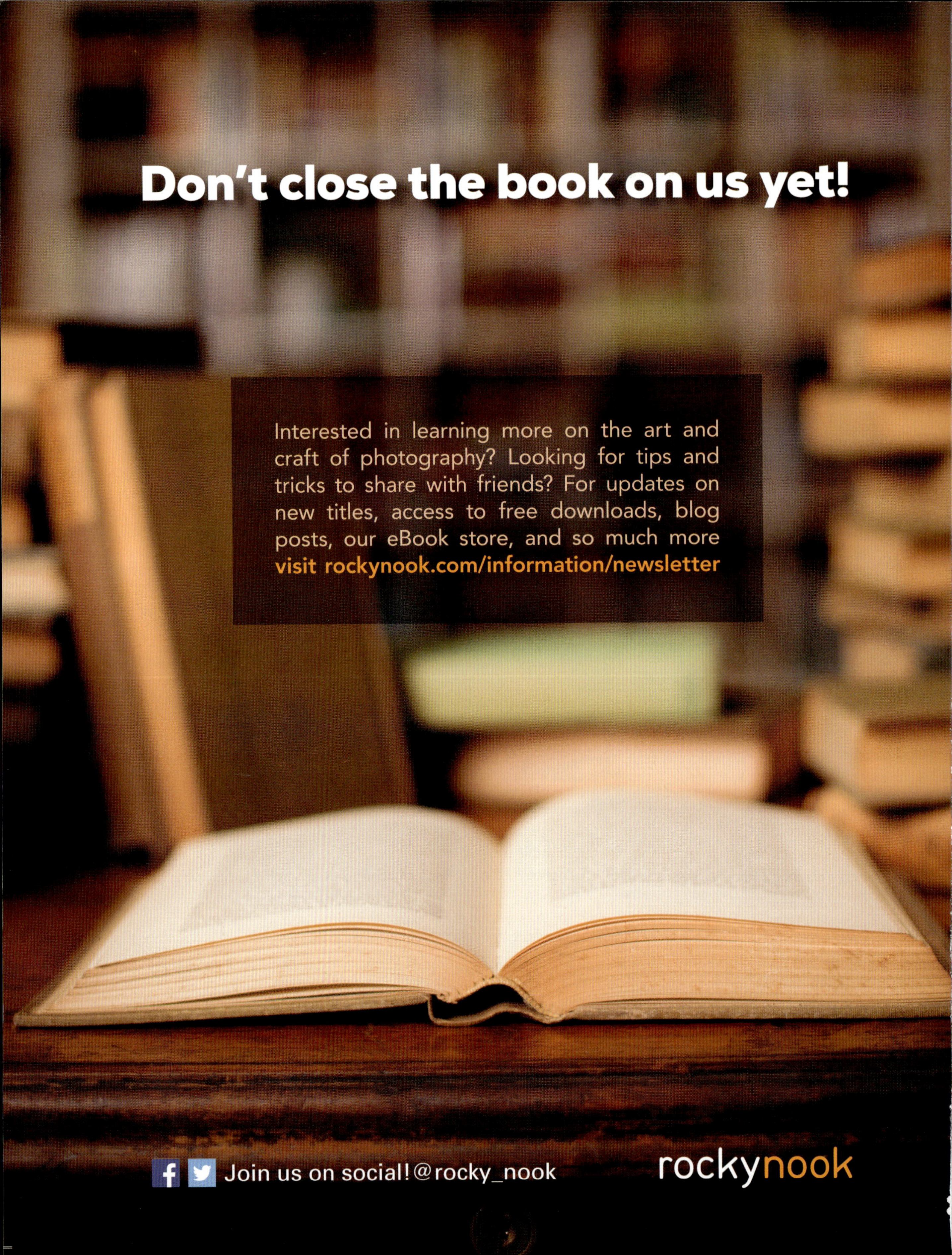
Don't close the book on us yet!
Interested in learning more on the art and craft of photography? Looking for tips and tricks to share with friends? For updates on new titles, access to free downloads, blog posts, our eBook store, and so much more visit rockynook.com/information/newsletter
Join us on social! @rocky_nook
rockynook